W9-BSZ-630

WALKING
THE
TIGHTROPE

WALKING
THE
TIGHTROPE

*The Private Confessions
of a Public Relations Man*

by
Henry C. Rogers

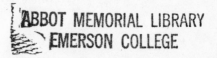
ABBOT MEMORIAL LIBRARY
EMERSON COLLEGE

WILLIAM MORROW AND COMPANY, INC.
New York   1980

HM
263
.R567

Copyright © 1980 by Henry C. Rogers

All rights reserved. No part of this book may be reproduced or utilized in any form or by any means, electronic or mechanical, including photocopying, recording or by any information storage and retrieval system, without permission in writing from the Publisher. Inquiries should be addressed to William Morrow and Company, Inc., 105 Madison Ave., New York, N. Y. 10016.

Library of Congress Cataloging in Publication Data

Rogers, Henry C   1914-
    Walking the tightrope.

    1. Rogers, Henry C., 1914-
2. Public relations consultants—United States—
Biography.   3. Press agents—United States—
Biography.   I. Title.
HM263.R567   659.2′092′4   79-24454
ISBN 0-688-03589-2

Printed in the United States of America

First Edition

1 2 3 4 5 6 7 8 9 10

To Roz, Marcia, and Ron
who were with me all the time
And Warren and Teme
without whose help it would never have happened

Foreword

Long ago, an acquaintance of mine—Hollywood artist John Decker, who counted among his close friends, W. C. Fields, John Barrymore, Gene Fowler—used to paint movie stars posing as historical figures. Decker's most brilliant rendering was a portrait of W. C. Fields posing as Queen Victoria. One evening the representative of a renowned whiskey company saw the portrait hanging in Chasen's restaurant, and immediately realized its publicity value. The representative conceived a whiskey ad that would feature the portrait of W. C. Fields as Queen Victoria with a boldfaced caption beneath reading:

W. C. FIELDS SAYS—"FIT FOR A QUEEN"

He went to W. C. Fields and John Decker to purchase reproduction rights to the portrait. They turned him down.

Had he hired Henry Rogers to acquire the portrait, I have no doubt he would have got it—and with it pulled off one of the most eye-catching promotional coups in modern times.

I have known Henry Rogers for most of the forty years he has been in the public relations business (in a solid partnership with Warren Cowan). In that time I have considered him the single best all-around public relations man in the United States. When Henry Rogers sets out to generate publicity for a client—a product, a motion picture or television show, an entertainment star—he almost always succeeds. I've seen him secure specialized publicity over the years for Rita Hayworth, Claudette Colbert, Joan Crawford, Frank Sinatra, Shirley MacLaine, Danny Kaye, Dean Martin, Audrey Hepburn, Tony Curtis, Dinah Shore, Doris Day, Paul Newman, Steve McQueen, Paul McCartney, and countless other headliners, including Princess Grace of Monaco and Prince Philip of Great Britain.

The man who handles luminaries like that, promotes them, helps win them awards and emblazon their names in headlines, surely would be the stereotype of a press agent—a fast-talking, wisecracking, bouncy, gaudy, stentorian pitchman. But in person, Henry Rogers belies the stereotype. He is understated in every way. He is handsome, an immaculate dresser, soft-spoken. He is thoughtful, intelligent, cultured. Among his avocations are reading (often a book a night), travel, classical music. He is also a good husband, a good father, a dependable friend. And, I repeat, the best public relations man in the entertainment world.

What makes him run—or, in his case, saunter?

Underneath, there is a man who loves his work, who loves to sell people (and shows and products). A man who, by some gift of talent or instinct, knows what the vast public—and therefore the media—wants. A man who is forthright and honest, yet a man of utmost tact, concerned for the feelings of others. He is a man of indomitable courage: he entered the communications field with a stutter, and overcame it; he went to the side of the victims of McCarthyism at the risk of his own career. If he has flamboyance, it is mental and muffled.

All of these factors have made him a success, a Gray Eminence behind the big names. Yet, I always knew there was more, and wondered what went on backstage, how he worked and achieved his triumphs in the Pygmalion profession. I always wanted him to write a book and tell it all, or at least tell a great part of it. In fact, several years ago, someone tried to write a book about him. It didn't work. I knew and Henry Rogers knew that only he could do such a book about himself and his mysterious work. And one day he did the book —did it himself—and here is that book. Now, at last, I know how public relations works, how Henry Rogers works, and now the public will know the truth about a little known, powerful field of endeavor for the very first time.

Henry Rogers's confessional will appeal to readers on three different levels.

Level one:—Great sections of this book are pure entertainment. They offer an inside glimpse at the behavior of famous persons when they think no one is looking or listening. These vignettes reveal celebrities at their best, their worst, their most human.

Level two:—The central thrust of the book is to show public relations as a force that affects the very fabric of our society.

Level three:—Finally, to a degree, this is a self-help book for anyone wishing to get into public relations or who has a nephew or niece who is eager to get into the field. Rogers tells precisely how a public relations person operates, what he or she is expected to do or should do to master the profession. I might add that many of Henry Rogers's credos and rules could be usefully followed when entering any busi-

8

ness, especially a business where communications and relationships with other people are important.

Anyway, it is all here, all the levels of interest, compressed between these book covers. And all told very personally and directly.

I will admit that what fascinated me the most were the constantly titillating, sometimes shocking glimpses—firsthand, through Henry Rogers's eyes—of certain aspects of international celebrities. Here, standing beside Henry Rogers, we see—

Rita Hayworth's husband, Edward Judson, depressed by the fact that his wife, starring in *Blood and Sand*, was having an affair with an unknown actor named Anthony Quinn. "Understand, Henry," Judson protested, "I wouldn't mind if Rita had an affair with Tyrone Power or Darryl Zanuck or someone else who could help her career, but Tony Quinn!"

Visitors to Joan Crawford's home forced to remove their shoes at the door so as not to soil her white carpets. Crawford kept a list of her planned activities for every hour of every day. On some lists she would note an hour and a half before dinner, "Time with Philip." When Rogers asked her what the notation about her current husband, Philip Terry, meant, she told him, " 'Time with Philip' is the time when we make love."

Frank Sinatra seeking advice on his bad image, and Rogers telling him he had a bad image because his behavior was outrageous and offensive—and, following that, Rogers getting fired by Sinatra.

Menachem Begin meeting with Rogers to learn how to improve his image and being told, "Don't take the advice of any American public relations expert who tries to change your image. Don't change anything. Be yourself."

Montgomery Clift lunching with Rogers—and sliding under their restaurant table in an alcoholic stupor.

Shirley MacLaine walking into the office of a Hollywood columnist who had slandered her and belting him with a right to the jaw.

The Beach Boys agreeing to hire Rogers only if he went into Transcendental Meditation. He agreed. They signed on.

Rogers ghostwriting Sheilah Graham's column when she was pregnant, having a falling out with Tony Curtis over an unpaid bill, incurring the wrath of Prince Philip of Great Britain after a successful American charity tour, helping Olivia de Havilland win a Motion Picture Academy Award.

Henry Rogers gives equal time to his promotion of products that

9

constitute the American Way of Life, products ranging from cosmetics to detergents to automobiles, and while doing this, he dissects the anatomy of public relations. As he states: "I try to influence the public on behalf of my client. I try, through the techniques I have developed over the years, through the experience I have acquired, to influence the public to buy a certain breakfast food, go to a particular movie, tune in to a particular television program, read a book, buy clothes, use certain fragrances. . . . I communicate a message to the public. Through that communication, I hope that I shall influence its behavior, its choice."

The strongest chapter in this book, to my mind, is Rogers's hard-hitting account of the relationship between the media and the public relations people. Rogers faults certain elements of the press for their dishonesty, irresponsibility, for the means they employ to mislead the public. But he is equally critical of certain members of his own peer group, those public relations people who are immoral, lacking in integrity, and who take advantage of the press.

I used to think it was love and money that made the world go round. But now, having read Henry Rogers's story, I know it is also public relations. Press agents are used by Presidents and Premiers, and an assorted number of lesser leaders in every field, to sell and manipulate the public—sometimes for the better, often for the worse.

Every reader's life, whether he or she knows it or not, is at some time dominated or directed by public relations persons in Washington, D. C., New York, Los Angeles, London, Paris, Moscow, Tokyo, Peking. For those who want to know how this hidden force affects them, affects what they like or dislike in their daily lives, this book is indispensable.

—IRVING WALLACE

Contents

CHAPTER 1

But What Do You Do?

It happens all the time. Whenever I tell people I am in the public relations business, the response is always the same. "Public relations? What do you actually *do*?"

No one ever asks a doctor what he does. They may ask him if he is an internist or a surgeon, or they might not even go that far. They may be satisfied with just the reply "I'm a doctor." No one ever asks "What is a shoemaker?" "What is a bricklayer?" "What is a dentist?" "What is an accountant?" "What is a stockbroker?" The one-word answer "I'm a bricklayer" is self-descriptive; there's no need to define his activities further.

In contrast, the term "public relations" is not easily defined, even in the field. Ask a hundred public relations men or women to define their business and you will get a hundred different answers, usually abstract or obscure. Here are just a few of them.

Public Relations News:

> Public relations is the management function which evaluates public attitudes, identifies the policies and procedures of an individual or an organization with the public interest, and plans and executes a program of action to earn public understanding and acceptance.

Dr. Rex F. Harlow, former professor at Stanford University:

> [Public relations is] a distinctive management function which helps establish and maintain mutual lines of communication, understanding, acceptance, and cooperation between an organization and its publics; involves the management in problems or issues; helps management to serve the public interest; helps management keep abreast of and effectively utilize change, serving as an early warning system to help anticipate trends; and uses research and sound and ethical communications techniques as its principal tools.

Effective Public Relations, written by Scott M. Cutlip and Allen H. Center:

> Public relations is the planned effort to influence opinion

through good character and responsible performance, based upon mutually satisfactory two-way communication.

Are you satisfied? Of course you're not. Those definitions are very difficult for a lay person to grasp. What does a public relations person do? In response, I shall tell you what this public relations man has been doing all of his adult life.

I have been in the public relations business since I was twenty-one years old. When I first started, I was in the publicity business. I was a press agent. Very simply, my job was to get the client's name in the paper. Over the years, as the business grew, as I became more worldly-wise, as my clients became more important and more sophisticated, the publicity business, the press agentry as it is also called, evolved into the public relations profession. I grew with it—a simple press agent (the middleman between my client and the press) to a public relations counselor, a practitioner, an advisor, a communicator, a marketing consultant.

Today, I communicate to the public the message that my client wishes to have communicated; I counsel with him on the best procedure to communicate that message. I try to influence the public on behalf of my client. I try, through the techniques I have developed over the years, through the experience I have acquired, to influence the public to buy a certain breakfast food, go to a particular movie, tune into a particular television program, read a book, buy clothes, use certain fragrances, attend art exhibitions, drink certain brands of whiskies and wines, and buy Swiss watches rather than Japanese watches. I communicate a message to the public. Through that communication, I hope that I shall influence its behavior, its choice. Sometimes it works. Sometimes it doesn't.

But then, you must ask, how does that differ from advertising? Aren't you describing what the advertising man does? The difference is that the advertiser pays the media to get his message into print or on the air, and the public relations man does not. A magazine is divided into editorial pages and advertising pages. The advertiser does his business with the advertising department; the public relations man does his business with the editorial department.

Each client presents a new problem, a new challenge each day. It is our responsibility to define each situation, arrive at a plan of action, come to an agreement with the client that our approach is the proper one, and proceed from there.

Paul Newman signs an agreement with Universal Pictures and it is our responsibility to make the announcement through the motion picture trade and consumer press. Pierre Cardin is about to launch a new bath powder. Before it arrives on the store shelves, photographs and press releases showing and describing the product must be placed with the fashion, beauty, fragrance, and general women's press. A new motion picture is about to open. The public must be told about it in advance through press and television coverage with the objective that the publicity will generate interest to see it. While the public relations man has been flooding the movie pages with feature material and photographs which will also stimulate interest in the film, the advertising man simultaneously has placed his advertisements in the advertising pages.

But long before the public relations man prepares his press material and approaches the media with it, problems must be faced up to and decisions made.

Will that Cutty Sark promotion we are planning help to stimulate sales in the New York metropolitan area?

Can we develop a new public relations program so as to make certain that Nina Ricci Fragrances (L'Air du Temps and Farouche) retain their leadership among French perfumes in the United States?

Will that segment we developed for the "Dinah Shore Show" where Jockey jogging clothes are featured achieve its purpose and increase the sales of our client's merchandise?

What can we do to inform the business community that Warren Avis has won the first round in his battle with David Mahoney of Norton Simon, Inc., to retain the use of his name? Warren Avis says that he is legally free to use his own name in the flower business, but Mr. Mahoney contends that when he bought Avis Rent-a-Car he bought the rights to the Avis name for all business enterprises. The courts will finally decide. Or will they? A number of well-placed articles in prestigious publications about the lawsuit may embarrass Mr. Mahoney to such an extent that he will seek settlement of the suit outside the courts. (That is what happened.)

Dr. Armand Hammer, eighty-year-old scion of Occidental Petroleum Corporation, wants to know if we can help him in his ten-year-old fight to get the Los Angeles City Council to approve oil drilling off the Pacific Coast Highway in Pacific Palisades. And if the City Council does approve, will Mayor Bradley approve or veto the bill?

How can we get the public to accept Steve McQueen as Ibsen's noble martyr in *Enemy of the People*? We know they would prefer

15

to see him in *Bullitt* or as a convict in *Papillon* but it is our responsibility to persuade them to accept Mr. McQueen as a character in an Ibsen play.

Will Jimmy Caan help promote *Comes a Horseman* since he had that argument with Alan Pakula while they were working together on the film?

Paul McCartney wants us to help him get recognition as a composer. One day his accomplishments will certainly rank with those of George Gershwin and Richard Rodgers as the work of one of the greatest composers of the twentieth century. But what can we do if McCartney won't cooperate with our plans? What do you do with a man who turns down a cover story in *Rolling Stone* because he doesn't want anything to interfere with his personal life? How do we solve the problem?

Names and companies, movie stars and movie moguls. Business executives and rock singers. Television producers and advertising sponsors of television programs. Liquor companies, perfumes, fashion. States—New York and New Jersey. Men's underwear and skincare lotions. Retail clothing stores. Record companies and bankers. All clients of Rogers & Cowan.

Rogers & Cowan is the twelfth-largest public relations firm in the United States. We are headquartered in Beverly Hills. We also have offices in New York and London. Our organization is comprised of approximately 100 public relations supervisors, account executives, secretaries, accountants, and office personnel. I am based in Beverly Hills, spend some 40 percent of my time in New York, and make two or three trips a year to our London office.

Is all this a bed of roses? Of course not. It is a series of ups and downs, highs and lows. Happy moments and frustrations. Pleased clients who become displeased the next day and fire the firm. Clients who are justifiably or unjustifiably critical, or clients who are satisfied with our services and remain satisfied for many years. And the media. Without the media, there is no public relations business. The public relations man has numerous messages he wishes to convey on behalf of his clients to many different publics—the moviegoer, the television viewer, the business executive, the financial community, the federal government, and many, many more. He cannot very well use the telephone or write an individual letter to everyone he wishes to reach. Instead, he uses the media to conduct, to transmit those messages.

But can he count on the media to convey the message? If he knows his business, in nearly every instance, the answer is yes. Since it is impossible for every newspaper, magazine, news service, television network to cover every source of news every day, they are ready and willing to hear from the reliable, experienced public relations man. Just as he is unable to reach each person who comprises the public individually, so the media is ill equipped to seek out every source of potential news. There are thousands of companies throughout the country that have earnings to report, mergers to announce, new products to bring to the attention of the public. Hundreds and thousands of federal, state, and municipal agencies have news to bring to the public and news which the public is entitled to receive. The entertainment world too generates news every day.

It is consequently impossible for the media to telephone or visit every news source every day and ask "What's new?" So the public relations man enters the picture. He sends his press releases to the media and out of the thousands of releases that pour in to the editor's desk every day, the editor decides which items are worthy of follow-up and checking through. He decides what goes into the wastebasket and what will be printed. Meanwhile, his own reporters are covering the White House, the State Department, the Governor's office, the Mayor's office, U.S. Steel, Ford and Chrysler. Gradually, through the weeding-out process, the most important news of the day is finally conveyed to the public. Maybe the public relations man has been successful in getting his story on the NBC news that day— maybe not. The final decision is in the hands of the editor, but only after the public relations man has entered the process.

In fact, few realize that the hand of the public relations man reaches onto virtually every page of any newspaper published. From page one of the *New York Times* to the cooking section of the *Long Beach Press Telegram,* to the real estate section of the *Los Angeles Times* and to the pages of *Time* and *Newsweek*, a simple investigation would reveal that a large percentage of the printed words in those and most other publications originated with a governmental press information agency, the public relations departments of our largest corporations, the White House Press Secretary, the Press Information Offices of our State Department, and a hundred other public relations sources. Each of the agencies, and each of these people are, in one way or another, in the public relations business.

The *Wall Street Journal* recently published an article about public relations men in Washington which indicates the ever-growing influence of the PR man on our society.

"They are known in the trade as 'government communicators.' They are better known around town as 'flacks.' No one knows how many government flacks there are in Washington; one estimate puts the number at 19,000, at a cost to the taxpayers of $400 million a year."

Then, just to give its readers an indication of where these estimated 19,000 public relations men work, the *Wall Street Journal* continues.

"The Transportation Department's public relations operation which costs about $8.5 million per year, isn't the biggest in Washington. That distinction probably goes to the Defense Department, which spends more than $25 million per year. The Agriculture Department at $24 million is in close pursuit. The Department of Health, Education and Welfare is a close third."

Let me not give the impression that the press accepts handouts as bona fide news. The responsible press uses the handout only as a source of information, and then develops its own story.

The influence of public relations does not begin to end with the printed media, either. Tune in the Johnny Carson show or Mike Douglas, or Dinah Shore, or "Today" or "Tomorrow," or "Good Morning America." Think for a moment as to how the guests happen to appear. Did Johnny Carson call Burt Reynolds and say, "Hi, Burt, I'm short a guest tomorrow night. Will you come on my show?" Did Burt Reynolds call Johnny and say "Johnny, old buddy boy, I have nothing to do tomorrow night. Can I come on your show?" Not likely. What is more likely is that when the time is close to the release date of Burt Reynolds's new movie, the publicity director for that movie will call the talent coordinator for the "Tonight Show," and suggest an appearance as part of the overall publicity effort on the film. The talent coordinator will check with the producer, the producer okays it and then gets the final approval from Johnny. Burt Reynolds then appears as a guest with Johnny Carson. During the course of the interview, Johnny and Burt will discuss the new movie. Here is the perfect example of how the media and public relations (in this case, the movie publicity director) work together for their mutual benefit. Johnny Carson has given his audience an amusing ten- or fifteen-minute interview. Burt Reynolds, who owns a large percentage of the profits of the movie, has an opportunity to reach millions of viewers who may well be influenced to spend four dollars the next night to see that movie. The PR man, in this case called the publicity director, has done his job well. Everyone is well served.

The individual entrepreneur—that is, the public relations man who runs his own company as compared with the man who works for a corporation or a government agency—has two major responsibilities if he is to be successful. First, he must have the ability to get clients. Second, he must have the ability to service those clients effectively, so that they remain as clients. In order to service his client effectively, the public relations man requires the cooperation of the media. In order to merit that cooperation, he must be trusted by the media. When the city editor receives a press release from a public relations man, he must have confidence in the veracity of that release. He looks at the letterhead to determine the source. If it is a reliable one, he gives it consideration. If the source has not been reliable in the past, then the press release automatically goes into the wastebasket. It is essential, therefore, that the public relations man acquire his credentials and establish his integrity, early in his career.

With the public relations man dependent upon the client for his livelihood and dependent also on the media, he finds himself serving two masters. He must. He walks on a tightrope from the moment he arrives at his office in the morning until he leaves in the evening. Walking the tightrope with the media on one side and the client on the other is one of the major problems that the public relations man faces every day.

Why the tightrope? Where is the conflict?

The media is on to a piece of news and wants to break it. The *New York Times* calls me for a confirmation. I have already discussed it with the client. It is not to his best interest to release the story right now. There is the conflict. I cannot tell the *New York Times* that they are barking up the wrong tree and that there is no story. Neither can I verify the news because the client has asked me not to. What to do? That is the dilemma of the public relations man.

The client wants us to release a story to the press which we know is not exactly true. If the story gets into print, it will be to the client's advantage. What to do? Another dilemma.

Time magazine decides to do a profile on one of our clients. The editor seeks my cooperation. The client doesn't want a profile in *Time*. He has too many skeletons in his closet, and knows they will be revealed by an investigative reporter. What to do? Problems, problems, problems.

To whom is the public relations man responsible? The most obvious answer would be the client but it is not that easy. Remember that without the cooperation of the media I will soon be out of business. The client may no longer be a client tomorrow, but the media will always be there. The answer to the question, "To whom is the public relations man responsible," is a complex one. There is no easy answer. I found mine many years ago. I decided that my responsibility must be primarily to myself. I must sleep with a clear conscience. I will not lie to the press. I will not lie to my client. I make my own decision as to what should be done. It usually involves a compromise between media and client. Then I try to convince both sides to bend a little. Sometimes I feel I must lean toward the media. Then I must try to convince the client to go along with my judgment. Or, if I lean toward the client, then the media must be convinced. Sometimes the problem is never put to bed satisfactorily. I have, over the years, lost clients because I could not convince them that they were wrong in a particular situation involving the media. There have been other instances where Rogers & Cowan has been "barred" by Associated Press, and other outlets important to us in the conduct of our business, because they objected to the way I had handled a particular situation. But, basically, if I make my own decision where there is a conflict, the odds are that the situation will eventually be resolved and both parties will be satisfied.

Media conflict is only one problem that the public relations man faces. There are many, many more. I have gone through a thousand experiences with hundreds of clients. I have conducted successful campaigns and unsuccessful campaigns. Clients have hired us and clients have fired us. Together with my partner, Warren Cowan, we built the most important public relations business in the history of Hollywood. We then expanded our business beyond the world of entertainment into the heady world of corporate and financial relations, product promotion, and various other activities that cover almost every aspect of our country's economy.

What has made us so successful? The answer is that the combination of our particular talents has made us into a formidable team. I could not have done it on my own. Warren could not have done it himself. There is an unspoken, healthy competition between us. Warren is younger than I am, and I had been in business for ten years before he went to work for me in 1945. In 1950, when the firm name was changed from Henry C. Rogers to Rogers & Cowan, I had already been in business for fifteen years. My attitude was "I'm not going to let my new young partner show me up." His attitude was "I'm going to prove that it wasn't a mistake when the name of the firm was changed." If I came to the office at eight o'clock, he would come in at 7:30. If I left at six, he would leave at seven. If I went to the office on Saturday, he would too. If he showed up on Sunday, I would be sure to be there.

The undeclared competition between us has proved to be beneficial to the clients as well as to us. We are both creative in the development of public relations programs for our clients, and they enjoy the advantages of two creative brains, instead of one. We meet to discuss a client and I throw an idea out to Warren for discussion. I say "How about this?" and describe an idea that has just come to me. "That's terrible," Warren replies. "But try this one on for size." Then it is time for his idea. I don't like it. Then we put both ideas together, juggle them around a bit, and *voilà,* we have what we were looking for.

Another reason for our success has been our willingness to break the rules. I have always been a maverick in the business and Warren never objected to my style. When I first started in business, the press agents of that day followed certain procedures, handled their clients and worked with the media in a prescribed accepted manner. I was skeptical when I examined what they were doing. I thought there must be a better way to represent a client, and that is what this book is all about.

As we developed our thinking on behalf of our clients, our reputation began to grow. Rogers & Cowan became more important than Henry Rogers on his own had ever been. Satisfied clients recommended their friends. Our clientele increased in both quantity and quality.

In the glamorous days of the fifties, we represented the most exciting and most glamorous stars of that era. Our business took us into the homes, into the studios, the private dressing rooms of Joan Crawford, Marlene Dietrich, Olivia de Havilland, Joan Fontaine, Jane Wyman, Maureen O'Hara, Anne Baxter, Bette Davis, Dick Powell, June Allyson, Frank Sinatra, Dean Martin, Danny Kaye,

Rosalind Russell, Danny Thomas, Red Skelton, Cary Grant, Sammy Davis, Jr., Shirley MacLaine, Elizabeth Taylor, Eddie Fisher, Tony Bennett, Tony Martin, Cyd Charisse, Lana Turner, and so many, many more. The representation of famous movie stars continued up through the sixties and the seventies and now, in 1980, we are still the leading firm in Hollywood. But, the late forties and the fifties were the glamour years with the true glamour stars.

It took a continuing learning process to represent Joan Crawford, Lana Turner, and the many, many others who were our clients at the time. There are no textbooks titled *How to Learn to Be a Successful Press Agent for a Successful Movie Star*. We had to learn it ourselves. We learned something from every client we represented, every press release we wrote, every encounter we experienced with the journalists of that day. It was this process of self-education, of questioning, of being a maverick in the time of conformity, that enabled us to get better and better at our job. Lawyers, doctors, and accountants learn from textbooks first, and personal experience second. We learned only from personal experience.

It was a constant learning process, and it still goes on. We are in an intensely personal, sensitive business. We deal with clients and the media every day. Each client has his own style. We must quickly size up the client and determine how we are going to deal with him on a day-to-day basis. The media we deal with is comprised of news press, television news reporters, columnists, magazine, and news-paper editors, syndicated reporters, television talk shows, radio net-works, local stations, and many other categories. Each one of them is as sensitive as our client. It is our responsibility to bring them to-gether to everyone's advantage.

For many years I have tried to write a book about my experiences in Hollywood publicity and corporate public relations. I have lived a life rich in dramatic, unique, and amusing experiences, all of which reveal the inner workings of the public relations business.

These experiences have involved some of the world's greatest celebrities, and some of the world's greatest industrial empires. I was certain that my story would be of interest to those many people who, over the years, have asked the question, "What does a public rela-tions man do?" Yet, I was unable to put the words together so that they were interesting enough to attract even my wife's attention. I was unable to find a theme, a thread, an approach, that would tie

22

together all of my experiences and my philosophy of business, into a readable book.

Then one day it came to me. Rogers & Cowan is unique in the field of public relations because of the broad diversity of our clientele. I decided that if I could explain what I had learned in creating and executing so many campaigns in so many different areas over the years, and how I had succeeded in walking the tightrope through so intensely personal a business, then surely I would create a clear view of this whole business we call public relations. While I hope my attempt answers the question, "What does a public relations man do?" I leave it to you to be the judge.

My *
value
is
variety

CHAPTER 2
How I Got to Buckingham Palace

The lobby of the Dorchester Hotel—London—4:45 P.M., November 12, 1965. I am a celebrity. I am surrounded by a half-dozen eager reporters who are plying me with questions. I try to remember all the public relations advice I have given to our celebrity clients for thirty years.

"I really can't say anything," I tell the press. "You all know the background. You printed it all in this morning's papers. I have an appointment to see him in fifteen minutes. No, I'm not sure whether I can tell you everything that happens when I get back. I'll ask him. If he says that our meeting is 'off the record,' that will be it. If he tells me there are no secrets, I'll tell you everything. Yes, I'm coming right back. I don't know how long I'll be. A half hour? An hour? I don't know. Now, if you will excuse me, I must get going. I'll see you later."

I step outside the hotel and the doorman, resplendent in green top hat, green frock coat and trousers, with gold braid on hat, coat, and trousers, opens the door of a waiting cab. I give him a shilling, step into the cab, and lean forward to the driver. "Take me to Buckingham Palace, please, the Privy Purse door."

Down Park Lane, around to the front gates of the palace where I see hordes of American tourists walking up and down in front of the fence, observing the fur-hatted sentries. A pause while the taxi driver mutters something to one of the guards. A right turn in the gravel-covered courtyard, a left turn, then another sharp left which brings us up to an unobtrusive door at the far right of the imposing-looking, centuries-old structure which has long since been the home of the kings and queens of the British Empire. The taxi stops. A uniformed guard opens the door.

"Can I help you, sir?" he asks politely.

"I'm Henry Rogers," I reply.

"Yes, Mr. Rogers, Prince Philip is expecting you."

I walk into a dimly lit, shabbily appointed ten-by-ten-foot reception room. Another uniformed guard, beribboned (World War II decorations, I surmise), is sitting behind a desk. He rises as I enter.

"Let me take your coat, sir. We'll keep it for you here nice and tidy until after your meeting. Please sit down and I'll have Mr. Thomas take you to his Highness's office." I allow him to help me off with my coat, sit down in a straight-backed chair and look around me. Old sporting prints decorate the walls. A small Victorian desk, not in particularly good repair, a well-worn chair, a two-seated threadbare velour upholstered piece, the room lit only by a low-hanging brass chandelier with twenty-watt bulbs. It is dim, but warm, comfortable. In a moment, before I have a chance to gather my thoughts, another uniformed gentleman, Mr. Thomas, enters the reception room. "Come with me, Mr. Rogers. I'll show you to Prince Philip's office."

We leave the reception room and enter what appears to be an interminably long hallway. I walk alongside my escort. I am in Buckingham Palace. I am on my way to meet Prince Philip to discuss plans for his historic goodwill trip to the United States.

Years before, the scene I have just described would have been a dream, not a reality—or the high point of my career. Indeed I viewed it as such, not from the standpoint of financial reward but in the contrast it presented between Henry Rogers, public relations man walking into Buckingham Palace, and Henry Rogers, the kid from Irvington, New Jersey, who thought he was destined to run his father's dry goods store on Springfield Avenue.

I had been in a royal palace before. My wife Roz and I had been entertained by Prince Rainier and Princess Grace at their palace in Monaco. I had made arrangements with their Paris public relations representative, Nadia Lacoste, to meet with the Prince about the premiere of *Kings Go Forth,* a United Artists movie which starred Frank Sinatra, one of my clients. We had discussed with Frank and the UA executives an idea which would launch the international promotion campaign for the film by staging the world premiere in connection with Princess Grace's annual Red Cross Ball. Would Frank sing at the ball if Princess Grace agreed to show the film to hundreds of her famous guests just prior to the ball? If he would, we knew that we could get tremendous worldwide publicity coverage for *Kings Go Forth.* Frank agreed. Now we must fit the other side into place. I had contacted Nadia, who received a tentative approval from Prince Rainier. She suggested that I come to Monaco and meet with the Prince, give him all the information firsthand, and work out the details with him. I expected to meet with him in his office. When we checked into the Hotel de Paris in Monte Carlo, a message was waiting. Would Mr. Rogers please meet the Prince and Princess at their apartment in the palace for tea and would Mrs. Rogers please join them? We certainly would.

On our arrival at the palace we were escorted to the private apartment of the Grimaldis and once there ushered into a cozy sitting room, where the Prince, dressed informally in slacks, a short-sleeved sports shirt, and espadrilles, and his beautiful wife, the former Grace Kelly, dressed equally informally in white slacks and blouse, rose to greet us. Handshakes all around. We were invited to be seated. The door opened and the butler walked in, a striking Nubian black, wearing a green satin jacket, a ruffled shirt, white satin knickers, white stockings, and black patent-leather shoes with silver buckles. I could only surmise that his costume was traditional and had been worn in the palace by other such servants for hundreds of years. The butler opened a bottle of champagne, poured a glass for each of us, and then left. We were not to have tea after all.

After the usual amenities of polite conversation, we got around to talking business. I outlined my plans. They were in general accord. By that time our champagne glasses were empty. The Prince stood up, walked over to the bar table, picked up the bottle, and refilled all the glasses. We had been there for an hour and I began to feel that we were overstaying our welcome. They had been very gracious, and I told them I thought we should be leaving. The butler magically appeared again and we said our good-byes.

Buckingham Palace was different, Prince Philip was different. Monaco seemed like a fairy tale; Buckingham Palace was real. Here I was right in the middle of London, surrounded by ten million people. This was the heart of what had been for hundreds of years the British Empire. I walked through the darkened halls, and as I looked at the oil portraits of kings and queens of the past lining the walls, I thought, *I wish my father could see me now*.

Thirty years before, I was about to have my twenty-first birthday. I had just asked my father to loan me $500 so that I could go into the publicity business.

"Of course I'll loan you $500 to go into business, but why the publicity business?" he asked. "I can understand the real estate business or the insurance business, but publicity—what is that?" My father was puzzled.

26

I was barely twenty-one years old. My only experience in publicity had been as an office boy for six months.

I explained it to him as best I could. "In Hollywood, there are actors, actresses, and directors, writers and producers who are all trying to make it big in the movie business. Everyone wants to better himself and get recognition for himself so that he can get a better job and make more money. One way of getting yourself better known is to get your name in the papers. The bosses read the papers, and read the client's name in the paper. This impresses them, and because of that, the theory is that their careers will be helped."

"Does it work?" my father asked.

"I don't know," I replied, "but I worked for a woman who makes a nice living because her clients believe it works, and there are quite a few other people in the publicity business in Hollywood who do very well too. I guess it must work."

"Let me get this straight," he queried. "Are you telling me that people will pay you money—good money—to get their names in the paper?"

There was a pause. "Yes," I answered. "It wasn't that way back in Irvington, but that's the way it is in Hollywood. Yes, people will pay me to get their names in the paper."

My family had arrived in Los Angeles some ten months before. The Depression of the early thirties had changed all our lives. My three sisters, father, mother, and I had lived in Irvington, New Jersey. My father had owned a dry goods store in that town of fifty thousand, and I was destined to take over and run that store when my father retired. I was sent to the Wharton School of Finance and Commerce at the University of Pennsylvania in Philadelphia to learn the retailing business. My life was all laid out for me—the thought of leaving Irvington and living anywhere else had never even occurred to me. But two and a half years into my degree at Penn, hard times began to affect us. My family could no longer afford to send me away to school. In January 1934, I left Penn and enrolled in night classes at New York University's School of Commerce, on the Washington Square Campus.

Five days a week I worked in our dry goods store, the establishment that was tied to my destiny. At 5 P.M. I took a bus from Irvington Center to the Hudson Tube Station in Newark; the tube in turn took me to the Ninth Street Station in New York City. From there a four-block walk brought me to Washington Square. A quick sandwich, classes from seven to ten, and then back home by midnight.

When the semester was over, I was able to get a nonpaying job as a counselor at Camp Cobbosee in Maine. That summer my father went bankrupt. On October 1, 1934, mother, father, two sisters, and I left for Los Angeles to join my older sister who had moved there with her lawyer husband two years before.

I did not want to finish my fourth year of college and earn my degree. I felt an obligation to take some of the financial burden off my father by supporting myself. A few months after our arrival, after having tried unsuccessfully to get a job as a salesman at May Company, Bullock's, Robinson's, and a number of men's specialty shops, I was hired by Grace Nolan, a Hollywood press agent, to be an office boy. At the time my sister, Estelle, was working for her as a secretary, and one day I got the job by pure chance. My salary was five dollars a week, and I was twenty years old.

It was my responsibility to read the papers, and clip out any items that appeared on Grace Nolan's clients. Every afternoon I drove Miss Nolan's car to downtown Los Angeles where I would deliver the press releases she had written on her clients to the movie columnists who worked at the *Times*, the *Herald*, the *Express*, the *Post*, and the *Daily News*. Then I would make a quick stop at the *Hollywood Citizen News* on Ivar Avenue and back to the office. We worked 5½ days a week. On Saturday morning, I would take the bus from our home in the Fairfax-Olympic area to Hollywood, pick up Grace Nolan's car, drop off the usual press releases at the downtown papers, leave the car at the office, take the bus home, and play tennis in the afternoon.

During the day, in addition to my messenger chores, I was teaching myself to write publicity copy. It came easily to me. When I was in high school, I was a member of the press club and reported Irvington High School athletic events to the *Irvington Herald*. At college, I prepped for the *Daily Pennsylvanian*, the university's newspaper. It was not difficult for me to adapt my reportorial style to Hollywood gossip columns and movie trade papers. It was a far cry from the dry goods business, and it was readily apparent that Hollywood held something more for me than had Irvington.

I was doing very well. After three months, Mrs. Nolan gave me an increase from five to twelve dollars a week. Even though I was just an office boy, I had already decided that publicity was going to be my career. Clients would come up to see Mrs. Nolan and she would introduce them to me. I remember Cesar Romero, a new actor in Hollywood at that time, shaking my hand one day and saying "Good luck, young man. Work hard and you'll make it big one day." I was thrilled. He was a genuine movie star.

I began to meet people in the movie business. Grace Nolan had an aged aunt, Grace Kingsley, who had just retired as movie critic and columnist for the *Los Angeles Times*. She must have been at least seventy years old. Though retired, she still wrote free-lance articles for the *Times*, and consequently was still invited to the movie premieres, the nightclub openings, and the big parties as well. One day soon after I started my job, Mrs. Nolan asked me if I minded taking her aunt to the Guy Lombardo opening at the Coconut Grove. "Would I mind!" Of course not. It was the biggest social event of the year. I picked up "Aunt Grace" in the family Buick and attended my first glamorous Hollywood opening.

I walked into the world-famous Coconut Grove in the Ambassador Hotel. I couldn't believe that I was actually there. When I went to Irvington High School and later to the University of Pennsylvania, I would put my homework aside to listen to the radio. The announcer would say, "And now, directly from the world-famous Coconut Grove in the Ambassador Hotel in Los Angeles, Guy Lombardo and his Royal Canadians." Then came the familiar sounds of the romantic music of Guy Lombardo.

And now here I was, in the Coconut Grove. The maître d' recognized Grace Kingsley. She introduced me to him. He looked briefly at me—just another young man, an unknown, escorting a former critic to an opening. There must have been many before me. But I didn't care. I was almost twenty-one years old and I was being shown to a ringside table, one of the best in the house. Grace Kingsley still commanded respect among the head waiters who remembered her in her days of fame and glory. As we approached the table, the other guests stood to greet us. If I was a "nobody" then, they were truly the most beautiful young people in the world of that day. Tom Brown, Anita Louise, Patricia Ellis, and Johnny Downs are the names I remember. I was introduced as "Henry Rogers, my niece Grace Nolan's new business associate."

I looked around me. It was hard to believe. Joan Crawford was dancing with Franchot Tone. There were Carole Lombard and George Raft, Norma Shearer, Wallace Beery, Dick Powell, and Joan Blondell.

Most of the names are now forgotten. In 1935 they were the biggest stars in the world.

Late one Saturday afternoon I returned home to a disastrous piece of news, reported to me by my mother. I had inadvertently put Miss Nolan's car keys in my pocket instead of leaving them in the car. As a result my boss couldn't keep an appointment with a prospective client in Santa Monica. She was furious, and I was fired.

Even though I had just lost my job, my resolve to become a Hollywood press agent was stronger than ever. Easier said than done. It was the Depression, I had just turned twenty-one, and my only job experience was that of office boy. There were six well-established Hollywood publicity firms at the time and when I approached each of them for a job I was turned down. I was not very impressive in an interview, owing to a speech defect I had had since the age of five. I stuttered badly. Both in high school and college, my grades did not reflect my IQ. On innumerable occasions I had shaken my head and not answered when the teacher had asked me a question. Even though I knew the answer, I would say "I don't know" because I was afraid to stand up, stutter, and make a fool of myself in front of my fellow students. As a result, life for me had been one moment of anguish after the next.

Years later, a distinguished speech therapist gave me his analysis of my stuttering and its source. I had been born left-handed, but forced by my mother and teachers to use my right. As I grew up, I picked things up with my left hand and wrote with my right. Playing baseball, I threw with my left hand and batted right-handed. I was ambidextrous, but I was the victim of the ignorance of my time. My parents and teachers thought that there was something abnormal and shameful about being left-handed, and the speech therapist theorized that this had set up a psychological block. It was this block that had caused my stuttering.

I could speak fairly well under normal circumstances, but I naturally got nervous at a job interview. Any twenty-one-year-old gets nervous in such a situation. My mouth closed shut. My jaws locked. My eyes closed. It was agony to get the words out. Prospective employers were sympathetic, but there were no jobs for me.

I still wanted to be a Hollywood press agent, even if I couldn't get a job. I realized there was only one answer: I would go into business for myself, stuttering and all.

I formulated a budget. I knew that $500 could hold me for six months. Office rent and telephone costs would be minimal, and I did not plan to hire a secretary until I could afford one. My day-to-day business expenses would be insignificant. Since I lived at home with my family, I would not have to worry about rental fees for an apartment. In six months' time, I should be able to generate sufficient income to support myself. It was that plan which I had proposed to my father and he was considering it.

Very patiently and sensitively he said, "I still don't understand why anyone will pay you to put his name in the paper, but I'll accept your word on that. But what are you going to do about your stuttering? You know how difficult it is for you to talk, particularly with strangers. You know that you have a psychological problem in answering the telephone—or even in picking up a phone to call someone."

I did not know how to answer him, because I knew my father had asked a logical question.

"I d-d-d-on't know," I replied. "All I ccc-an do is try. I'm n-n-not going to s-s-sit home and worry about it all m-m-my life. I'll just have to f-f-ight it through."

A few minutes later he wrote out a check for $500. Three days after that, I put a one-inch ad in *Daily Variety* and the *Hollywood Reporter*. It ran as follows:

HENRY C. ROGERS
announces the opening of his
Publicity offices at
6605 Hollywood Boulevard, Hollywood, California
Phone HO 9-6146

I was in the publicity business. I had a one-room office on Hollywood Boulevard which I shared with another press agent, Hal Weiner. We paid twenty dollars a month rent—ten dollars each. I sat at my desk waiting for the telephone to ring, for Hollywood to break down my door. I sat for one day. Two days. On the third day, the telephone rang. It was Joe Fine, Advertising Director of *Daily Variety*. I had placed my four-dollar ad directly with him.

"Henry," he said, "I have a client for you." I could scarcely believe it. Now I was really in business.

The client was the dance team of Kirby and De Gage, who had just finished appearing in a dance sequence in a Warner Brothers musical. They believed that if they hired a Hollywood press agent

31

they would be on their way to stardom and to achieve it paid me fifteen dollars a week. My job was to get their names placed in the Hollywood columns and trade papers, on the theory that mention of their names in print would remind producers and directors and casting directors of their recent Warner Brothers assignment, and that when their agent went in to try to get them another job, the publicity would have made the potential employer more amenable to their cause.

Three weeks elapsed. I was working industriously for Kirby and De Gage, but they had not yet paid me.

My father said, "Are you sure you want to be in the publicity business? You've been working for three weeks on those dancers and they haven't paid you anything yet. When are you going to get your money?"

"I don't know, Pop," I replied. "They finished their movie at Warner Brothers and now they're working at the Agua Caliente Hotel in *Tijuana*—that's across the Mexican border near San Diego."

My father thought for a minute.

"I don't know anything about your business, but I do know human nature. Your clients will never get around to paying you unless you keep after them. Let's all go to *Tijuana* on Sunday. We'll have lunch there and you can see your clients and collect the money they owe you."

This seemed to me like a good idea. I agreed to it. On Sunday morning, father, mother, sister Estelle, sister Lillian, and I piled into the family car and drove to the Agua Caliente Hotel. It was a magnificent Mexican hacienda-style hotel, with red-tiled roof, dark-stained tile floors, Spanish colonial furniture, large, lazily turning fans overhead, the discreet click of a roulette ball falling into place emanating from a small gaming room off the lobby, and a bougainvillaea-covered outdoor dining area where we decided to eat our lunch. A moment after we ordered, there was the blare of a trumpet and a troupe of mariachi musicians came out to play the inevitable "La Golondrina." Then, preceded by another blare of the trumpet, Kirby and De Gage—*direct from Hollywood*—ran out on the floor and began to dance right in front of our very eyes. It was an exciting moment for me. They were my clients, my very first clients. They spotted me and smiled. Sister Estelle leaned over in my direction and whispered, "Gee, I'm impressed. They really know you." I was impressed too. I was really in the publicity business, involved in the

32

world of entertainment, and here I was sitting at the world-famous Agua Caliente Hotel, watching my very own clients.

After the show I went backstage to greet them. They were delighted that I had driven down to see them and congratulated me on the fine job I had been doing. Then Kirby said, "By the way, Henry, I owe you some money. Here it is." He handed me forty-five dollars in cash. It was a dramatic moment for me. This was the first money I had earned in the publicity business.

I went back to the table, and proudly showed the money to my family. They were all as proud of me as I was. As we strolled through the lobby after lunch, we heard the clicking once more of the roulette ball, and sounds that were obviously coming from a craps table.

"Let's stop in here for a minute," said my father. "I'd like to take a look at what's going on."

Fifteen minutes later we finally left the hotel, dejected and morose. My father had lost fifty dollars, and I had lost the forty-five Kirby had just given me.

As I started up the car, my father, who was sitting next to me, turned and said, "Are you really sure that the publicity business is for you? This would never have happened if you had gone into the insurance business."

I looked at him. We both started to laugh.

"Don't worry, Pop," I said. "I'll get it back. There are other people who will soon be paying me forty-five dollars for three weeks' work."

Kirby and De Gage did not last very long as clients. At best, they were mediocre nightclub dancers, and the publicity I got for them did not enhance their careers. I was not off to a very auspicious start.

In 1937, I married Rosalind. I was twenty-three, she a few years younger. By that time, my income had jumped astronomically to seventy-five dollars a week, even with my stutter. I handled actors, actresses, nightclubs, and restaurants. I was paid by each client a fee of ten dollars, sometimes fifteen dollars a week. Marc Lawrence paid me fifteen dollars a week when he was working and ten dollars a week when he wasn't. The trouble was that he never worked, so he never paid me. The fees I was able to command inched up gradually, twenty-five dollars, thirty-five dollars, then fifty dollars a week. The progress was slow, but I felt that I was advancing.

The stuttering was increasingly proving to be a problem. In order to get new clients, it was necessary for me to meet new people. In order to meet new people, it was necessary for me to call them on the telephone. I was terrified of the telephone. When the phone rang on the other end and a voice said "Who's calling please?", I was in trouble, I couldn't say Henry. I would say "H-H-H-H-H" and then came a long gasp. Somehow I couldn't get the H-H-H-H over to the *en*. It always seemed an interminable length of time before I got to H-H-H-H-*en*. Once I got there, the *ry* was easy and the R-R-R*ogers* flowed relatively well. Often, by the time that what I felt was minutes—more likely seconds—had elapsed before I was able to tell the person at the other end of the phone my name, he would have hung up. Then I would start all over again. I used a lot of underarm deodorant—I sweated a lot. When I finished a conversation on the telephone, not only was my shirt dripping wet but the telephone and my hand were soaking wet as well. I used up a lot of handkerchiefs in those days.

In 1939, I met Rita Hayworth. She changed my life. If it had not been for her, now, twenty-six years later, I would not have been walking down that long corridor, deep in the recesses of Buckingham Palace, on my way to meet with Prince Philip to plan an historic goodwill trip that would take us to Miami, Houston, Palm Springs, Los Angeles, Chicago, and New York. But, more on that later. First things first.

CHAPTER 3
Rita Hayworth Makes Me a Star

Every man can look back and pinpoint the turning point in his life when fate stepped in and set him on the path which determined his future. Fortunate is that man who is set on the path to success— and stays on it.

In 1939 Roz and I would pass the time by playing in a five- and ten-cent poker game. One day Rita Hayworth and her husband, Eddie Judson, joined the game. She was eighteen or nineteen, a Mexican nightclub dancer, recently put under contract to Columbia Pictures, and married to a man much older than she. Rita was ambitious, but Eddie was *fiercely* ambitious for her. They both wanted her to become a movie star, and both were worried about her career. Although she was under contract to Columbia, the studio had done very little with her. Her option was coming up shortly, and they were concerned that the option would be dropped. They thought that the twenty-five-year-old publicity man, Henry Rogers, whom they had met through some mutual friends at that poker game one night, might be able to impress on her own studio and other studios as well, that here was a beautiful and talented young lady who deserved recognition.

Rita could not afford to pay me a normal fee, so we worked out a deal where I would receive 5 percent of her income. We signed a three-year contract. She received $300 a week, so I was to receive $15 a week from her earnings.

I had no idea what was about to happen. I did not realize that fate was about to change my life and hers. I wish I could say now that when I signed my contract with Rita Hayworth, I knew one day she would become a big star. I wish I could say that in 1939 I told Rita Hayworth that if she put herself in my capable hands, I would build her from comparative obscurity to the most talked-about woman on earth. It wasn't so.

Rita had just finished a picture with Howard Hawks and Cary Grant, titled *Only Angels Have Wings*. She had a comparatively small role in that picture, and no one expected that anything would come of her appearance in it. Eddie Judson was Svengali to Rita's Trilby, and we decided that we had to do something dramatic, something

35

exciting, that would make movie producers aware of her. One day Eddie started talking to me about Rita's clothes, and how important he felt a dramatic wardrobe was for the success of an actress. From this discussion, I developed an idea.

I took my idea to Gene Herrick, West Coast Editor of *Look*.

"Gene," I said, "I have a very exciting idea for you. Rita Hayworth—"

"Who?" he asked.

"Rita Hayworth," I continued, "is an actress at Columbia who receives a salary of $15,000 a year. She spends every cent of it on clothes. She is comparatively unknown here in Hollywood, and yet her wardrobe ranks beyond that of any of the big stars. Her wardrobe is fabulous because she feels that being well dressed is one of the most important things a girl can do in her struggle to become a big star.

"Interestingly enough," I continued, "her wardrobe is already gaining recognition because she has just won an award." I took a telegram out of my pocket and showed it to him. It was addressed to Rita Hayworth at Columbia Studios, Hollywood, California. The telegram was signed by Jackson Carberry, President of the Fashion Couturiers Association of America.

The telegram said that members of the group had been polled, and the poll revealed that they had just voted Carole Lombard the best-dressed on-screen actress, and Rita Hayworth the best-dressed off-screen actress.

Everything I told Gene Herrick was a lie. Rita Hayworth didn't spend $15,000 on her wardrobe. She did not have a fabulous wardrobe. The telegram was written by me and sent to Rita at the studio. There was no such person as Jackson Carberry. There was no such fashion group. I had made it all up.

Gene Herrick liked my idea. I convinced him that Rita Hayworth was a beautiful girl, that her clothes were magnificent, that the story angle was good, and that it would make an exciting feature for one of his upcoming issues. He was convinced, and immediately assigned his top photographer, Earl Theisen, to shoot the layout I had described.

Now came the problem. Where could we get the clothes for the "fabulous wardrobe"? Eddie Judson and I scurried around town borrowing the clothes. We borrowed from Hollywood designers, department stores, and specialty shops. By the time Earl Theisen arrived at the modest bungalow on Veteran Avenue in Westwood, where the Judsons lived, Rita Hayworth actually had a "fabulous" wardrobe.

Earl Theisen shot hundreds and hundreds of pictures. At one point, he said, "I have an idea for a shot that might be a cover possibility." He had Rita do her hair in Spanish style and bare her shoulders, put Rhumba gourds in her hands, and had her strike an exotic flamenco pose.

Some six weeks later, Rita Hayworth was on the cover of *Look*. The magazine carried ten pages' worth of photographs of the fabulous wardrobe of the Hollywood actress who spent all of her $15,000 yearly salary on clothes. The cover and the layout became a sensation in Hollywood. Everyone began to talk about her. Rita was on her way to becoming a star. As a result, Columbia Pictures picked up her option.

I have often been asked whether I have a guilty conscience about lying to Gene Herrick. The answer is "No." My lie, or series of lies, really didn't hurt anyone. If Gene Herrick had found me out at the time, he would have been furious and barred me from his office. But I had nothing to lose. I was young and struggling. None of my other clients were important enough to get into *Look* anyway.

I have also been asked "How would you have handled the Gene Herrick matter if you had a chance to do it all over again?" Taking into the consideration the times (1939), my age (twenty-five), my experience (four years), and the quality of press agentry that was practiced in Hollywood at the time, I would, given a second chance, have done exactly the same!

But I wouldn't do it today, even if I were twenty-five years old, and had only four years' experience in the business. We live in a different world. All our standards are different, some better, some worse, but certainly different. The standards of journalism are different as are the standards of press agentry. We live in a more sophisticated world, and both the journalist and the press agent are more sophisticated. Today Gene Herrick would put a telephone call through to Jackson Carberry, President of the Fashion Couturiers Association of America. Quickly discovering that no such person or organization existed, Henry Rogers would have been brought to task by the sophisticated editor, and it is doubtful that their association would have continued from the time that the hoax was revealed.

But there is another difference today. Even the experienced press agent would cover his tracks. He would never put himself in the position of being caught in an apparent lie. He would not try to make up news, concoct it, dream it up and invent it out of pure imagination. Instead, he would actually go out and *make* the news. Starting with the same idea that I had, he would find an organization and a president of an organization who will lend himself to the idea, because he is looking for publicity for himself and his organization. The press agent would convince the president that the publicity coverage will be as beneficial for him and his organization as it will be for Rita Hayworth. The first organization may turn him down, as will the second. Eventually someone will decide to go along. Then the press agent makes his move. The telegram is sent from the fashion organization to the starlet. News is officially out and the press agent now relays it to the editor's desk, inviting the editor to call the president of the organization for verification. The editor will probably do just that. He will receive verification and hopefully run the story. That is the way Hollywood press agentry is practiced today.

The *Look* cover and ten-page layout was the beginning of a tremendous publicity campaign. The Columbia publicity department saw that Rita Hayworth had caught the imagination of the press and they jumped on the bandwagon. Rita, Eddie, and I worked closely together, trying to think up ideas to submit to the columnists. Every day Louella Parsons, Jerry Starr, Harrison Carroll, Read Kendall, Edwin Martin, and the gossip columns of *Hollywood Reporter* and *Daily Variety* would receive items from me about Rita Hayworth. The movie magazines, very powerful in those days, began to run stories, articles, and covers on Rita Hayworth, Hollywood's new glamour queen. Ann Sheridan, Warner Brothers "Oomph Girl," was filmland's number one sex queen in those days, but Rita Hayworth was moving up quickly on the outside, as they say in horse-track parlance. Then came the clincher. *Life* became interested in Rita. Maggie Maskell, in charge of magazine publicity for Columbia Pictures at that time, came up with the idea of posing Rita in a black and white, lace and satin nightgown. We were at the Judson house, shooting "Rita Hayworth at Home," when the photographer said, "Rita, get on the bed— yes—on top of the bed cover—get on your knees, give your body a half profile to the camera, and give me a provocative look." Rita, always willing to comply, jumped on the bed, and struck the proper pose as Maggie, Ed, and I stood by watching. Click, click, click, went the camera. Three weeks later the photo was on the cover of *Life*—and Rita became the pinup girl for millions of American service men all over the world. Rita Hayworth had become a star.

It wasn't the publicity alone. While all this was happening, Harry Cohn, President of Columbia Pictures, could see that he had a potential gold mine in Rita.

Although she was still under contract to Columbia, Warner Brothers hired her to costar with Ann Sheridan in *Strawberry Blonde*. Twentieth Century-Fox hired her to costar with Tyrone Power in *Blood and Sand*, a bullfighter epic featuring a relatively unknown actor named Anthony Quinn.

Three years elapsed, and my contract expired. Miss Hayworth, still under contract to Columbia on an old seven-year agreement, was by this time still making only $600 a week. My income from this one client had jumped 100 percent to an astronomical thirty dollars a week. Fortunately, I was not entirely dependent on her. I had other clients.

Rita and Eddie decided not to renew my contract. They appreciated everything I had done, but I was no longer needed. She had become a star, and the Columbia Studios publicity department was geared to the continued buildup of one of their most important properties. A staff of publicists in Hollywood and New York were pounding their typewriters to help build what was to become one of the greatest of all Hollywood legends. My friends were deeply resentful that Rita had not signed another three-year contract. I was too, although I put up a good front. "What the hell," I would say, "maybe I did help her become a star, but she made me a star, so I have nothing to complain about." It was a cover-up. I was deeply hurt. I had done my job, and at the peak I had received thirty dollars a week for my efforts. I reasoned that if Rita had kept me on for another three years, I would have eventually received $150 or $200 a week, which was enormous money in those early days. Although she had no legal obligations to me, I felt that she had a moral one. In contrast her attitude was "We made a three-year deal in good faith and we both lived up to the agreement. I don't owe him anything." From her standpoint she was right.

That all happened in the years 1939 to 1942. Rita Hayworth went on to become one of the most famous movie stars in the world. After Edward Judson, she married two of the world's most prominent and desirable men, first Orson Welles and then Aly Khan. There were others after that. Rita Hayworth has had more than the usual share of torment and unhappiness in recent years, and I think I know why. In those early years of her career, Rita was in the ruthless hands of Edward Judson who exploited her unmercifully. I have no doubt that such treatment had an adverse effect on her entire life. I was there, and I saw what was happening to Rita. Two incidents will give you an indication of their life together in those days.

One day Eddie came into the offices with a dejected look on his face. He said, "You know, Henry, that Rita has just started to work on *Blood and Sand*."

"Yes, I know. How is it going?" I replied.

"Well, the picture has scarcely started and Rita is already having an affair with Tony Quinn."

I was shocked. A man telling another man that his wife was having an affair was not something to be taken lightly in 1940.

"Eddie, that's ridiculous," I replied. "You have been listening to idle gossip. Who told you silly drivel like that?"

"She did," said the cuckolded husband. "You must understand, Henry, I wouldn't mind if Rita had an affair with Tyrone Power or Darryl Zanuck or someone else who could help her career, but Tony Quinn!!!!"

It seemed to me Eddie would have sold his wife to the highest bidder if it would have enhanced her career.

It was only a few months after that that Eddie came to see me again. "Henry," he said, "I need your advice. You know that Rita's option is coming up at Columbia. Everything seems to be going nicely but I'm not sure that Harry Cohn is going to exercise that option. He invited us to spend the weekend on his yacht. He said we would all take a cruise to Catalina. What would you think if I took conveniently ill just before we were ready to leave? Then I would insist that Rita go alone. If Rita and Harry Cohn spent the weekend together, there is no doubt that he would exercise her option for another year."

I advised him not to get conveniently ill and that he should accompany his wife on the yacht. I told him that Rita had already displayed enough talent and that her career was moving ahead quickly enough. She didn't have to sleep with producers to get ahead. I never asked whether Rita went on that weekend trip alone or with her husband. The fact is that her option was picked up and she went on to great fame.

Once Rita received the opportunity there was no stopping her. Her unique glamour lit up the screen. If you have ever seen Rita on late-night television in *Gilda*, if you ever saw her dance with Fred

Astaire and Gene Kelly in some of her memorable films, you know that somehow or other, with or without Henry Rogers or Eddie Judson, she was destined to make it big.

It is most likely that she would have become an important star even if she had never met me. It is also possible that I would have achieved the same level of success if I had never represented her. It is a fact, however, that we met at the beginning of our respective careers, and each was able to make a contribution to the other at a time when help was needed.

There were those who said then that I had made Rita Hayworth a star. I always denied that. I gave her a little push. I started the ball rolling. But there have been literally hundreds of other men and women in Hollywood over the years who have had big publicity buildups at one point or another in their careers. The publicity never helped them to achieve real stardom because they never had the talent, or the indefinable magic that marks a star. Rita had the talent, the magic, the spark. If I hadn't started the ball rolling, then it would have started to roll by itself. I am convinced of that.

What about me? What did she do for me? She, without knowing it, gave me the push when I needed it most. I had been struggling in the publicity business for some four years. I was one of the many young men who were trying to make their mark in Hollywood in this field. It was difficult for me to make an impact when I represented restaurants, nightclubs, struggling actors and actresses who didn't have that magic, and consequently never could make it big. Fortunately, for me, some of Rita's magic spilled over onto me. Suddenly it was Rita Hayworth, movie star. Rita Hayworth appearing in films with Cary Grant and Tyrone Power and James Cagney. The obscure nightclub dancer, Rita Cansino, almost overnight became the talk of Hollywood. "How did it happen?" they asked. Then came the speculation. "I hear that young fellow, Henry Rogers, is her press agent," said someone. I became associated with a Hollywood phenomenon. Suddenly people knew who I was. Suddenly the name Henry Rogers became recognized. Maybe it would have happened without her. I'll never know. I do know that Rita Hayworth made me a star.

CHAPTER 4

And Then Came Claudette Colbert

No one makes it alone. Everyone needs help. There are those to whom help comes automatically, but there are others who realize that they must seek it out and take advantage of it when it finally comes.

If I had not been playing in that poker game with some friends, I would never have met Rita Hayworth. It readily became apparent to me that the key to success was to meet as many people as possible in the movie business, to broaden my scope of acquaintances.

But how does an ambitious young man with only a Rita Hayworth to his credit get to meet a movie star, no less represent her or him as a press agent? One doesn't just telephone Clark Gable or Cary Grant and say, "Hello, I'm Henry Rogers. You don't know me, but I'd like to be your press agent."

The stuttering would come and go. If I could remain calm, I could carry on a conversation with a prospective client or a business associate and he would never know that I had a problem. As a teenager, I had found a speech therapist who had helped me. His treatment involved utilizing a pattern of breathing which maintained the flow of sound coming out of my mouth by starting each phrase with a long "u-u-u-h-h-h." By starting with this unintelligible sound, it was easier to get the first syllable of the first word started. If I used that method, I could speak fluently, although it did sound peculiar. The problem would come when I anticipated a word which I knew I couldn't say. If I were forced to say "lily of the valley" I knew I was in trouble. I knew damn well I couldn't say "lily," and as the word drew closer and closer, I would try to think of another word to take its place. A rose is a rose is a rose but it ain't no lily, and when that fatal word finally arrived, I was the proverbial dead duck. I would say "l-l-l-l-l" but I couldn't cross the bridge between the "l" and the "ily." It was hell but I toughed it out.

I knew that I had to meet new people, stuttering or not. I found that getting in through the back door was the answer. I could not go directly to the movie star but I could go to his agent, his business manager, his lawyer. He was the person who knew whether Mr. or

Miss Movie Star was dissatisfied with his publicity and might be interested in discussing the subject with a young, ambitious publicity man. The next step was—how would I meet the lawyer, the agent, the business manager?

I learned that one contact opened the door to the next. One agent, if he liked me and respected me, would introduce me to his friend, the business manager, whose office was down the hall. So it was that Rita Hayworth's agent, Tom Somlyo, introduced me to Claudette Colbert's agent, Charles Wendling, who also happened to be her brother.

At that time, Claudette Colbert was recognized as the highest-paid actress in Hollywood. In 1934 she had won the Academy Award for her performance in *It Happened One Night* and then went on to even greater fame with such films as *Since You Went Away, Skylark, Arise My Love*, and many, many more. Now, in 1940, she told her brother that the time had come for her to hire a press agent. Claudette Colbert, at the height of her career, was worried. Under long-term contract to Paramount Pictures, she was about to start her first film away from her home studio. She had just signed an agreement with MGM to costar with Clark Gable, Spencer Tracy, and Hedy Lamarr in *Boom Town*. She was concerned that the MGM publicity department would be devoting its attentions to her costars for the simple reason that they were each under contract to Leo the Lion. Claudette worked for the competitor on the other side of town. Would she be ignored in the publicity campaign on the film?

Charlie Wendling agreed with his sister that there was cause for concern. He told Claudette that he had met a young man named Henry Rogers a few weeks before. Perhaps she had heard of him— the one who had done that fabulous publicity job on Rita Hayworth. Yes, she had heard of him. Yes, she would like to meet him.

Claudette lived with her husband, Dr. Joel Pressman, in a magnificent "movie star" home on Faring Road in Holmby Hills—a Los Angeles suburb a few minutes from Beverly Hills. I often pass that home now and vividly recall the day I first stood at the front door, pressing the door bell, nervously awaiting a response. A white-jacketed butler received me and showed me into my first movie star's home. Even then I knew the difference between good taste, bad taste, and no taste, and it was readily apparent that I had entered the home of a tasteful lady. Later I discovered that the home had been decorated by William Haines, a former silent movie star who had turned his talents to decorating. His style was a contemporary one, and he had a way of fitting the decor and furnishings to his client's taste and personality. In the case of Miss Colbert's home, he had succeeded in spades. The tasteful lady walked into the tastefully decorated drawing room and gave me a warm greeting, extending her hand and then offering me tea.

Her graciousness put me at ease. I knew that I would stutter very little, if at all. She sat back in her chair, looked at me, smiled, and said, "Charles says you are the new bright young man on the block. If you're the one who is responsible for all the publicity I've been reading about Rita Hayworth, then he must be right."

I smiled and modestly told her that it had all been a team effort. Having dispensed with the preliminaries, Claudette got down to business. "Charles has told you of my problem. What do you think you can do for me?" she asked.

I had done my homework. I had checked back over the newspaper and magazine files, had talked to journalist friends, and knew how to reply.

"Miss Colbert," I replied, "I do not believe it is a difficult problem. You had a tremendous splash of publicity in 1935 after you won the Academy Award for *It Happened One Night*, but there has been comparatively little press coverage on you in the past few years because you haven't encouraged it. You live a comparatively quiet life. Your home studio publicity department [Paramount] is busy working on other stars and other films, and you have allowed yourself the luxury of doing without publicity. The press is interested in Claudette Colbert. They just won't exert any great effort to knock down your door, because everyone else is knocking down their door. If you are interested and will cooperate, you will get as much publicity in connection with *Boom Town* as will Clark Gable, Spencer Tracy, and Hedy Lamarr."

"What do I have to do?" she asked.

"Nothing, really," I replied. "Just cooperate. I'll bring the press to you. Just work with them."

She sat up in her chair, and looked at me skeptically. "Just a minute," she said. "When you say 'cooperate,' you don't mean that you're going to ask me to pose in my bed in a black and white satin nightgown with my boobs hanging out?"

I laughed. "Of course not," I said. "What's right for Rita Hayworth is wrong for Claudette Colbert. You have a very special image. You're a lady, you're an outstanding actress, you're one of the biggest stars in the world. I will represent you accordingly."

She relaxed. She put down her teacup, took out a cigarette from a Chinese cloisonné box that was on the table in front of her. I fumbled for a match and lit her cigarette.

"So far so good," she said, "give me some examples of what you would do."

"My first move," I replied, "will be to set up a Sunday feature for you with Louella Parsons. I've checked the files and she hasn't interviewed you in three years. Of course, there is one catch."

"What's that?" she asked.

"She doesn't go out to interview *anyone*. You'll have to go to her house and do the interview there."

"Oh, I don't mind," Claudette replied. "I've done it before. She takes a couple of good belts and gets sloshed, then Dorothy Manners or Ruth Waterbury sits in and actually does the interview. That's okay. What else?"

Then I outlined my plans. New glamorous photography for the movie magazines, interviews on the set during the shooting of the film with Associated Press, United Press, International News Service, local columnists to visit on the set to chat with her, the development of ideas for *Life*, *Look*, *Collier's*, and the women's magazines, interviews with movie magazine writers, column items on a regular basis, and many other details that comprised a publicity campaign for an important movie star back in 1940.

"It sounds fine," she said. She rose from her chair, signaling that the interview was over.

"I'll think it over and then I'll talk with Charles. He'll let you know."

I left feeling very pleased with myself. I felt that I had made a very good impression. I had been at ease, and consequently stuttered very little. In fact, I was certain that Claudette had not even noticed my speech defect.

An hour later Charlie called. "Claudette was very impressed with you," he said. "She would like you to represent her. What is your fee?"

It was an important moment for me. At the time, Rita Hayworth was paying me a fee of twenty dollars a week which was 5 percent of her salary. Most of the other clients were paying twenty-five dollars a week. Some were paying thirty-five. I knew that Claudette Colbert was the highest-paid actress in the world. This was my big chance to increase my fees, set a new plateau. How high could I go? I gulped. "My fee is $100 a week," I said. There must have been a quaver in my voice. Charlie knew that that was much more than other clients were paying at the time. He knew, though, that if his sister paid more than other clients, she would get more of my time. He was right. "Okay, you've got a deal," he replied. "Claudette will pay you $100 a week. You can start tomorrow."

It was a big breakthrough. Today our actor-actress clients pay us $20,000, $25,000, $30,000, $35,000 a year as a fee depending on the work load involved. Other clients pay us $50,000 and $100,000 and $150,000 a year. But in 1940, to establish the fact that someone was willing to pay a fee as high as $100 a week gave Henry Rogers new stature and respect in Hollywood.

But the addition of Claudette Colbert to my client roster proved to be even more important than just establishing a fee increase. Charlie Wendling worked in a theatrical agency headed by the distinguished Charles K. Feldman. Today there is a Charles K. Feldman Library in the Beverly Hills headquarters of the American Film Institute. Back in 1940, Charles Feldman already had an exalted position in Hollywood; he represented many important film stars, and was highly respected by studio executives. He entertained in his Coldwater Canyon home the most important people in the motion picture industry—and Charlie Feldman took a liking to me and admired what I was doing for Claudette Colbert, one of his favorite clients. Then other agents and business managers began to take notice of me. In a few years time I was representing Dick Powell, Marlene Dietrich, Maureen O'Hara, Anne Baxter, and of course many lesser names as well.

The publicity business did not command a great deal of respect in those days. With a few exceptions the practitioners were a seedy lot. The few exceptions were Margaret Ettinger and Helen Ferguson. Margaret Ettinger had status and social position. It helped that she was Louella Parsons's cousin. Helen Ferguson had been a silent movie star, and, as such, had established personal relationships with many important film personalities. When I was breaking into the business she already had an illustrious clientele which included Barbara Stanwyck, Loretta Young, Joel McCrea, Jeanette MacDonald, and Gene Raymond. How was I ever going to break into that exalted company?

First of all I was not the same as the seedy practitioners of my craft. I looked for more in life and wanted more out of it. I liked the heady atmosphere of success. If I wanted to be successful, I knew that I would have to move up the social ladder as well as the business ladder. With that in mind, I looked at Hollywood in those years of the forties.

There were the creative people in the business. The producers, directors, writers, studio executives, actors, and actresses. Those were the people who made the business run. But in back of those people were the "service" people whose contribution to the business was essential if it were to run smoothly and efficiently. The "service" people were the lawyers, the agents, the business managers. Far down the list were the publicists, the press agents. The more successful lawyers, agents, and business managers were accepted socially. With the exception of Margaret Ettinger and Helen Ferguson, the press agents were not. Social acceptance would give me an added edge if I were to move up that elusive ladder to business success and I knew I had certain attributes that gave me an edge in this respect. I was fairly attractive. I was well educated, well read, well informed. I had already developed an interest in art and music. My conversation was concerned with more than just the most recent gossip as revealed in those days by Louella Parsons, Hedda Hopper, and Jimmy Fidler. And very important to the total picture was my wife Rosalind. She was beautiful, personable, a talented conversationalist, well read and well informed. Moreover, she genuinely enjoyed her husband's business. She enjoyed entertaining clients and prospective clients. She was a helper, a partner.

With all that in my favor, then, I began to take my place as one of those "service" people in the movie industry who became accepted on the social as well as the business level. The advantages to this were obvious. As a social equal I conducted my business on a higher level than a social "unequal." Take two young men with equal talent, drive, and ambition. The young man who operates on the same social level as the people he hopes will some day be his peers has a decided edge over the other young man who returns right home in the evening. The young man who has entertained or been entertained by the prospective client the night before is treated with just a little more respect at the next morning's meeting than the other young man who stayed at home and mowed his lawn.

So, taking my cue from the successful agents, business managers, and lawyers in the motion picture industry at that time, I added social nights to business days to enhance my position as a publicist in the movie industry. From 1935 to 1945, the business grew steadily. I may have gotten in through the back door, but personally and professionally, I was *in*.

CHAPTER 5
Louella, Hedda, and Sheilah

When you are an ambitious nobody, you must develop a clear strategy to gain access to and develop relationships with those people who are essential to your success. In the years between 1940 and 1950 there was no smog in Los Angeles, and under the clear skies and bright sunlight, I knew that in order to become a successful publicist, I must educate myself in the workings of the motion picture industry. Hollywood and Vine had lost the glamour of the twenties and the thirties and gradually the movie crowd had stopped going to the Hollywood Brown Derby and moved westward some eight miles to Romanoff's, Chasen's, and the Mocambo. The Hollywood streets were jammed with service men throughout the forties, but Beverly Hills was serene and movie stars reigned supreme. Never in the history of the world had so many truly beautiful movie stars— women and men—lived and worked so closely together in a twenty-mile radius.

In those halcyon days of the motion picture industry, when the studios not only produced their own films but owned the theaters in which they appeared, each studio had its own large roster of actors under exclusive contract. Each studio had its own publicity department, some with hundreds of employees. These publicity departments had a twofold purpose. First, they were charged to publicize the movies, so that when they were about to open and the advertising had begun to appear, the public, as a result of the publicity, was already primed to see them. Second, they had the responsibility of publicizing the stars who were under contract. The theory was that the more personal publicity an actor received, the more desirable he would be in the eyes of the public. The more desirable he became, the more people would go to see his movies. The movie would net more profit, and the studio would become more successful. That was the theory.

In those days Clark Gable, Robert Taylor, Norma Shearer, Rosalind Russell, and Greta Garbo were under contract to MGM. Tyrone Power, Alice Faye, Sonja Henie, and Don Ameche were the big stars at Twentieth Century-Fox. Bette Davis, James Cagney, and Pat

49

O'Brien were the kingpins at Warner Brothers. Bob Hope, Bing Crosby, and Dorothy Lamour were already doing their *Road* pictures at Paramount, and William Holden, Glenn Ford, Evelyn Keyes, and Rita Hayworth were among Harry Cohn's chattels at Columbia.

Where did that leave me, the Hollywood publicity man who ran his own business? I had to look for clients among those actors, actresses, directors, and producers who were not under long-term exclusive contract to one of the major studios. I could also look to the actor who was dissatisfied with what his studio was doing for him. Although studio executives and studio publicity department heads frowned on their contract actors seeking outside publicity counsel, there were some strong-willed actors who defied the movie moguls.

I had long been convinced that the only way I could become successful was to "build a better mousetrap." In order to build one, I had to study what the other publicity people were doing for their clients. My study confused me. By that time I knew who among both the studio and independent press agents represented each of the important actors and actresses in the industry. I could not understand the point of what they were doing. I read endless items in the movie columns day after day:

> Loretta Young has built a new rose garden and spends her days off from the studio pruning her roses.
> Have you heard that Alice Faye has taken to cooking and has developed an omelette recipe which includes oysters and mussels?
> Tyrone Power is taking fencing lessons.
> Dick Powell bought a new motorcycle.
> Sonja Henie sharpens her ice skates in her spare time.

The unwritten, accepted rule of that day was to stick to trivia because that was what the public wanted to hear. I knew there was something wrong with this. What was the *purpose* of all this drivel that appeared in print? I looked at things differently. I did not want to spend my life dealing with nonsense. I felt that if a client paid me a fee I should be able to accomplish something for him besides just getting his name into print with no purpose. What could I accomplish? I decided to break the rules. I decided that if I was going to represent an actor, it was my responsibility to impress the top film executives, producers, and directors in the business with the talent,

50

the glamour, and the box office appeal of my client. I was not concerned about reaching the moviegoer in Cleveland. If I could impress the industry to the extent that it would give my clients better roles and higher salaries, then I didn't have to worry about the moviegoer in Cleveland.

I started to talk with my clients and prospective clients about the fact that just getting their names into print was not important in itself. What the item, paragraph, or article said was important. Did it help meet *their objective*? Did it help impress the industry and consequently help the client get better roles and higher salaries? Who should interview the client? What should the client say to the interviewer to help reach the objective? Each client had a problem that creative and well-thought-out publicity could help to solve, and I decided that this was the manner in which I wanted to run my business and represent my clients. I did not care whether Loretta Young had a new rose garden!

Rita Hayworth had wanted to become an important star and she had known that she first had to convince her boss, Harry Cohn, that she had the requisite capabilities and "star quality." She hired me for that reason.

Claudette Colbert was concerned that her stature in the industry would be lessened if she appeared in a film with Clark Gable, Spencer Tracy, and Hedy Lamarr, who she feared would outshine her. She engaged my services.

Joan Crawford was branded "box office poison" by the theater owners of America. M-G-M fired her. She was concerned that her career was going downhill. She became a client.

The list of clients began to grow.

Kirk Douglas was beginning to attract attention in Hollywood as a result of his role in *Champion*. He was not under contract to any particular studio. If we could help him win an Academy Award nomination for *Champion*, his price would jump astronomically and he would be sought after by the most important producers and leading ladies in town.

Maureen O'Hara was not getting roles at RKO she felt that she deserved. A publicity campaign on her behalf might attract the attention of other studios.

Tony Curtis knew that he could go no farther in his career if he continued to play *Thief of Bagdad* roles–especially with his Brooklyn

51

accent. The right kind of publicity should make other studios think of him as a straight leading man, with sufficient talent to play both drama and comedy.

Each had a problem that really involved Hollywood and the motion picture industry—not the public. Each had a message about his ability to bring to the bosses and each paid a fee to the Henry Rogers office to communicate that message.

It was my responsibility to convey these messages to the industry. How? I couldn't very readily write Harry Cohn a letter and say, "Rita Hayworth is going to be a big star. Take my word for it."

I couldn't very well tell every studio executive, producer, and director in the business that the nation's theater owners didn't know what they were talking about. Joan Crawford's decline was due to the lousy parts she had gotten of late. Give her a good part in a good script and she would become an even more important star in the late forties and the fifties than she had ever been before.

All of this was fine in theory, but how could I accomplish my objectives on behalf of my clients? The answer was obvious: I must use established vehicles—the Hollywood columnist and the Hollywood trade papers. But rather than nonsense, I would give them substance.

All of Hollywood believed and was influenced by what they read in the columns. What they read influenced their business decisions the next day and took up many hours of speculative discussion. It was always incredible to me that the very people who employed publicists would accept as gospel that which appeared in print as a result of the efforts of someone else's press agent.

Perhaps not so incredible. Early on, I developed a theory about why all of us believe everything we read. How many times have you heard some one say, "I just read an article in the *New York Times* and I didn't believe a word of it"? Very rarely, if ever, do we doubt the veracity of anything that is in print. My theory is that we believe everything we read as a result of the method which taught us how to read. The teacher would hold up a picture of a cat. Under the picture in bold letters would be *cat*. When we went out into the schoolyard, there was a real *cat*. We never doubted what we had read in the book because it had been proved true. Example followed example as we went through the first grade, the second grade, and all the way through school. Indelibly implanted in our minds was the notion that what is in print is truth, what is in print must be considered gospel.

52

If you have never seen Barbra Streisand on the screen, and I tell you that she is a great actress, you will not necessarily believe me, but if you *read* it in *Time*, you will automatically accept it as a fact. And those who live in sophisticated cities are no different than those in rural areas.

Right from the outset I perceived my need to develop a close personal relationship with the Hollywood columnists. I knew that if I could make them into my friends instead of just business associates, I would be a step ahead of my competitors. This move was no different from the one I had already made in my development of personal relationships with agents, business managers, and lawyers. Because the columnists exerted such tremendous influence, they were feared and revered. If they liked you it could help your career. If they didn't like you, your efforts to become a successful actor on the Hollywood scene was just that much more difficult. Hollywood moguls from L. B. Mayer to Samuel Goldwyn to David Selznick catered to the top columnists and because of this their egos were enormous. They knew that a flattering item in their columns could help a career; a nasty, bitchy one could destroy one. There was no doubt that I needed the columnist to help me do a good job for my clients. My problem, in those early days, was that I had very few clients who were important enough to warrant attention from the columnists. What did I do?

I began by representing, and frequenting, nightclubs and restaurants because that's where the stars went and "stars were news" for Louella Parsons and the others.

It was also a good source of income for me in the early days. I would receive twenty-five or thirty-five dollars a week as a fee, but in addition, 50 percent off on food and drinks. The restaurant and nightclub client also served other purposes. It allowed me the opportunity to go out in the evening—to see and be seen. It was my primary job to spot the film actors, producers, directors, and writers who were dining out that night and dutifully report that news to the press the next day, but if Rosalind and I went to Sugie's Tropics in Beverly Hills, one of the "in" places in the late thirties and early forties, which I represented, there was also always the chance that I could get an opportunity to chat with a prospective client. After having had my dinner and conducted my business by table-hopping around the restaurant, I would sign the check, add the tip, and the cost of the dinner would be deducted from my fee at the end of the

53

week. The deductions were not too great. For $1.75, Sugie's Tropics served a five-course dinner, which included shrimp cocktail, chicken noodle soup, steak with potatoes and a vegetable, and pineapple upside-down cake. I paid 50 percent of the check.

First and foremost, however, was the fact that nightclubs and restaurants helped me establish my relationships with the important columnists. When I telephoned Louella Parsons's office to report that Clark Gable was having dinner with Carole Lombard at Cafe Lamaze or Alice Faye and Tony Martin were smooching together at the Century Club, her assistants would welcome my call. It may have been trivia but it was the kind of trivia that columnists needed to fill their columns at that time in Hollywood history, and I knew that it was the only way for a young "nobody" to develop a personal relationship with these powerful columnists. I always received a warm reception at the Parsons office even before I began to get clients who were important enough for Louella's column, and for her personal attention.

When I finally got to the point when it was no longer necessary for me to represent nightclubs and restaurants, it was a welcome relief. I was always uncomfortable about being an employee rather than a guest in a restaurant, and there was always a problem about collecting my fee. I still shudder when I recall that my daughter Marcia was almost born in the Swing Club off Hollywood Boulevard one night early in my career. It was 3 A.M. on a Saturday. Rosalind, pregnant and two weeks overdue, and I had been sitting there since ten o'clock waiting to get paid four weeks' fee—$140. The boss kept stalling me. We sat and waited, assailed by liquor fumes, smoke, and brassy music. Suddenly Roz gasped. "It's started," she moaned. "My labor pains just started. Can't we get out of here?" I jumped up from the table, pushed my way through the crowd, and accosted the owner. "I have to have my money—now! My wife just went into labor. She's going to have her baby right here in your goddamned nightclub. Now!—the money—now!" The owner panicked. He ran to the cash register. He counted out $140. "Get out of here," he said. I did. We sped to Cedars of Lebanon Hospital. Two hours later Marcia was born. A few hours after the birth, Roz opened her eyes and saw me sitting beside her bed. She put out her hand and said, "Do you think you'll ever make enough money so that we won't have to go to nightclubs anymore?"

Who were the columnists? They were a varied lot. Louella Parsons was the Queen, ruling with the proverbial iron hand. Soon after I arrived on the Hollywood scene, Hedda Hopper gave up a dubious acting career to become a columnist. For years she tried to wrest the crowd away from Louella and came close to succeeding. Then there was Sheilah Graham, the former London music hall girl who came to Hollywood, became F. Scott Fitzgerald's mistress, and soon became number two contender for Louella's crown. It never rested on her head but there were years when she was feared and disliked just as much as her two competitors. There were others too—among them Harrison Carroll and Jimmy Starr. But they never acquired the stature and importance of their women counterparts.

It was years before I met Louella Parsons, years before she even knew who I was. When we finally met, I found her to be sweet, warm, kindly, and addleheaded. She couldn't remember details too well, always seemed a bit tipsy, and invariably fell asleep at parties. The Louella Parsons stories are legendary and I shall only add one, since it gave me a shocking insight into the power of the press columnist.

When Warren Cowan first joined me right after World War II, we decided that he should dedicate himself to wooing the columnists. His biggest target, of course, became Louella. He wooed her by becoming an important source of news for her. In addition to giving her material on our clients, he constantly looked for other movie news that she might feel was important. Being a natural reporter and a natural publicist as well, with his eyes and ears open all around the town, he always managed to give Louella exclusive tips which delighted her. She became very fond of him and as a result, we both developed a personal relationship with her that was rare among the young press agents of that time.

One of our clients was opening in a play at the Biltmore Theater in downtown Los Angeles. A kind word from Louella Parsons would move mountains. Warren and I invited her to go to dinner with us and then to the theater opening afterward. She accepted, and at dinner we all had a few drinks. Shortly after the curtain went up, I heard a strange noise close to me in the hushed theater. Roz was on my right, Louella on my left, and Warren on her left. I looked over and there were Louella and Warren, both fast asleep—and snoring! I reached across Louella and poked Warren. He opened his eyes, became aware of what had happened, and gently awakened Queen Louella. The same thing happened three times during the course of the evening. After the curtain went down on the last act, we all went backstage. Louella embraced our beaming client and cooed, "Darling, you were just wonderful. You gave a superb performance." Two days later Louella Parsons ran two paragraphs in her column in which she extolled the performance of our client in glowing terms, even though she had slept through a good deal of it. Why was she so kind? She liked Warren and liked me. She had had a pleasant evening. She neither liked nor disliked our client. She was not a theater reviewer. Her integrity could not be questioned. It was just a kind gesture.

Louella was always kind to her friends. They could do no wrong, just as her enemies could do no right. The press agent who double-crossed her was in trouble. She would not only disregard any of the news he gave her, but she would also bad-mouth him in the industry. She could easily cost him his job or his client. The actor, the producer, the executive, and even the studio head who incurred her wrath, found that life was very unpleasant.

Hedda Hopper used her power without mercy. Her life was devoted to unseating Louella from her throne. In her early days as a columnist I was able to develop a favorable working relationship with her, but in 1946 she cut me off.

"Don't ever speak to me again," she said. "Don't ever call my office, and don't ever try to get any of your clients into my column. Just tell them that Hedda isn't talking to you anymore—and if you won't tell them, I will."

That wasn't easy for me to take, particularly because it was unjustified. Joan Crawford had just announced that she was divorcing Philip Terry. I represented Joan Crawford. Louella Parsons, Miss Hopper's deadly enemy, had broken the story as an exclusive. Hedda had been "scooped" as we said in those days, and as a result was furious. Although I tried to explain to her that I was not responsible for giving the story to Louella Parsons, she didn't believe me. Who had given it to her rival, if I hadn't? I didn't know and Joan didn't know either. The latter wasn't true, but I had to protect my client, even if it did mean risking Hedda's wrath. The truth of the matter was that without my knowledge, Joan had given the tip to Ruth Waterbury, one of her closest friends, who also happened to work for Louella Parsons. Hedda Hopper thought I had double-crossed her. The fact was that my client had double-crossed me. She should have discussed it with me, and we should have decided jointly as to how to release the story. It is difficult to comprehend today how

56

important a Joan Crawford divorce story was then to the Hollywood columnist. Today, neither the Hollywood press nor the public is that interested in who is marrying who or who is divorcing who.

Back then, however, the publicizing of personal trivia was as important to the stars as to the columnists, and for many years, before I started a discussion with a prospective client, I explained that I was not one of Hedda Hopper's favorite press agents, and because of that fact some of these clients took their business elsewhere. It wasn't until her waning years that Hedda relented in her wrath at me. She finally had to admit that Rogers & Cowan would continue to exist, with or without her, and so we resumed our professional relationship. But I just couldn't forgive her for her arbitrary, unfair treatment and gave Warren the responsibility of working with her.

Sheilah Graham was also regarded as a bitch but I got along with her very well. In one of her early books, Sheilah related an incident where she approached Constance Bennett on a movie set. "Don't speak to me," said the blond movie star. "You're the biggest bitch in town." "No, darling," cooed Sheilah, "I'm the second-biggest bitch in town."

She was too, but despite her sharp tongue, Sheilah and I struck up a close personal relationship. In the columnist-press agent relationship, the press agent is the pursuer, the columnist the pursued. She had to work harder for news because she was number three in the pecking order, after Louella and Hedda. She knew that I was a good source of news, not only from what I knew and could tell her about my clients, but also because of what I could tell her about nonclients as well. She would call almost every day and pump me for news. What was happening? Who was doing what to whom? Was there a new romance in the making? Was Joan Crawford feuding with John Garfield on the set? What was really happening between Humphrey Bogart and Betty Bacall? Did Bette Davis really tell off Jack Warner at Edie Goetz's party last night? Sometimes I would know the answers to her questions, and sometimes I would volunteer information.

Once or twice a month Sheilah would ask me to take her to Romanoff's for lunch. It was the "in" place in Beverly Hills at the time and everyone who was anyone in the movie business would make it a point to have lunch there very often. The procedure was always the same. Sheilah was there for business reasons, not to socialize with me. She was always on a diet, which gave her the excuse to order the most expensive cut of meat on the menu. After devouring it, she would eat what was left on my plate and at the same time she also managed to look constantly around the room to see who was there, making notes on the pad that she always carried with her. After pumping me for whatever news I might have for her, she would stand up, look around the room once again to determine in what order she would do her table-hopping, turn to me and say, "I'll be right back, Henry. I just want to talk to Bogie for a moment."

Then she was off, for at least a half hour. She would chat with Humphrey Bogart for a few minutes, then bounce over to Greer Garson's table for a moment or two (depending on whether or not Greer was in a confiding mood that day), and on to Herbert Marshall, Lana Turner, Darryl Zanuck, or even the great Louis B. Mayer himself. News, news, news, that was what she was after. Hollywood gossip—gossip that kept the Hollywood wheels spinning. Finally, her day's chores finished, she would return to my table, and I would pay the check and drive her home.

What did I get out of all this? I had the number three columnist 100 percent on my side and in those days that counted for a lot. While we had a reasonably good working relationship with Louella Parsons, she treated us much as she did the other press agents in the business—impartially and fairly. We had no relationship at all with Hedda Hopper so having Sheilah in our "back pocket" was a plus. What did that mean? It meant that we got preferential treatment. If on account of space problems, Sheilah had to choose between using a story that came from our office versus a story that came from another source, she would use ours. The Sheilah Graham column, although it appeared locally in the *Hollywood Citizen News*, a comparatively unimportant daily, was widely syndicated. It ran daily and Sunday in the *New York Mirror,* a high-circulation tabloid which also carried Walter Winchell's column. This made Sheilah a very important contact for us. Getting a client into her Sunday column, which featured a full interview with a Hollywood personality, was considered a prestigious accomplishment for a Hollywood press agent, and it was the rare Rogers & Cowan client who didn't make that column. Finally, when an unfavorable story was about to break on one of our clients, a call to Sheilah would result in her giving the story a more favorable slant than did the other journalists.

We had a quid pro quo relationship—you help me and I'll help you. It was advantageous for both of us and transcended professional considerations. When Sheilah was in her last month of pregnancy and confined to her bed, she could not write her column—I wrote it for her. But no one ever knew. It was our secret.

So Louella, Hedda, and Sheilah were important in my life at that time, because what they had to say about my clients featured prominently in the newspapers that all of Hollywood read and Hollywood believed everything it read.

But those were the days when columnists were most important and more influential than they are today. Louella and Hedda have both passed on. Sheilah retired from the Hollywood scene and today we have Rona Barrett at 7:45 A.M. on ABC-TV's "Good Morning America." We have Army Archerd in *Daily Variety* and Hank Grant in the *Hollywood Reporter.*

But it just isn't the same. The movie stars of 1980 are not the movie stars of 1948. When Norma Shearer or Cary Grant or Clark Gable or Marlene Dietrich walked into a restaurant, the other diners would turn around and gape. Today when Paul Newman or Jimmy Caan or Al Pacino or Robert di Niro walk into a restaurant, they might get a casual glance. It is likely that they are not even recognized—to some extent because they prefer not to be. The world has changed. Hollywood has changed. The glamour is gone.

A number of factors contributed to the demise of the Hollywood columnist. The ever-growing importance of television news as a means of communication was of course the primary factor. The changing nature of public taste coupled with the changing nature of today's movie star contributed equally to the change that has taken place. Once the public waited breathlessly for the news of Lana Turner's latest husband or lover. Sidney Skolsky, one of the lesser lights among the columnists, for many years earned his living by telling his readers that Marilyn Monroe slept in the nude or flannel pajamas or lace nightgowns—or whatever her sleeping habits happened to be. The columnists wrote about glamorous people in a glamorous time.

Today the *National Enquirer* or *The Star* and a few movie magazines are among the few outlets for Hollywood gossip. Coupled with all this change is the fact that Hollywood film stars are no longer glamorous and the public is no longer as intensely interested in their personal lives as it once was. Audiences know little about the personal lives of Al Pacino, Robert di Niro, Nick Nolte, James Caan, and seem to care less. If they hear good things about their latest movie they'll spend four dollars to go see it, but that is the extent of their interest. Even when there is some interest, as in the case of Barbra Streisand's romance with Jon Peters, there is none of the lip-smacking anticipation and eagerness for news that there was even as recently as the days of Elizabeth Taylor and Richard Burton. The world has changed, movie stars have changed, the motion picture industry has changed, and the publicity business has changed too.

Today Hollywood is more of a business community than the glamour capital of the world. Today we are more apt to read page 1 news in *Daily Variety* or *Hollywood Reporter* about Dennis Stanfill's, Chairman of 20th-Century Fox Studios, acquisition of Pebble Beach real estate with the profits from *Star Wars* rather than a personal story about Barbra Streisand or Steve McQueen. The trade press is filled with business and financial news, and the days of the power-hungry Hollywood columnist are over. Today Roderick Mann, formerly of the *London Express*, writes a very sedate column for the *Los Angeles Times*. There is also a movie production column in the same paper which runs a few times a week. James Bacon, formerly of Associated Press and basically a news man, writes a syndicated column for the *Los Angeles Herald Examiner*. Hank Grant writes a chatty column for *Hollywood Reporter* and Army Archerd one for *Daily Variety*. There are syndicated columnists who write Hollywood news such as Marilyn Beck, Dick Kleiner, and Colin Dangaard. Jack Martin writes a column for the *New York Post*, and Liz Smith writes one for the *New York News*. There is comparatively little gossip.

The press is more sophisticated than it once was. Consequently the Hollywood press agent of yesterday has become the Hollywood publicist and public relations counselor—better informed, working on a higher level with clients who are more business oriented than they used to be. The publicist is more business oriented too.

CHAPTER 6
Joan Crawford Wins an Academy Award

Human beings being what we are—that is, too lazy to decide for ourselves about anything—our attitudes and thinking are determined every day not by ourselves, but by influence wielders and opinion makers, whether we want to admit it or not. The classic example of how the motion picture industry was subconsciously influenced by the press involved a publicity campaign that I conceived for my client Joan Crawford in connection with her performance in *Mildred Pierce*, the movie that brought her an Academy Award for Best Performance of the Year by an Actress in a Leading Role.

It was 1945. I had been in business for ten years and represented many important Hollywood stars. Still it was a particular thrill when the call came in from an agent acquaintance telling me that Joan Crawford, one of the most glamorous and exciting actresses on the screen, had suddenly been fired by MGM, and that she wanted to meet me.

Women all over the world copied Joan Crawford's hairdos, her exaggerated lipsticked mouth, her walk, her throaty voice, her erect, sensuous walk, and the provocative turn of her head as she traded flippant remarks or romantic endearments with Clark Gable, Franchot Tone, Melvyn Douglas, Robert Taylor, and her other dashing leading men of the day. Dress, coat, millinery, and shoe manufacturers stormed the theaters on the first day each of her films opened with sketchbooks in hand, rapidly copying the latest Adrian designs, so that still another version of the Joan Crawford padded-shoulder suit, strapless shoes, and dramatic hats could appear in the nation's department stores a few weeks later. Joan was a phenomenon. Her fan letters poured in by the thousands every week. Rarely, if ever, has an actress so captured the attention and adoration of women throughout the world, as did Joan Crawford in the thirties and early forties.

But MGM, with whom she'd been under contract since the late twenties, fired her on the grounds that her last few films had been failures. She was now considered "box office poison"—a devastating indictment of a woman whose box office appeal had resulted in millions of dollars pouring into the coffers of MGM Studios and the very same theater owners who had now so branded her. Louis B. Mayer, who ran the company in those days, decided that he had had enough of Joan Crawford. He would look for other, younger actresses, whom he would build into stars.

Joan Crawford was devastated. Having tasted the ultimate in success, it was difficult for her to even contemplate failure. She never once thought that her career was finished, but she was angry, bitter, and determined to show L. B. Mayer that he had made a mistake. She would become a bigger star away from MGM than she had ever been during the years when she was under L. B.'s watchful eye.

She had long become adept at press relations. Both the studio where she worked and her home were always open to journalists who wished to interview her. She would pose for photographs for hours on end. Members of the MGM publicity department worshiped her, not only because she made their job easier, but because she treated them as equal human beings. She always said, "There are no little people. There are only people." As equal human beings, she sent them gifts on their birthdays, flowers when they took ill, and lunched with them in her dressing room suite at the studio.

When she went off the MGM payroll, her friends in the publicity department were no longer available to her. There was no one to set up interviews, arrange for photographic sittings, talk to magazine editors about her. Realizing how important the press had been in helping her career, she now decided to engage a press agent. Publicity had never cost her anything—it was a service supplied by the studio. Now she had to hire someone to render that service. Fortunately, my reputation had preceded me. I did not have to seek her out. She had asked to see me.

In 1945, Joan Crawford lived the movie star life that her fans envisioned. She had a large, magnificently furnished home on Bristol Avenue in Brentwood, a Los Angeles suburb some ten miles west of Hollywood on the way to the beach at Santa Monica. I drove up to the house, was buzzed through the locked auto gate, parked my car, briskly strode to the front door, and rang the bell. An English butler answered.

"You're Mr. Rogers?" he asked in a whisper.

"Yes," I replied.

"Please take your shoes off and come in," he whispered.

As long as he whispered, I would whisper too.

"Why?" I said so quietly that he could scarcely hear me.

"Because the carpets are white throughout the house and Miss Crawford asks all her guests to take off their shoes before they come in. If they don't, the carpets will get soiled, and we wouldn't want that, would we?"

"We certainly wouldn't," I replied.

I was still standing outside. The butler looked at me, and I looked at him. I shrugged. I had been a Hollywood press agent for ten years. I had come to expect anything. I took off my shoes, and the butler picked them up.

"Come in," he said.

As I did so, he placed my shoes gingerly in the guest closet.

"Follow me," he whispered, "Miss Crawford is expecting you."

I looked down at his feet. He was wearing shoes. I gave him a quizzical look.

"I only wear these shoes in the white-carpeted sections of the house. You see?"

He stopped and showed me the soles. They were new and shining. I followed him through room after room of white carpeting. I walked up white-carpeted stairs, down a white-carpeted hallway, through a sunlighted, magnificently feminine white-carpeted bedroom, into a white-carpeted dressing room with mirrored walls. Joan Crawford was sitting at her dressing room table, reading a script. She wore a white satin robe, modestly buttoned to the neck. A young woman was crouched on the floor giving her a pedicure. Another woman was giving her a manicure. Standing in back of her, a young male hairdresser was putting her hair up in curls. They were all in their stocking feet.

I had seen movie stars at home before, but nothing as luxurious or as movie star-ish as this.

"Good afternoon, Miss Crawford," I said.

"Call me Joan," she said. "I'll call you Henry. Meet Sidney Guilaroff, my darling friend and hairdresser, and this is Julie and this is Marie."

There were acknowledgments all around.

"I've heard a lot about you," she continued, "and without even meeting you, I have decided that I want you to represent me. Call my business manager tomorrow and work out the financial arrangements with him. We don't have to bother about that now. Now let me tell you what I want to have done."

In my previous experiences, I had first had to sell myself to the prospective client, and then outline a plan in which I explained what I felt could be accomplished. Not so with Joan Crawford. She slipped a neatly typed sheet of notepaper which she had prepared as an agenda for our meeting out from the pages of the script she had been reading. Using the notes as a reference, she told me about her plans for the future, how she planned to align herself with another studio, and how a publicity campaign, using her strategy and executed by me, would help bring her back to her former exalted position in Hollywood. I took notes furiously as she talked.

When she was finished, I started to say something, but she interrupted me.

"I know this is unusual for you, Henry, but trust me. I know what I'm doing. You were planning to give me your ideas, but I don't need them now. That sounds presumptuous but take my word for it that I'm a better press agent for Joan Crawford than anyone else is. I'll need your help, of course, but let me do the thinking and you do the doing. I'm getting ready to go out for dinner now, so I won't have any more time to talk to you. Call me tomorrow and we'll get together in a few days when I have more time to talk. In the meantime, please get started and follow through on what I've discussed with you."

My meeting was over. I stood up, ready to leave, when suddenly a nurse appeared in the dressing room.

"Excuse me, Miss Crawford," she said, "the children are ready for bed now."

"Thank you, Nurse, would you bring them in please."

A moment later two beautiful, towheaded youngsters, wearing what I remembered to be Dr. Denton's, stepped timidly into the room.

"Good evening, Christina. Good evening, Christopher," she said, and turned to me.

"This is my daughter, Christina, she's seven. And this is Christopher. He's two.

"Kiss Uncle Henry good night, Christina. And Christopher, come and shake hands with Uncle Henry."

Christina came close to me and curtsied. Then as I bent down to greet her, she kissed me on the cheek and said very softly, "Good night, Uncle Henry."

"Christina," her mother reproved her, "you didn't curtsy properly. Do it again, please."

Christina looked at her mother. She started to do her curtsy again.

"Christina," again reprimanded her mother, "what do you say?"

64

"Yes, Mommie dearest," said Christina, and the shy seven year old went through the whole process again.

Two-year-old Christopher struggled through the same routine, except that he bowed at the waist instead of curtsying as his sister had done.

Christina then dutifully kissed Sidney, Julie, and Marie and waited patiently while Christopher bowed and shook hands with everyone.

Then kisses and hugs for their mother and the ritual was at long last over. All of us were embarrassed but said nothing.

Finally Joan asked, "And now what do you say, children?"

"Good night, Mommie dearest," said Christopher.

"Good night, Mommie dearest," said Christina.

The nurse led them quietly away. For ten years Uncle Henry participated in the same ritual every time he went to see Joan Crawford —except for the six or seven times that Christopher had run away from home.

I started to work for Joan, following her guidelines. She was right —she knew exactly what had to be done. She was the most well-organized person I had ever known. She had lists for everything. She was always out of bed by six in the morning, and her daily calendar accounted for every moment until midnight. When she wasn't working in a film, she was even more organized and scheduled. There was half an hour for her agent, an hour for her business manager, another half hour for Henry Rogers, a two-hour script conference, time for lunch, time for the children, time for dictation to her secretary, and usually late in the day before dinner one and a half hours was scheduled for "Time with Philip."

I once casually and naively asked her what "Time with Philip" meant. She was married to Philip Terry at the time.

She smiled. "Well, we're good friends, Henry, so I'll tell you. 'Time for Philip' is the time when we make love." I left that meeting, shaking my head in disbelief. Being well organized was admirable, but scheduling on paper in advance time for lovemaking with one's husband was just too much for me.

But Joan Crawford's organized mind and determination to prove that L. B. Mayer was wrong when he fired her, paid off. Jack Warner, production chief of Warner Brothers Studios, never liked L. B. Mayer. It would delight him to show up his old rival. He had confidence in Joan Crawford's ability to make a comeback, and he signed her to a new contract. Soon there came an announcement that Joan Crawford

65

would star in the screen adaptation of James Cain's successful new novel, *Mildred Pierce.*

Whether Joan Crawford would have gone on to win the coveted Oscar for her performance in *Mildred Pierce,* if it hadn't been for the efforts of Producer Jerry Wald and me, will never be known.

It all started one day when I received a call from Jerry, who was the producer of *Mildred Pierce* for Warner Brothers. Jerry, a former New York press agent, a former gossip columnist himself for the old *New York Graphic,* was wise in the ways of publicity and how it could be used effectively to play the Hollywood game. We were personal friends and he knew that I represented Joan Crawford. He had an idea. Let us start a campaign, he suggested, get into print that Joan Crawford was doing such an outstanding job on *Mildred Pierce* that she would be a strong contender for the Academy Award. I respectfully replied, "Jerry, you're crazy." Joan Crawford had only been working on the film for a few weeks. It was illogical to talk about an Academy Award at such an early date. Besides, what columnist would believe such obviously concocted trivia?

"Listen to me," he said. "Call Hedda Hopper [this was before our feud] and tell her you were talking to me. Tell her I was raving to you about the great performance that Joan Crawford was giving in *Mildred Pierce.* Tell her that I am so impressed with her that I'm certain that she is already a strong contender for the Academy Award. She will pay attention to what you tell her. She will telephone me for confirmation. I'll repeat to her what I just told to you."

Skeptically, I called Hedda Hopper. Skeptically, she listened to me. Then, Jerry told me later, she followed the plan as he had predicted.

The next day, there was an item in her column which stated, "Insiders at Warner Brothers Studios are saying that Joan Crawford is giving such a great performance in the early stages of *Mildred Pierce* that she will be a strong contender for next year's Academy Award."

Jerry Wald's brainstorm had paid off. I decided that his idea had merit and that I would keep it going. I would develop a long-range campaign to call the industry's attention to Joan Crawford's performance in *Mildred Pierce* with the objective of making her a contender for next year's Academy Award.

First, I decided I had better talk to my client. After all, she called the shots, not me. I went out that same afternoon to see her at the studio. She was in her dressing room, going over her lines for the next scene. I knocked on the door.

"Come in," said the unmistakable resonant voice of Joan Crawford. I walked in and she greeted me warmly.

"I've been meaning to call you all day," she said.

"My telephone has been ringing since early this morning. Everyone is congratulating me on my performance. I didn't know what they were talking about until one of my friends told me to read Hedda Hopper's column in this morning's paper. Where did that story come from? What's going on?"

"That's what I want to talk to you about," I replied.

I closed the door and sat down.

"We've been working together for a few months now, and you've been calling the shots. That's fine with me because you told me that you knew better than I what was right for you in publicity, and you've been right. But now I want to strike off on my own, and I want you to have faith in me."

I told her about the call from Jerry Wald, and the item in Hedda's column that day which had come as a result.

"I wish I could take credit for this idea," I said, "but it's not mine. It's Jerry's. I want your approval to start a campaign right here in the industry that will get people thinking well in advance that you are going to be an Academy Award contender next year for *Mildred Pierce*."

I looked at her, and she returned my look.

"Go on," she said, "I'm listening."

"I don't think anyone has ever done this before, but it's possible. If Hedda ran the kind of item she did this morning, I'm sure I can get other columnists to jump on the Joan Crawford bandwagon. You know as well as I do that members of the Academy vote emotionally. How can you select one performance as 'the best'? It's impossible. There are always two, three, four, or five outstanding performances every year. How can anyone evaluate them? I'm confident that people in our business can be influenced by what they read and what they hear. Word of mouth is just as important as the printed word. You have a tremendous advantage. You have cultivated the press all these years, and they love you. They are all indignant over the way you were treated at MGM, and they are already caught up with the idea that you are going to be a bigger star here at Warner Brothers than you ever were before. With the press on our side, they may well influence enough votes so that you would get a nomination. You would then be one of five. After that, if it happens, we'll worry about getting the award."

She didn't say anything. She took a cigarette from her gold cigarette box. I started to light it for her. She shook her head. She could light her own cigarette. She lit it with her gold Dunhill, inhaled deeply, stood up, and paced up and down the small portable dressing room.

"I'm worried about one thing," she said. "It could kick back and I could become a laughingstock if it ever got out that Joan Crawford's press agent was plugging her for an Academy Award."

"It won't get out."

"Why not?"

"Because you are under contract to Warner Brothers. Everyone knows that the studio is behind you. It is understandable and acceptable for the studio to put on a publicity campaign for *Mildred Pierce*, and you are the star of the film."

"Are you going to work with the studio?"

"No," I replied.

"Why not?"

This was really unheard of at the time. I had always worked closely with the studio publicity departments.

"Because if they knew what I was doing, the word would soon get out all over town and then it could kick back. Besides, there are hundreds of votes right here at Warner Brothers. I want everyone here at the studio to think that the publicity is spontaneous, not instigated by me, and I want to generate enough enthusiasm for you right here so that you will pick up the great majority of the Warner votes."

"It sounds good," she said, "but I don't think it can work. I've never been well liked in our business. I've given performances before that I thought deserved Academy consideration, but I never had a chance. People in Hollywood don't like me, and they've never regarded me as a good actress. They grudgingly admit that I'm a personality, and that I have a worldwide appeal, but it's hard to find anyone who will agree with me that I'm a damned fine actress."

"Maybe it won't work as you say—but maybe it will," I replied. "This reminds me of the people who wear copper bracelets on their wrists to cure arthritis. They all admit that it might not do any good, but it can't do any harm, so why not try it? What do you say, Joan, will you let me try it?"

She laughed.

68

"Go ahead," she said. "Try it. We'll see what happens."

"Fine," I concluded. "I'm going up to Jerry's office and tell him what I'm going to do. Remember, only Jerry, you, and I will know about this."

She smiled, waved good-bye, and went back to studying her script.

I began to place other items in print mentioning Joan Crawford as a possibility for the Academy Award. The campaign began to build in momentum. Here was a woman who only the year before had been branded as box office poison by the theater owners of America. It was a dramatic idea to bring her back into the limelight after she had been put down so badly. The press, who had always liked her because she had always been so cooperative with them, responded as I had predicted they would.

Late one night, shortly after the production of the film had been completed, Jerry telephoned. "Sorry to call you so late," he apologized, "but I knew you would be interested in what just happened. I just came from a party at Hal Wallis's house," he explained. (Hal Wallis was then and is still considered one of Hollywood's greatest producers.)

"Hal pulled me off into a corner and said, 'Jerry, I hear that Joan Crawford is so sensational in *Mildred Pierce* that she will be a strong contender for the Academy Award. If that's true I'll certainly want to use her in my next production.'

"It's true," replied Jerry, "but I'm curious as to where you heard about it."

Mr. Wallis paused. "I don't know. I'm not quite sure," he said hesitatingly and thoughtfully. "I guess I must have read it somewhere!"

Hal Wallis, one of the most sophisticated and knowledgeable producers in the business, a man who hired his own staff of publicists, had reacted exactly the way the producer of *Mildred Pierce* and Joan Crawford's press agent had hoped he would. We had delivered the message to him through the Hollywood columnists and trade press, and his subconscious had received it for him.

Some six months elapsed between the time that the film was completed and the day it opened in the nation's theaters. During that six months the momentum of my campaign accelerated. Warner Brothers, caught up in the enthusiasm of the press, decided that *Mildred Pierce* was an even more important film than they had originally anticipated. They began to advertise it much earlier than was the norm. Finally, the picture opened. Fortunately, for all of us, the reviews were excellent. Joan Crawford had given a brilliant performance. Warner Brothers, delighted with the big business that the movie was doing throughout the country, delighted that Joan Crawford had audiences lined up at the box office to see her just like in the old days, and even more delighted that L. B. Mayer had been proved wrong, decided to go all out for the Academy Awards. They started an advertising campaign in the Hollywood trade papers, quoting the great reviews that Joan and the film had received. They set up special screenings for those Academy members who had not yet seen the film. I continued to work quietly behind the scenes, influencing the press to continue their constant coverage of Joan Crawford's performance, talking to people in an effort to send the word-of-mouth message of the campaign throughout the industry.

As everyone knows, Joan Crawford went on to win the Academy Award for her performance in *Mildred Pierce*. In those days, there were only some 2,000 members of the Academy of Motion Picture Arts and Sciences who participated in the voting as compared to some 3,500 today. A few hundred votes, sometimes as few as twenty-five or fifty, one way or the other could determine the winner. No one ever knows because the accounting firm of Price, Waterhouse keep their tabulations a closely guarded secret. So Jerry and I never did find out whether our efforts actually resulted in placing the Oscar on Joan Crawford's mantelpiece.

But there is a footnote to the story.

It was Academy Award night. The award ceremonies were over—Joan had won! I called on her in her home and was promptly escorted upstairs to her bedroom by the familiar butler. She was sitting up in bed, coiffed, perfumed, resplendent, radiant. "Henry," she said, "isn't it exciting? I can't believe it!"

I looked at her, healthy, glowing, and never more beautiful. Seeing her like that confused me. She had called that morning to ask me to cancel her tickets for that night's Academy Award event. She said she had suddenly gotten a cold and the doctor had told her she was too ill to attend.

I smiled, walked over to the bedside, kissed her, and said, "Congratulations, I just knew you would win. The photographers will be here in a few minutes, so get ready for them. Mike [Mike Curtiz, the director of *Mildred Pierce*] will be here too. He's carrying your Oscar with him. But before everyone arrives, look at me and tell me the truth. You really don't have a cold. You really weren't too ill to show up tonight. You were just too frightened to get up on the stage and receive the Academy Award if that Price, Waterhouse envelope had your name on it. Come on now," I said. "Confess!"

Joan laughed. "Henry, you can be so suspicious at times. Of course I've been ill. The doctor absolutely forbade me to go out tonight." Then we both laughed.

There was a buzz of voices downstairs. The photographers had arrived. I had invited twenty-six of them. They were preceded by Mike Curtiz, triumphantly marching to the bedside of the new Academy Award winner with the golden Oscar in his hands. As he handed it to her, he bent over and kissed her on the cheek, and twenty-six flashbulbs lit up the room. Someone called out "Another one please." The two principals struck their pose again—and again and again. "Okay," I said, "that's enough. Miss Crawford has been ill and this is a very trying experience for her. Let's break it up."

With voluminous congratulations and waves, they left the room. She held Mike's hand and waved me toward her. She smiled, and with her eyes invited me to kiss her again. I did. She whispered, "Thank you, Henry." I returned her smile. We both knew.

"Everyone else we invited will be here in a few minutes," I said. "I had better ask the butler to bring in the champagne."

I left her alone with Mike. A few minutes later the fifty guests arrived who had been scheduled to have a glass of champagne with Joan, "win or lose." Joan may have been afraid to attend the Oscar ceremonies that night but she was also a great showwoman. The photo of her in bed clutching the Oscar pushed all the other winners off the front page. She was there all by herself.

CHAPTER 7

I Drop the Magic Wand and Learn a Lesson in Humility

It is only logical that a successful young man can readily become impressed with his own "brilliance," but I was fortunate enough to find out early in my career that humility is a virtue, not a handicap.

In 1945, after a big publicity buildup, Joan Crawford won the Academy Award for her performance in *Mildred Pierce*. In 1946, Olivia de Havilland won the Academy Award for her performance in *To Each His Own*. Joan Crawford was my client. Olivia de Havilland was also my client. Was it a coincidence that both these distinguished actresses had won the coveted Oscar at the time that they were clients of Henry Rogers? I didn't think so. In fact, I was convinced that those Oscars really belonged to me. In each case, I felt that I had started with the odds against me. In a competition against four other actresses who I believed were better liked, more respected, more admired than my clients, my clients had won the award for two successive years. Each of them had won, I was convinced, because, through my publicity and promotional efforts, I was able to convince the members of the Academy of Motion Picture Arts and Sciences that Joan Crawford in 1945, and Olivia de Havilland in 1946, gave the best performance of the year.

The validity of the Academy Awards has been questioned since their inception more than fifty years ago. How is it possible to select "Best Actress in a Motion Picture"? Is there a yardstick to measure Joan Crawford versus Bette Davis versus Claudette Colbert versus Loretta Young versus Irene Dunne? Of course not. The only equitable way to select a "Best Actress" would be to have each actress play the same role, and then determine who gave the best performance. Even in such an absurd instance, you would not get a consensus of opinion. People are still arguing as to who was the greatest Hamlet of them all. John Barrymore, Sir Laurence Olivier, Sir John Gielgud, Nicol Williamson? There is no one answer.

All of which leads up to the point that the Academy Awards are more of a popularity contest than a talent contest. If you have five brilliant actresses each of whom has given a brilliant performance in a brilliant motion picture, how does the Academy voter decide who he will vote for?

Whether Hollywood likes to face up to it or not, the voter casts his ballot emotionally, and not critically. Unable to decide which performance he feels is the best, he allows his emotions to take over —he has no choice. So it comes down to a number of emotional and sometimes practical considerations, none of which have to do with the quality of the performance which is being judged.

A maelstrom of thoughts whir through the mind of the voter before he affixes his pencil to the ballot which is lying on the desk in front of him. Best actress? Who shall I vote for? I don't like Bette Davis so I'm not going to vote for her. Loretta Young? She snubbed me at that party the other night. Olivia de Havilland? Maybe she's the one. Her sister, Joan Fontaine, with whom she often feuded, has been treating her abominably. I feel a little sorry for her. I've been reading about her a lot lately. I didn't like her as a person a few years ago, but she seems to have changed for the better recently. She's much nicer to everyone than she used to be. I heard that everyone on the set at Paramount was very impressed with her behavior on that last movie she did. Those were very interesting ads on her performance that have been running in the trade papers in the past few months. I like her image—and she certainly gave a fine performance in that movie, certainly as good as any of the other contenders. In fact, as I think about it, she was better than the others. Yes, that's it. I'm casting my vote for Olivia. The pencil check mark then goes next to Olivia de Havilland's name on the ballot, for her performance in *To Each His Own.*

And so, Academy Awards are won. Does it really happen that way? In my opinion—yes. Just as haphazardly, just as emotionally. It is not difficult to understand then that after Olivia had won her Oscar, I was convinced that it was largely because of the image I had helped to create for her in the industry. I had created the image, through publicity, of her as cooperative toward her coworkers in the industry and the press at that time, as well as through an advertising campaign in *Hollywood Reporter* and *Daily Variety* which constantly reminded Academy voters about the performance she had given.

I was convinced that a publicity campaign, conceived and executed by the Henry Rogers publicity organization, could result in an Academy Award for my client. Who was the next person I would touch with my magic wand?

In 1947, producer Fred Brisson came to me with a proposition. His wife, Rosalind Russell, had never had a press agent. She had just completed a picture called *Mourning Becomes Electra*. Fred offered us a substantial fee to conduct an Academy Award campaign on her behalf. In addition, he offered us a small bonus if she won a nomination, and a big bonus if she won the award.

This was an interesting and exciting challenge—the first time that we had ever been asked to conduct an Academy Award campaign for someone who was not a regular client.

Fred Brisson put an interesting obstacle in our path. Roz Russell was in the East. The arrangement he had made with us had been done without her knowledge. She would never be available to us for interviews or any other promotional purposes. We would have to conduct our campaign without the cooperation of the principal involved. This made the challenge even greater.

I was young and cocky. I had hit two home runs. I was about to hit a third. Warren Cowan had already been working with me a few years, and his creative thoughts and ideas flowed consistently.

Mr. Brisson, our client, set up a private screening for us of the film. Having been preconditioned to love the film and Rosalind Russell's performance, we came away convinced that hers was the best of the year. Neither of us remarked that we had dozed a couple of times during the film's screening. All we had to do now was convince the Academy's voting members to feel as we did.

How to do this? We had to establish the idea that Rosalind Russell was the front-runner in the race. Hollywood loves a winner. Don't we all?

One day Warren said, "Let's get one of the casino owners in Las Vegas to announce that his experts have established the betting odds for this year's Academy Awards."

"How are we going to do that?" I asked.

"I don't know," he replied. "I haven't gotten that far."

Two days later he had. We drove to Las Vegas together, a 300-mile, six-hour drive from Los Angeles, and had a meeting with the casino owner who Warren had previously contacted. He had convinced the operator that his casino hotel would get worldwide publicity if his own press relations department would release to the wire services and the movie trade papers the proper gambling odds on the upcoming Academy Awards race. The operator agreed that Warren could write the press release, establishing the odds that he thought

74

were proper. After all, Las Vegas hotel owners are not supposed to know anything about Hollywood Academy Awards. Warren wrote the release, and the hotel publicity department then sent it out to the press. The story broke big. Rosalind Russell, according to the Las Vegas "experts," was the front-runner in the race. She was a 6–5 favorite. Susan Hayward for *Smash-Up* was 6–1, Dorothy McGuire for *Gentleman's Agreement* 8–1, Loretta Young for *Farmer's Daughter* 8–1, and Joan Crawford for *Possessed* 12–1. (She had won two years before and tradition had it that she could not win in such rapid succession.)

We had begun to establish the climate we were seeking. Las Vegas proclaimed Rosalind Russell the favorite. Everyone in Hollywood read the story. Everyone was impressed. After all, didn't Las Vegas know more about establishing odds than anyone else? Of course they did. Rosalind Russell must be the favorite. Obviously, the logic ran, she must have given the best performance if Las Vegas favored her.

Articles instigated by us began to appear in the Hollywood columns touting the great career that Rosalind Russell had had in motion pictures. Mention was made of other outstanding performances she had given over the years. My reasoning was that if voters were in a quandary as to who to vote for, they might reason that even though they were not so enthusiastic about *Mourning Becomes Electra*, they had loved her in *The Women* and *Sister Kenny* and many other notable films. It was about time that she won an Academy Award.

We convinced a local PTA chapter to announce Rosalind Russell as the "Actress of the Year." A local drama group did the same. We convinced a fraternity on the USC campus to announce that Rosalind Russell was the outstanding actress of the twentieth century. Two weeks later a UCLA sorority made a similar-type announcement and the press used that too. These announcements were not coming from the Henry Rogers publicity office. They always came from the organization. No one knew that the articles which appeared in print were inspired by us, and that the press releases were written by us.

The momentum built. There was a gradual, steady buildup by word of mouth. People were talking. That's exactly what we wanted.

Then we received unexpected help from legitimate sources. The National Board of Review selected Rosalind Russell as the Actress of the Year. The New York Film Critics gave her their annual award for the best performance of the year for *Mourning Becomes Electra*. Everyone thought she was a cinch. There seemed to be no competition.

Just at that time, my own Roz and I had begun to furnish our new home. The living room stood empty. Furnishing it would have to come last, because we just couldn't afford to spend the $5,000 it would take to do it the way we wanted.

I came home one night about a month before Award time and said to my wife, "Start to furnish the living room. We will be getting that big bonus from Freddie Brisson when Roz wins the Award, and I'll give you $5,000 out of it to do the room exactly the way you have planned it." Rosalind was ecstatic. She went right to the telephone to make an appointment with her interior decorator for the following morning.

Day after day the momentum built. It seemed as though we couldn't lose. The day of the Awards, *Daily Variety*, in the pre-Oscar poll they conducted in those days, announced that as a result of polling a representative number of Academy voters, Roz Russell was an odds-on favorite to win the Academy Award for her performance in *Mourning Becomes Electra*. That afternoon, I went to Rosalind Russell's home. Fred Brisson had long since told her about the deal he had made with me. Although she had been embarrassed about it at first, she had become accustomed to the idea that a press agent had originally stimulated much of the interest in her performance.

"After all," Freddie had said, "look what he did for Joan and Olivia. That's the way Academy Awards are won in Hollywood."

I had written her acceptance speech. She looked at it, and went off to her bedroom to rewrite it in her own style.

Freddie and I sat in the bar discussing the upcoming evening. He had booked a "victory" table at Mocambo, a Sunset Strip nightclub, where he and Roz would go with a few of their close friends after the Awards ceremony. I told him that I also had reserved my own "victory" table in the back, because my Roz and I were going to celebrate too.

"If all goes as planned," Freddie said, "come by about noon tomorrow. We will celebrate together with our own private glass of champagne and I'll write out your bonus check. You've done a fine job, Henry. I want you to know how much Roz and I appreciate your efforts."

A few hours later we were all in the Shrine Auditorium. The evening seemed to go on interminably. First there came the technical awards. Then the writing awards. Then the best supporting awards.

On and on and on. I was not the least bit nervous since I knew nothing could go wrong. If I fidgeted, it was because I was getting weary waiting for the great moment. At last from the stage the master of ceremonies announced, "And here is Olivia de Havilland who won the award last year for her performance in *To Each His Own* to present the award for Best Performance by an Actress in a Leading Role." Olivia walked onto the stage to an enthusiastic round of applause. She read off the list of the five nominees.

It was a tense moment. I could see Rosalind Russell a few rows in front of me, leaning forward in her seat. She was getting ready to run down the aisle to seize the coveted Oscar.

The Price, Waterhouse representative walked onstage with an envelope grasped in his hand. He gave it to Olivia. She started to open it. Roz Russell began to stand up.

Olivia read, loud and clear, "Loretta Young for *Farmer's Daughter!*" Roz Russell's beads broke and scattered all over the floor. The audience gasped in surprise. Loretta Young, with a radiant smile on her face, was walking down the aisle, the spotlight on her. The audience broke into belated applause. My wife was running up the aisle.

The award ceremony was over. Everyone rushed out for their cars —but I had lost my wife. At last, in the lobby, in a crush of people I spotted her. She was pale; she was wiping her lips. "Where were you?" I called. "Where did you run to?"

"I went to the ladies' room," she replied. "I threw up. How are we ever going to pay for our living room?"

To her credit, Roz Russell was a wonderful sport. She went to the Mocambo and entertained her guests.

I was a good sport too. I went to the Mocambo, and got very drunk. I was in a state of shock. I couldn't believe it.

But how could the polls have been so far wrong? Why did *Daily Variety*, whose reporters had polled at least 25 percent of the membership of the Academy, come up with the wrong answer? Polls are a tricky business. Generally, I believe that when people are polled they have a tendency to give an answer that is not necessarily their own opinion. This is what happened in our Academy Award campaign. When Academy members were asked who they had voted for in the "Best Actress" category, they said "Rosalind Russell." They hadn't voted for her. They said they had, because the publicity had convinced them that she was going to win, and they wanted to be on the winning team. When they had cast their ballots, they had actually voted for Loretta Young because they felt that she deserved the award more than the other candidates.

The experience may have proved to have been the best thing that had happened to me up until that time in my career. Someone had given me a swift kick in the ass. It hurt, but it served an important purpose. The arrogance of youth left me the night Loretta Young walked up on the stage to receive her well-deserved Oscar. Henry Rogers learned that he could strike out too. He would hit some home runs but in baseball parlance a .400 average is astounding. In reflection, I thank the Academy voters in 1947 for teaching me humility when I really needed it.

I learned humility and I also learned something about publicity. It can accomplish just so much and no more. Roz Russell didn't win the award for her performance in *Mourning Becomes Electra* because audiences, including Academy members, just didn't like the picture. They were bored by it. They admired Roz's performance but they just wouldn't vote for a performance in a movie that lulled them to sleep.

As the years go on, I watch young people make it big quickly and then the word gets out that "success has gone to his head." It happens in Hollywood every day, of course, but it happens in every business, in every town, in every community in the country, and throughout the world as well. A young man finds himself successful at an early age and says to himself, "What's all this malarkey about it's being so tough to be successful? It's easy. I guess I'm just smarter than those other guys out there." He makes a killing in the stock market and wonders why others go broke. He builds a better mousetrap and everyone beats a path to his door. The jury listens to his plea and agrees that his client is innocent. The newly appointed university professor receives a standing ovation from his students.

Then one day the stock market unexpectedly takes a sharp drop and our young friend is wiped out. Someone builds a better mousetrap, the attorney loses a few cases, and the university professor finds that his students are dozing. What happened? Was it luck the first time around? Did the roulette ball fall into the wrong slot by mistake? Was there an evil supernatural force at work? More likely, the laws of average began to work and Hank Aaron started to strike out.

That first kick in the ass is difficult to take. You begin to feel that you can do nothing wrong, that God is smiling down on you twenty-four hours a day, and that His smile will never turn to wrath. He is

78

looking out for you in a special way because you just happen to be just a little bit smarter than anyone else. Then, wham! The roof falls in, someone kicks you at that precise moment, and then (if you're lucky), it dawns on you that you're just an average guy, like everyone else. You're really not different at all. I know all this very well—it happened to me.

I worked on other Academy Awards in the years that followed. Jane Wyman, a Henry Rogers client, won the Academy Award the following year for *Johnny Belinda*. There were other winners and other losers too. But however favorable the signs were, I never had the misplaced assurance I had in those Rosalind Russell days. That experience taught me humility, and I am a better public relations man for it.

CHAPTER 8

Do I Stay Warm by the Fire Or Take Sides in the Cold War?

While there are few willing martyrs in this world, there are lots of those who, when controversial situations arise, say "screw security" and jump to their feet to take a supportive stand. Such a stand is seductive, but the consequences must be anticipated.

In answering the question, "What does a public relations man do?" most of my examples have indicated business procedures that I have developed over the years. It has usually been a clear-cut case of "This is what I must do" or "This is what I must not do," and the decision is based on my own experience and gut feelings.

My decision making was not clear, however, during the days of the McCarthy Era and those which just preceded them. Those days were known to all of us in Hollywood at the time, as the days of J. Parnell Thomas and the House Committee on Un-American Activities.

Personally and professionally, most of us in business, at one or more points in our lives, must face up to the critical decision of choosing between uninvolvement and the risks that come with involvement in controversial causes. For me, that decision loomed large in 1947. Did I want to stay home by my own fireside or did I want to join the crowd in dumping King George's tea in Boston Harbor? It was not an easy decision to make.

I was never an automaton, motivated only by a desire for success and money. I am a human being, and there have been times when I have said, "Forget the business—I want to do what I want to do, and if my business is damaged by my own personal conduct, well, I'll just pick up the pieces and start all over again." I said *damaged* and not *destroyed*. I am much too practical a person to act so irrationally that my business would be destroyed by something I did politically. I have always recognized that my first responsibility is to support my wife and children, but I always felt that I could survive some damage, and that is why I have never had too many qualms about the stands I have taken on controversial issues.

Let me make an analogy to stress the importance of the McCarthy

80

Era and the influence it had on the lives of concerned citizens at the time. If I were thirty-five today, meeting someone my own age, we would ask each other, "How were you involved in the Vietnam War?" "Where were you in the hippy days of the sixties?" "Were you part of the Haight-Ashbury scene in San Francisco?" "Were you involved in the Chicago convention riots or the Martin Luther King bus sit-in?" We would want to compare our experiences about how we were involved in these historic events because of the great influence they had on us. For my generation, the McCarthy Era was as stormy and as dangerous in our lives as the events mentioned above were to young people today.

So with that as background, let me now tell you of my experiences during this turbulent time.

The McCarthy Era found hundreds, yes, thousands of people throughout the United States weighing personal values against personal risks. I was one of them and it all came back to me one night in November 1978, at a dinner party in a magnificent Bel Air home with ninety other guests. It was an occasion celebrating the fortieth wedding anniversary of William and Tally Wyler. William Wyler, retired, had long been recognized as among the most distinguished and most successful directors in Hollywood. His *Ben Hur* had won more Academy Awards than any other motion picture in history. The long list of memorable achievements to which his name is attached, includes *The Letter, The Heiress, Funny Girl, Roman Holiday, Friendly Persuasion, Wuthering Heights, The Best Years of Our Lives*, and many, many more.

It was a night of nostalgia for me. At my table sat Billy Wilder, director of *Some Like It Hot* and *The Apartment*, two films which were energetically publicized by Rogers & Cowan. At the next table was John Huston, director of *Treasure of the Sierra Madre, The Night of the Iguana*, and numerous other film masterpieces. I had worked closely with John on *Moby Dick* and recalled, as I waved to him across the room, staging a press junket from Dublin to Cork when that production was filming in Ireland. Across the room was Danny Kaye, longtime friend and client, Frank Capra, friend, former client, longtime giant of our industry, and so many more familiar names and faces.

My past as a Hollywood public relations man flashed before me as I looked around the room. Then I thought, more than nostalgia there is something else very special about this group. After so many years,

81

there still seemed to be a tie that held us together. As I looked around I realized that at one time we had all taken risks together. Even though we might not see each other for months or years at a time, people who take risks together form a lifetime bond stronger than iron. Ours came back to me as clear as day. Back in 1947 we had all been active members of a politically oriented organization—the Committee for the First Amendment. If that vile demagogue, Senator Joseph Mc-Carthy of Wisconsin, had had his way, many of us might not have been at that lovely party almost thirty-one years later. We might have been driven out of the industry, or worse, gone to jail.

The Committee for the First Amendment was founded by William Wyler, John Huston, and writer-director Philip Dunne. I was invited to attend one of the first meetings along with some fifty of Hollywood's most distinguished producers, actors, directors, and writers. I was invited because I was politically sympathetic, and the founders felt that they would need a publicist to espouse their cause with the press and the public.

It was a time when Hollywood had become increasingly apprehensive about the political pressures which were being put on movie creators. Although the industry had been subjected to a statewide Communist witch-hunt, now the anti-Communist hysteria had moved to Washington, and the House Committee on Un-American Activities was directing its attention to Communist influences in the motion picture industry.

The time had come to fight back and although I was concerned about being tainted with the Red brush, I volunteered my services. Early in October 1947, I issued a statement to the press on behalf of the Committee for the First Amendment which had been written by the three founders of the Committee. It stated:

> We the undersigned, as American Citizens who believe in constitutional democratic government, are disgusted and outraged by the continuing attempt of the House Committee on Un-American Activities to smear the motion picture industry.
>
> We hold that these hearings are morally wrong because: Any investigation into the political beliefs of the individual is contrary to the basic principles of our democracy.
>
> Any attempt to curb freedom of expression and to set arbitrary standards of Americanism is in itself disloyal to both the spirit and the letter of the Constitution.

As the fury engendered by the hearings in Washington began to mount, our ranks grew to 500, and at a meeting one night it was decided that a group of our committee members should go to Washington to protest the manner in which the investigation of the House Committee on Un-American Activities was being conducted.

Before the evening was over, David Hopkins, who worked in the publicity department of one of the independent motion picture companies, and I were asked to join the volunteers on the chartered plane to handle the relationship between our group and the press. We both accepted. David was prominent and well liked in the industry. He was the son of the late Harry Hopkins, confidant of Franklin D. Roosevelt. He grew up in the White House in his preteen years. We agreed to work together to make certain that our committee's action in going to Washington was properly understood by the press, the public, the government, and our own industry.

David and I had our work cut out for us. We did not have the problem of attracting the press. There were already headlines all over the world about what the House Committee on Un-American Activities was doing. Hollywood had always been in the spotlight since the days of Charlie Chaplin and Mary Pickford. This spotlight was the most intense that the industry had ever been in, and it provided a field day for the press. A governmental body was attacking the motion picture industry. The industry was accused of allowing Communist doctrine and philosophy to infiltrate the content of movies. The most important movie moguls and film stars in the world had been called as witnesses. Some were in favor of what the committee was trying to do. Some were opposed. We were the opposition, but our public relations strategy was to make certain that our motives were recognized and understood, and that no one would infer that we were Communist dominated or influenced. We were good Americans who protested the manner in which the House Committee on Un-American Activities was conducting its investigations. We believed that their procedures were unconstitutional and it was for that reason that we had called ourselves the Committee for the First Amendment.

I was proud of having been selected for this assignment. It was apparent that even back in 1947, I had already become recognized as a member of the community who was willing to lend his talents, without remuneration, to causes about which I felt strongly. And I did feel strongly on this issue.

When I told Roz that I was going to Washington she was frightened and nervous, though supportive. She was worried that all of us would be branded as Communist sympathizers. My business would suffer. She would suffer. Our children would suffer. I explained to Roz that it was unlikely, as some 500 important people had lent their names to advertisements which had appeared in the *Hollywood Reporter* and *Daily Variety*, acknowledging their membership in the Committee For The First Amendment. They couldn't brand *all* of us as Communist sympathizers.

What were our objections to the procedure of the House Committee? We objected to the fact that the hearings were not hearings at all, but rather de facto trials. The accused were denied their normal constitutional rights. The prosecution's witness couldn't be cross-examined by the accused. The committee acted as prosecutor, judge, and jury. The function of a House Committee is to investigate, we contended, not to stage trials. A House Committee's ultimate objective is to recommend legislation. This Committee had been in existence for ten years and had never recommended one piece of legislation to Congress. We contended that their activities were *Un-American* and eventually would be declared unconstitutional.

On October 28 we took off for Washington. Our public relations strategy had been planned. We had decided that John Huston and Philip Dunne should act as spokesmen because with a plane-load of fifty important Hollywood figures, the press would be interested in talking with everyone and could conceivably come out with a myriad of different points of view. We knew the impression we wanted to create, and there was a better chance that we could get our views across by using two articulate, well-informed spokesmen rather than fifty. However, I anticipated a problem and immediately after takeoff, David and I met with Huston and Dunne in the back of the plane.

I opened the conversation.

"I think we're going to have trouble and should figure out what we're going to do about it before it happens."

"What do you think will go wrong?" queried John.

"It's great for you and Phil Dunne to be our spokesmen but I don't see how we're going to keep some of our other people quiet. And once they start talking, there is no way that we can control what the press is going to print."

"Who worries you?"

"Bogie for one," I replied. "He feels that he's the most politically sophisticated guy in our business and you know how he goes off half-cocked some times. And let's face it, reporters are going to be much more interested in talking to Humphrey Bogart than they are going to be in talking to John Huston or Phil Dunne. I'm not worried about the others. Danny Kaye, Gene Kelly, Evelyn Keyes, Betty Bacall and the others will all shift the questions put to them over to the two of you."

John said, "Betty's the answer. If we make a big deal out of all this with Bogie, he'll think we're trying to censor him. I'll talk to Betty. She'll get him to keep his mouth shut. Anything else? How about you, David, anything worrying you?"

David felt everything was in good shape, and with that we went back to our seats.

When we stepped off the plane in Washington, we were besieged by a horde of press photographers and reporters. We wanted publicity —publicity would influence the public and the Congress as to our cause, and we had alerted the press as to our arrival time before we had taken off from Los Angeles. In alerting them, we had also informed them that they could photograph our arrival, but there would be no interviews at the airport. We told them that we planned to proceed from the airport directly to the Statler Hilton Hotel, where we would hold a press conference. When we arrived at the private meeting room off the main lobby of the hotel, which we had reserved in advance, we were not surprised to find almost a hundred media representatives waiting for us. Newsreel cameras (this was before television) were set up, radio reporters had clustered their microphones around the dais, and the reporters were gathered round with pencils poised.

John and Philip stepped up to the dais and delivered their prepared statements. Then they opened up the press conference for questions and answers. As I had predicted, the reporters were naturally more interested in making headlines by questioning Humphrey Bogart, Danny Kaye, and Gene Kelly. To their credit, our actor friends dutifully remained silent and referred all questions to our spokesmen.

It immediately became apparent to us that the press was divided into two camps. Reporters from the *New York Times, Washington Post, St. Louis Post-Dispatch,* and other liberal newspapers were sympathetic and understanding of what we were trying to accomplish.

85

The Hearst papers, *Chicago Tribune, New York Herald Tribune, New York Daily News*, and the reporters representing the other newspapers which comprised the conservative press, were antagonistic. Huston and Dunne handled them brilliantly but we knew what the contents of the articles would be even before we read the newspapers the following morning. The liberal press was favorable. The conservative press implied that we were Communist sympathizers.

After agonizing over the morning newspapers, we went en masse to the old House Building where seats had been held for us in the hearing room where the House Committee on Un-American Activities was about to begin another session.

There were two sets of witnesses. The press had taken to calling them "friendly" and "unfriendly." The friendly witness was in general accord with the committee's contention that the Communists had infiltrated Hollywood and that Communist propaganda was being slipped into motion pictures. The unfriendly witness was the one who in simple terms thought that the committee was all wet.

The House Committee had already questioned its friendly witnesses and the interrogation of unfriendly witnesses was about to begin.

The next few hours were agonizing for all of us. I felt particularly squeamish because, although I did not profess to be an authority on constitutional law, I genuinely felt that my constitutional rights were being threatened. I sat there, squirming on the uncomfortable wooden benches on which we were all sitting, and watched and listened to the proceedings as they took place. Personally, I was listening. Professionally, I was thinking about my responsibilities for the rest of the day. There would be more questions from the press, more requests to pose for the newsreel cameras, and additional remarks to be made into radio microphones. The visit to the House Un-American Activities Committee by a group of the world's most glamorous movie stars was the most important news in Washington that day, and the media remained close to us without a moment's respite. Each reporter waited for a slipup, something untoward to happen that would give him another headline for the afternoon papers. Would Gene Kelly do a buck and wing up the Capitol steps? Would Bogie lose his temper and take a swing at a photographer? Each member of our group was on his or her best behavior.

John Howard Lawson, Hollywood screen writer, one of those who supposedly was responsible for slipping Communist propaganda into such movies as *Action in the North Atlantic, Sahara, Algiers,* and

86

Four Sons, all of which he had written, was the first to be called to the witness stand.

The strategy of the committee was to ask each witness two key questions:

"Are you a member of the Screen Writers Guild?"

"Are you now, or have you ever been, a member of the Communist Party of the United States?"

Lawson's answer to the first question, according to the record of the proceedings, was:

"The raising of any question here in regard to membership, political beliefs, or affiliation is absolutely beyond the powers of this committee."

The Lord High Executioner, committee Chairman J. Parnell Thomas, wanted only a "yes" or "no" answer. Mr. Lawson would have none of it.

Mr. Lawson reminded the committee that it had allowed the "friendly" witnesses who had appeared on previous days to answer questions more fully. We scarcely could hear him. Mr. Thomas had begun to pound his gavel at the first word. The jarring sound of the gavel bounced off the marble walls of the room. Our ears rang with the clamor.

It was Mr. Thomas's turn to speak.

"Mr. Lawson, you will have to stop or you will leave the witness stand. And you will leave the witness stand because you are in contempt."

Once again, Mr. Lawson was asked the question, "Are you now, or have you ever been, a member of the Communist Party of the United States?"

He responded, "The question of Communism is in no way related to this inquiry, which is an attempt to get control of the screen and to invade the basic rights of American citizens in all fields. . . ."

All Mr. Thomas wanted was a "yes" or "no" answer and he couldn't get it. He started to pound his gavel again over Lawson's statement. I strained to hear what Lawson was saying.

When Mr. Thomas finally had quiet, he ordered Lawson away from the stand and addressed the proceedings as follows:

"John Howard Lawson refused to answer the question, 'Are you a member of the Communist Party?' and other questions put to him. Therefore it is the unanimous opinion of this committee that John Howard Lawson is in contempt of Congress. Therefore this subcommittee recommends to the full committee that John Howard Lawson be cited for contempt of Congress and that appropriate resolution be referred to the House of Representatives."

As J. Parnell Thomas stepped angrily down from the stand after the contempt citation was read at the hearings, all of us left, our hearts heavy with this firsthand knowledge of the way in which our government was running its business.

J. Parnell Thomas sent ten Hollywood witnesses, including John Howard Lawson, to jail for contempt of Congress in the next few days.

That night I telephoned the city desks of the New York papers, the assignment desks of the wire services, and each of the newsreel and radio networks, to inform them of our arrival in New York the following morning, where we had scheduled another press conference. We held it right on the steps of the plane, the press having been given permission to come out on the field to meet with us. Twenty minutes after our arrival in New York, questions having been asked and answered, and hundreds of photographs having been taken by the news lensers, we took off for Hollywood on our TWA Constellation, hoping that we had accomplished what we had set out to do.

We did not yet know that we had succeeded. We knew that we had been on the front pages, but what had the media coverage achieved? We did not yet know that our appearance in Washington had definitely influenced public opinion in our favor. A great majority of the headlines we had made were favorable. With the exception of the right-wing press, editorial comment was also decidedly on our side. We did not yet know that our appearance in Washington had sparked a ground swell of press and public reaction against what we had called the Un-American procedures of the Thomas Committee. With few exceptions, the press began to attack Mr. Thomas, his fellow Committee members, and his tactics.

We had completed what we had set out to do in Washington. We had told the public, and through our appearance at the hearings, we had told Congress, that we protested the manner in which the hearings were being conducted, and our voices had been heard. We had made the headlines we had hoped for and as we arrived back in Hollywood, with reporters and photographers waiting for us at the Los Angeles airport, we felt that we had achieved our objectives. I was particularly gratified, because I knew that my years of experience in dealing with movie stars and the media had paid off. Everything had gone off smoothly and effectively. Our group thanked David and me as we finally left the L.A. airport for the professional manner in which we had handled our assignment during our three-day excursion.

A few days after we returned, we were delighted to read in our morning papers that Mr. Thomas had adjourned the hearings indefinitely. We had won, to an even greater extent than we had hoped for. We never thought that Mr. Thomas would feel the pressures that had been applied to him so intensely as to call off the hearings completely. This was a total victory for our side. We were even more gratified to learn that Eric Sevareid himself was quoted as saying that the pressures of press and public opinion which had been instigated by the Committee for the First Amendment had forced the hand of the infamous J. Parnell Thomas.

Ironically, Mr. Thomas, who had sent ten Hollywood witnesses to jail for contempt of Congress during his brief appearance in the limelight, soon was sent off to jail himself. Shortly after our experience with him, he was convicted of putting his family on the government payroll. He died soon after that.

The one frustrating aspect of public relations is that it is always difficult to evaluate the results. David Hopkins and I evaluated our own performances, and, as objectively as we could, we decided that we had done our job well. However, we both knew that the success of a venture cannot be attributed solely to a public relations effort. There are many different factors that contribute to such a success, and my most recent campaign was a perfect example of this.

We were faced with a situation that required public relations strategy. A group of us decided on that strategy. The "client," in this case everyone who was on the plane, had to agree with the strategy and abide by it. They did. Then we needed the cooperation of the media. We got it. All these elements, and a hundred more, had to work together in order for the entire operation to be successful.

For myself, I had made a small contribution to combat injustices which I felt were being perpetrated in Washington. I offended certain people by taking a stand in a political battle and someday those people could adversely affect my business. But it was a time when I felt that I had to walk away from the warm fire of security and take sides in a cold war.

CHAPTER 9
John Wayne and Hedda Hopper
Gang Up on Me

Standing up in a crowd to be counted is not too dangerous, but when you're out there all by yourself and the enemy starts shooting at you, it gets kind of scary.

That's what happened to me. Despite the demise of J. Parnell Thomas, McCarthyism accelerated in the years following my trip to Washington with the Committee for the First Amendment, and in 1951, anti-Communist activity in Hollywood had reached a crescendo. Blacklisting was in effect: The movie moguls had run scared, and were quietly not hiring anyone who was even remotely associated with a leftist organization. Filmmakers who were acknowledged members of the Communist Party were automatically out of the business, even though there was no law making it a crime to be a member of the Communist Party. Those who were named as having attended meetings or discussion groups with Communists were named as "fellow travelers" and they too found themselves on the blacklist. If you had an enemy who dropped your name as one who associates with black-listed moviemakers, you could wake up one day and find that there were no job offers. You were on a blacklist and didn't even know it. Careers had been ruined; talented writers and directors had gone to prison. Creative people had left Hollywood and taken up other professions in other cities. Fear was everywhere and pervaded everything. Where would the axe fall next?

There had been no repercussions either on a business or personal basis as a result of my involvement with the Committee for the First Amendment some years before. Hollywood was politically oriented in those days. There were those in the middle of the political spectrum. Then there were different groups that went from slightly left of center all the way over to Communism. There were also those on the opposite side who started slightly right of center and went all the way over to Fascism. I was slightly left of center. Extremists on both sides of the political spectrum never saw in me a potential ally. Besides, most of my clients were too wrapped up in their own careers to worry about how I cast my ballot on election day. After my Washington experience, even though I had been apprehensive at times, I did not think that my political beliefs could ever hurt me, until I found that there were pressures other than blacklisting that could be used against me. I never dreamed that a time would come when the press would threaten to put me out of business, nor that my entire business career would be threatened because of McCarthyism in Hollywood.

In May of 1951, the House Committee on Un-American Activities, revitalized by that time, arrived on the scene in Los Angeles to hold another series of their seemingly endless hearings . . . and to serve subpoenas on those Hollywood people who were suspected of being members of the Communist Party. In June, writer Carl Foreman was handed a subpoena. I knew about it because Rogers & Cowan had a close relationship with the Stanley Kramer organization in which Carl was a partner. We had been engaged by Stanley and United Artists to work on the publicity campaigns for *Champion, Home of the Brave*, and *Cyrano de Bergerac*, all of which were produced by Kramer and written by Foreman.

At the time he received the subpoena, Carl was working on the screenplay of *High Noon*, which he was scheduled to produce, Fred Zinneman to direct, and Gary Cooper and Grace Kelly had already been signed to star in. Carl was not a close friend. I would describe him as a friendly acquaintance . . . like a hundred others whose paths cross yours when you work in a small world like Hollywood.

Carl, on being served with a subpoena, had told Stanley, Fred Zinneman, and Gary Cooper about the problem, and that he would not cooperate with the committee.

A week later Carl appeared before the committee and took what was known as "The Amended Fifth" position. Carl stated freely that he had been a member of the Communist Party in his youth until 1948, but refused to "name names" in his testimony. Dinner party conversation had it that Carl would not go to jail as had ten others a few years before because he had not been cited for contempt. He had retained his principles by not naming names but he had also left himself open to be blacklisted.

The very next day all of us who were aware of the close relationship which existed between Stanley Kramer and his friend and partner Carl Foreman, were shocked to read a headline on page 1 of the

Los Angeles Herald Examiner. Stanley Kramer, as President of the company, had fired Carl Foreman. Everyone took sides in the resultant controversy. There was the Kramer position. Then there was the Foreman position. Dinner party conversation became more and more heated. Rifts developed. Husbands and wives stayed up all night arguing. Whose side were you on?

I was naturally on the Foreman side. Having declared myself for freedom and justice, I respected the Foreman position. I didn't condone his having been a Communist in his early youth, but that was all in the past. I believed in the position he had taken with the investigators. He had been willing to tell everything about himself but had refused to mention others. I felt that it was unjust of Stanley Kramer to have fired his partner.

While this was happening, *High Noon* had started filming. When it was finally completed, Carl Foreman called me. I had neither seen nor talked with him during the months that the controversy had been raging. Carl was one of the principals. I was just an observer on the fringe.

"Henry, would you do me a favor?" he asked.

In those days, when everyone was fearful of even signing a pledge for a Red Cross donation, I didn't say "Of course, Carl." I cautiously said, "What is it?"

"I would like you to handle a press release for me," he said. "I'll be glad to pay you for it, naturally."

I was still cautious. "What kind of press release?" I asked.

Carl then went on to explain that Kramer and his partners were buying out Foreman's interest in the company. Foreman understandably didn't trust Kramer to make the proper press release. He wanted me to release the announcement simultaneously on his behalf along with the announcement that would be coming from the Kramer office. In that way he would know that his former partner-friend would not double-cross him again.

I agreed to handle the press release. Carl wasn't a friend as such, but I had empathy for his plight. I knew he was about to be blacklisted, joining a long list of other friends and acquaintances. But empathy was one thing; sticking my neck out was something else again. Was this the time to stick my neck out? To what extent would it be out, I asked myself. Not at all, I concluded. No one could criticize me for just sending out a press release.

"Of course, Carl," I said, "I'll be glad to work out the press release. What's the next step?"

"We're going to meet in the company attorney's office tomorrow morning to sign the papers. That would be a good time for you to draft the release. Would you mind meeting me in Sam Zagon's office in the Taft Building in Hollywood tomorrow morning at ten?"

I didn't mind at all. Carl was in trouble—or at least he was about to get into trouble. It was the least I could do to handle a simple press release for him. The following day we all met. The announcement was drafted, approved by Carl and Stanley, and the following day it was released to the press. No one was surprised. The announcement was expected. It stated that Stanley Kramer had arrived at a financial settlement with Carl Foreman and Carl was no longer associated with the Kramer organization.

Carl called to thank me. "Glad to be helpful," I said.

A week later, Carl Foreman was on the telephone to me—again. "Henry, I need another favor. I have to ask you to make another announcement. I'm going into business, I'm setting up my own company. I think I can lick this blacklisting crap and I'm ready to announce Carl Foreman Productions. As soon as we get set up, I'll become a regular client of Rogers & Cowan. Gary Cooper wants to be my partner and his father-in-law has agreed to put up the initial financing. That's the announcement I'd like you to make."

"Gary Cooper?" I was amazed. "Carl," I said, "are you telling me that Gary Cooper is joining forces with Carl Foreman? I can't believe it. Coop is one of our leading right wingers. He and his family are the leaders of the ultraconservative set in Hollywood. I don't get it."

"Coop's lawyer, I. H. Prinzmetal, called me," Carl explained. "He said that Coop wanted to know what I was planning to do. When I told him that I planned to fight the blacklist by forming my own company, he said that Coop wanted in. I was as amazed as you are."

"I still don't understand," I said. "Why does he want in?"

"According to Prinz, he admires and respects me for the way we worked together on *High Noon*. Even though he's a tough-minded conservative Republican, he feels that the House Committee on Un-American Activities has overstepped its bounds. He says that there's no reason why Hollywood should be knuckling under to those guys. He believes because he is one of 'them' and not one of 'us' that if he joins forces with me, it might break the back of this whole ridiculous Red-baiting business."

My mind started racing. I had long been powerless to do anything about Red-baiting even though I had expressed my indignation on the subject a hundred times. Maybe this was an opportunity for me to do something. No one had ever tried to fight the blacklist before. Carl was not going to wait for studios to offer him a job. He was going into business for himself. With Gary Cooper as an ally he could get private financing which would allow him to write and produce his own films. Here was an opportunity for me to do something constructive. Would I be sticking my neck out? Well, maybe. I really didn't know. I knew that in my heart I wanted to align myself with Carl Foreman, but did I dare? Was this a moment where my personal feelings were getting in the way of my business priorities? I had worked for many years to build a business. I had a good reputation in the Hollywood community, and that reputation had given me the luxuries that go with success. Did I want to endanger that position by doing something foolish? I wasn't a hero. I wasn't a martyr. I wasn't going to let "them" destroy me. What could "they" do to me? Well, some of the press could take potshots at me. I considered my client list. They all seemed to be apolitical. What would their reaction be when they read that their press agent had gone into business with Carl Foreman, certainly a controversial writer-producer at that time, but also with Gary Cooper, one of the most respected actors in the world. Was it worth the risk? I asked myself again. It was. I made a decision.

"Carl," I said. "Don't ask me for a favor in planting this release. Don't worry about when you will get the money to pay us a regular fee. Why don't you just invite me to be a partner in your company? Let me join the team."

"I'm not sure that's a good idea for you," he replied. "You'll really be sticking your neck out. You could get into a lot of trouble."

"I'm willing to take that chance. If a conservative Republican like Gary Cooper is willing to set up a company with Carl Foreman, then a liberal Democrat like Henry Rogers can join them. What's good enough for Gary Cooper, is good enough for me." I didn't want Carl to think I was taking a heroic position.

"Henry, I'm very grateful. This is the time when very few men are willing to stand up and be counted. If you're really willing to come in, I'm delighted to have you. But if you get into any trouble, I want you to get out immediately. I've told Cooper the same thing! This is my battle and I don't want to cause trouble for anyone else."

"Carl, I'm in," I said. "Let's draft the press release."

The following day a meeting was set up attended by Carl, his attorney, Sidney Cohn, I. H. Prinzmetal representing Gary Cooper, and myself. We all became members of the board of directors of Carl Foreman Productions.

Two days later an announcement appeared on page 1 of *Daily Variety* and *Hollywood Reporter*. It stated that Carl Foreman had announced the formation of a new motion picture production company. Gary Cooper, I. H. Prinzmetal, Sidney Cohn, and Henry C. Rogers were named as members of the board of directors.

At 9:05 that morning, Warren walked in. "I've gotten three phone calls in the last five minutes. Everyone is asking me if we've gone crazy getting mixed up with Carl Foreman," he said. As he was telling me who had called, my phone rang. It was Hedda Hopper.

"Now I know why I got mad at you years ago," she said, the first words she had spoken to me since barring me from her column because she thought I had given Louella Parsons the exclusive story on Joan Crawford's impending divorce from Philip Terry.

"You're just no good. You've gotten yourself mixed up with that Commie bastard, Carl Foreman. As far as I'm concerned, that washes you up in this town. I'm going to personally see to it that you're driven out of the business."

Before I could answer, she hung up.

I didn't panic but the call did make me awfully nervous. I didn't panic because Hedda Hopper, in her vindictiveness toward me, had already done everything she could to harm me. Everyone knew that she didn't like me and offhand, I could not see how she could hurt me any more than she already had.

My secretary said that Mrs. Rogers was on the telephone.

"What's going on?" she asked. "My mother said her telephone has been ringing all morning. Her friends are telling her that they didn't know her son-in-law was a Communist."

"Tell your mother not to answer her telephone, that her son-in-law is as much of a Communist as she is, and that all the excitement will be over in a few days. As for you, please don't worry about it. I know I have stuck my neck out, but sometimes a man just has to do what he feels is right."

When she hung up I knew that she was worried. I was getting

worried too. Was this just a temporary crisis, or would it become more serious? I would have to wait and see.

Then the phone rang again. This time it was John Wayne. I knew him fairly well, although he was not a client. Rogers & Cowan represented a number of enterprises in which he had a financial interest.

"Hi, Duke," I said in a cheery voice, even though I sensed what he was calling about.

"Henry, I like you," he said. "You're a very well-liked guy. You have a good reputation. That is why I'm calling you. I'm not going to tell you how to run your business, but you made a big mistake when you put yourself on Foreman's board of directors. His name is mud and you're going to get splattered. Think about it."

Next call was from Jimmy Fidler. He was a powerful radio newscaster and syndicated columnist in those days. He wasn't fooling. He was mad. He threatened me by telling the movie world I was a "commie sympathizer."

These weren't idle, haphazard telephone calls. They were part of a pressure plan which was directed against anyone who had the audacity to associate with a person who had been subpoenaed and had not been established by the House Un-American Activities Committee as a "friendly witness." Much of the pressure was applied by members of a group called Motion Picture Alliance for the Preservation of American Ideals. Among the members of the Alliance were John Wayne, Ward Bond, Adolphe Menjou, Ginger Rogers, Robert Taylor, and many other distinguished Hollywood citizens.

Next Carl Foreman called inquiring as to what was happening at Rogers & Cowan. When I told him, he said "I told you so" and then went on to say Gary Cooper's lawyer had also called. Coop was up in Montana hunting with Ernest Hemingway. Hell was breaking loose in his own camp too. Warner Brothers had a contract with Cooper that they were trying to break. Prinzmetal had been holding them to the terms of the deal. Now Warner Brothers claimed that they had legal grounds. Mr. Cooper's alignment with Carl Foreman had given them the opportunity to use the "morals clause" to break the contract. In addition, the Hollywood movie moguls had found out where Coop was and he was being bombarded with threatening telephone calls. Louis B. Mayer, Harry Cohn, Walter Wanger—all had called. The phone hadn't stopped ringing. A few days later, Cooper admitted defeat. The pressure was too great.

Prinz came over to my office and we drafted a press release from

Gary Cooper. It stated that Mr. Cooper had the highest respect for Carl Foreman's talent, his integrity, and his character but that as a result of "the pressures that have been applied, I am forced to submit my resignation as a member of the board of directors of Carl Foreman Productions."

I told Carl that I wasn't backing down. Even though I was being pressured by the Alliance, Roz and Warren were both supportive. Roz had said, "I admit I'm scared but you have to do what your conscience tells you to do. I'm with you." Warren had literally said the same.

I was mad as hell. I was no hero. I wasn't even an idealist. Then came the one call I feared. It was Bo Roos, a Beverly Hills business manager. He had taken a liking to me many years before, and had developed a great respect for what Rogers & Cowan did for its clients. He consistently recommended his clients to us. He represented John Wayne, Red Skelton, Fred MacMurray, Ray Milland, Joan Crawford, Lloyd Nolan, and many more important stars, producers, and directors. We represented many of his clients. In fact, his clients represented some 25 percent of our entire business.

I met with him in his Camden Drive office. He was not his usual jolly self. Grim-faced, he shook hands with me.

"Henry," he said, "you're in trouble. One of my most important clients, and I'm not going to tell you who, is pressuring me to pull all of our clients out of your office. I have been trying to protect you for the past two weeks, but I can't hold him off anymore. You represent eight of our clients. You know that I brought them to you. You know that I can take them away from you. I don't want to do it, but my decision rests with you. It's your decision, not mine. This is bigger than both of us."

God, it sounded like a scene from a "B" movie. "This is bigger than both of us." He was telling me that the powerful Alliance was bigger than the both of us. It was beginning to look that way. I thanked him for warning me in advance of the axe that was about to fall on my head. He agreed to wait a few days for an answer.

I called Carl and told him what had happened. He was shaken. "I can't let you do this anymore, and I can't let them blacklist you. I'm going to call John Wayne and ask to meet with him.

"It's obvious what has happened," he continued. "Wayne saw that you hadn't buckled under immediately with the phone calls you received, and then he figured out the spot where you are really vul-

nerable. He went to Bo Roos, who he knows likes you and has been responsible for bringing you a sizable number of clients, and he has pressured Roos to pressure you. These guys won't stop at anything."

John Wayne and Carl Foreman met in Bo Roos's office at 11 A.M. that Saturday morning.

Carl said, "John, I can't prevent you from trying to put me out of business. I'm asking you, however, to take Henry Rogers off the hook. You have no beef with him. You're about to destroy his livelihood. You're about to destroy a business that took him years to build."

Wayne replied, "Of course I have a beef with Henry. He's in business with you. We have to fight fire with fire."

The conversation lasted for hours. These two men who stood at opposite ends of the political spectrum faced each other and argued politely but firmly their points of view about the American way of life, freedom, liberty, principles, and justice. In the end, Carl managed to persuade or shame Duke Wayne into taking the heat off me and Rogers & Cowan. And that afternoon Carl called me. "It's okay, Henry," he said. "You can call Bo Roos. Tell him that his very important client won't be pressuring him anymore about you. You're off the hook, Henry."

As it happened, Carl Foreman Productions didn't break the blacklist, and a few months later he went to London. He intended to stay for a few weeks, but instead stayed for twenty years. He wrote the screenplay for *Bridge Over the River Kwai* for producer Sam Spiegel, but never personally received the Academy Award which was given for the screenplay. It was still blacklist time for Carl Foreman and his name was not even on the screen credits.

When Attorney Joseph Welch, the Boston Brahmin, took up arms a number of years later on behalf of the U.S. Army and confronted Senator Joseph McCarthy on June 9, 1954, before millions of television viewers and asked, "Senator, have you no shame?" it was the beginning of the end for Senator McCarthy and for the Hollywood blacklist as well. Hollywood at long last began to feel its own sense of shame.

Carl Foreman went on to become recognized as one of the world's great filmmakers. As producer and writer over the years he has been responsible for such films as *The Guns of Navarone, Young Winston, The Key, The Victors, Born Free*, and *Living Free*. He received Academy Award nominations for *Champion, The Men, High Noon,*

The Guns of Navarone, and *Young Winston,* and as I mentioned previously, his screenplay for *Bridge Over the River Kwai* won the Academy Award, but he never received it.

Now he is back in Hollywood. He survived those terrible black-listing years and when he was ready, returned to a more sensible Hollywood.

The question of principle versus that of security is one that has been argued for thousands of years. In this instance, the decision was taken out of my hands. Carl Foreman talked John Wayne out of destroying me before I was forced to make the decision as to whether it would be Carl Foreman and principle versus Roz Rogers, my children, my partner, my business, my career. I am not ashamed to admit that if the pressure had ever gotten too great, I would have followed the path of Gary Cooper. At the same time, it pleases me that Carl disagrees with me. He says I did enough, more than enough in a fight that was not mine to begin with. I hope he's right.

There I had been, walking the tightrope again. Maintaining my balance had not been easy. I had personal motivations and influences on one side, and business considerations on the other. On the personal side, I had two conflicts. First, in the interest of justice and personal conviction, I wanted to help Carl Foreman who I felt was being unfairly treated by the motion picture industry. Had he committed a crime? No. He was just another victim of the McCarthy Era. In contrast, I was pulled, although through no pressure from them, by my wife and children whose virtual existence depended on my bringing home clients' fees every week. Was I doing anything to endanger their existence? I had employees who were dependent on me, and a partner who was justifiably worried about what my actions might do to our business. It was a frightening experience to have members of the press threaten to put me out of business, and to feel the hot breath of John Wayne on my neck. Would other clients have left if the powerful Mr. Wayne had given the word? I don't know. Fortunately, Rogers & Cowan was not hurt by the experience. If we had been, I am confident that my partner and my family would have backed me up, and we would have started to build our business and our personal fortunes all over again. I am grateful that we weren't hurt. I am also pleased that at a time when it was important, I had made a personal stand, telling myself and the world that there are times when personal considerations outweigh sound business judgments.

CHAPTER 10
Blazing the Way into Television Publicity

When someone said that getting there was half the fun, he should have also added that it's also most of the anguish, the frustrations, the torments, and the sleepless nights. As I continued to climb the ladder of success, the problems became greater and the climb more difficult.

If my experiences with Rita Hayworth from 1939 to 1942 had taught me that you could get lucky with your timing in launching a successful public relations campaign, by the early 1950s I realized that we had to stay ahead of the rapidly changing climate of the public relations business if we were to stay on top of it. David Susskind once said to me, "In the business you are in, Henry, you better keep running faster and faster because your competitors will always be barking at your heels." At the time, the competitors had not yet started to bark, but Warren and I both knew we could not sit back on our heels if our business was to continue to grow.

Our breakthrough into television was the first new challenge we faced. It marked a personal turning point in my life, and taught me, stutter and all, to laugh at myself, for I didn't simply break into television, I toppled into it.

By 1952 Rogers & Cowan had become the biggest and most successful publicity firm in Hollywood. There were many days, however, when I thought I would give it all up. I would find another profession that did not call for so much verbal communication. I still stuttered badly. As I became more successful, as our organization expanded, as I became responsible for the employment of more and more people, and as the number of clients increased, so too did the pressures—and my stuttering problem. I was more sensitive than ever about my speech.

People were kind. They were patient while I tried to get the words out, but I always felt that I was imposing on their time by taking so long to get my point across. Yet while it may have obsessed me, my stutter didn't seem to bother anyone else.

I had been in business for seventeen years. My stuttering followed no pattern. There were people whom I had known for years who never even knew that I had a speech affliction. Yet, inexplicably, there were times when I even had trouble speaking with Warren and my other associates. I would call a meeting of our employees. Six of them would come into my office to discuss a problem we had with a particular client. I tightened up. I couldn't get the words out. They would sit and fidget and wait until the words finally spilled out. They were embarrassed because the boss was having difficulty in communicating his thoughts. I squirmed in agony, embarrassed because they were embarrassed.

At home my speech patterns were as unpredictable as they were in the office. There were times when I would sit at the head of the dinner table with my wife Roz, and children Marcia and Ron and preside with equanimity and confidence. On other occasions I would keep a sullen silence because I feared I would start stuttering that night. It was simpler for me to be quiet and not intrude on the conversation that was taking place around me.

Despite these personal difficulties, I was determined that Rogers & Cowan would continue to grow and that television would be the next mountain to climb. We began to plan a strategy for breaking in. We knew we could do it: after all, in catching the attention of the public a television show struck us as being no different than a movie, and we were considered experts at conducting publicity campaigns for motion pictures.

The most important television shows in the early 1950s—and these included "The Bell Telephone Hour," "Ford Theater," "Colgate Comedy Hour," the "Philco Playhouse," among others—all had something in common: a single advertiser whose commercials were the only ones used on the show. In the examples given, the advertiser's name was built right into the title of the show. We knew the advertiser had more to gain from the success of a television program than did the network. The advertiser was seeking to reach the largest possible audience with his commercial messages. He was interested in selling more soap, toothpaste, breakfast cereals, and automobiles. Television advertising stimulated sales. Therefore, the larger the audience the larger the sales. If a show did not click, then sales were adversely affected. We were convinced that publicity campaigns on the shows, conceived and executed by us, could definitely influence television-viewing habits. We were convinced that a publicity blitzkrieg could get audiences to tune in to a particular television program. Here was our great opportunity. We would try to convince advertisers, Philco,

101

Bell, Ford, etc., that if they engaged us to conduct publicity campaigns on the shows they sponsored, they could get higher ratings, and consequently enjoy increased sales for their products.

Prior to television, many advertisers had sold their wares through radio advertising. Jack Benny, Edgar Bergen and Charlie McCarthy, Fred Allen, Eddie Cantor, Amos 'n' Andy, Fibber McGee and Molly, Burns and Allen—all the great radio shows of the thirties and forties were sponsored by national advertisers. These advertisers had engaged publicity firms to help attract audiences, but at the time I had never sought out the radio advertisers as possible clients. First, they were based in New York and we were not in business there. Second, I was too busy building our movie business in Hollywood.

But now Warren Cowan had become my partner. He could take care of the Hollywood end of the business, while I tried to break into television. If I could get to the sponsors of the leading television programs, I felt that I could convince them that Rogers & Cowan could help to increase their sales. We were showmen, finely tuned to methods of showmanship in attracting audiences. I would try to convince them that although they were advertising experts, they were not in show business. In order to attract the largest audiences to their shows, show business experts were essential. We were the show business experts. There was no other public relations firm in the country that could boast of our success in show business, and there was no other Hollywood-based public relations firm that had yet thought to approach the world of television. The field was wide open.

I was certain that I could sell this concept if I could get to the right people. The right people were in New York, and so the first step was to open an office there. Warren and I decided that if we were really to break into television, I would have to spend a great deal of my time back there. Who did I have to see? How would I get to them? I had the obvious answer. The way to get to the advertiser was through his advertising agency. The "client," that is General Motors, Procter & Gamble, Lever Brothers, Colgate, U.S. Steel, Ford, Philco, Du-Pont, and many others, left most decisions on television programing as well as publicity/promotion, to their advertising agencies. If Rogers & Cowan was to get into television, then my first step would have to be to establish relationships with the ad agencies.

The advertising agencies recommended to their clients that they buy certain television programs. They then supervised the production of those programs, and prepared the commercial messages that ap-

102

peared intermittently throughout the program. Most of them did not have publicity or public relations departments. They felt that publicity, publicity which could command the attention of the public to a particular program and thereby influence added viewers, was the responsibility of the network. Those few agencies which had their own public relations departments concentrated their efforts on their clients' products, rather than on publicity for television shows. This was a job which called for show business experience. The agencies were specialists in advertising, not in show business publicity. We were.

My contacts were primarily in Hollywood. How to get to the advertising agency? From my very early days as a Hollywood press agent I had learned that the Hollywood agent could open the right doors for me. I remembered Tom Somlyo who represented Rita Hayworth, and Charlie Wendling who had represented his sister, Claudette Colbert. I remembered how helpful Charles Feldman had been in opening up the doors for me to meet and represent film stars. It immediately became apparent that the Hollywood agent could also open up the Madison Avenue ad agency doors for me. I knew that most of the network television programs at that time had been put together, had been "packaged," by Hollywood theatrical agencies. Music Corporation of America and William Morris were the two leading agencies in television. They represented most of the top talent. With their Jack Bennys, Edgar Bergens, and Arthur Godfreys, they sought out writers and would develop with them the format of a television program. Then it was the agent, not the star himself, who would sell that show to NBC, CBS, or ABC. There were also times when the agent would bypass the networks and sell the show directly to the advertising agency for its client.

The William Morris Agency, as an example, would develop a format for a musical variety show to star their client Eddie Cantor. They would take it to the Lennen & Newell Agency for their client, Colgate-Palmolive. Colgate would decide that this format, if they could get it on a network on Sunday night at eight o'clock, would be an ideal vehicle to advertise their soaps and toothpastes. They would go to NBC, who would agree to fit what was by now called the "Colgate Comedy Hour" starring Eddie Cantor into their programing schedule. So, that was how the "Colgate Comedy Hour" starring Eddie Cantor was seen on NBC Sunday nights at eight. The William Morris Agency received 10 percent of the total budget of the show

103

for their efforts. Certainly, the Hollywood agent could help open up the doors of television for me.

George Gruskin was my friend at the William Morris Agency. I met with him one day and told him my theory. He said it made perfect sense and wondered why no one else had thought of it before.

"If you could get yourself into that world," he said, "you would find very little competition. The publicity offices that used to represent the advertisers in the radio days are long gone. Publicity for television shows is now done by the network press information departments, and some of the ad agencies have their own publicity departments which aren't very good. It's really a wide-open field for you. You should really go after it."

"I want to," I replied, "but I don't know anyone on Madison Avenue. Could you help me meet some of the right people?"

He thought for a moment.

"Terry Clyne is a friend of mine," he said. "I'll set up a meeting with him for you. Terry is head of television for the Milton Biow Agency. Biow has a big chunk of the Procter & Gamble business. P & G is the biggest advertiser in television. If you're going to do this, you might as well start right at the top."

A week later I met with Terry Clyne in his plush offices at 666 Fifth Avenue in New York. He was an attractive, relaxed man in his mid-forties, who greeted me warmly and after offering me coffee, invited me to tell him what I had on my mind.

I explained to him about Rogers & Cowan and our prominence in Hollywood, and then told him my theory that television was show business, that show business had long recognized the advantages of aggressive publicity campaigns, and that I was convinced that if we could sell the television advertiser on the idea of a publicity campaign, conducted by show business experts, it would make a huge impact: a television program backed up by a Rogers & Cowan creative publicity campaign had the opportunity to attract a larger audience than a television program which depended solely on the routine publicity which emanated from the network press information departments or ad agency publicity departments. I was on safe ground. I knew that the Biow Agency did not have its own publicity department and that Terry would not be offended by my sales approach.

"It all sounds very interesting," he said. "As you know, P & G is our most important client. They spend more money sponsoring television programs than any advertiser in the business. I'll mention this to Bill Craig. If Bill is interested, I'll set up a meeting for you. I'll let you know."

"I hate to appear stupid," I said, "but who is Bill Craig?"

Terry laughed.

"He's the number two man at P & G in television advertising, actually the client we deal with. Gail Smith is over him, but Bill is the guy for you to talk to. If he likes your thinking, he'll take it farther up the line."

The meeting was over. I thanked Terry for his time and his interest. I left his office—elated. It was my first attempt to get into television, and it appeared as though I was on the right track. Terry Clyne had thought enough of what I had to say to suggest a meeting with his client. I was on my way.

A few days later Terry Clyne called.

"Bill Craig just came in from Cincinnati. I told him about our conversation, and he's agreed to meet with you. I made a date for you to meet him for a drink at 21 today at six o'clock. Can you make it?"

Of course I could make it. At exactly six that evening, I entered the world-famous 21 Club for the first time.

"I'm Henry Rogers," I said to the receptionist. "I'm here to meet Mr. Craig."

"Bill Craig?" he questioned.

"Yes, Bill Craig."

"He's in the bar waiting for you, Mr. Rogers. Go right in." He waved me in the direction of the bar. I realized that for those who were "in," 21 was a very informal watering hole. The maître d' was waiting for me at the entrance to the bar.

"Come in, Mr. Rogers," he said. "Mr. Craig is down there at the end of the bar. He's expecting you."

He pointed me in the direction of Bill Craig. I spotted him. He was talking to a distinguished-looking gentleman.

"Excuse me," I said, addressing Craig. "Forgive me for interrupting. I'm Henry Rogers."

"Not at all," he replied. "Meet Lewis Titterton, he was just leaving."

I extended my hand. Mr. Titterton, very sedately, very properly, shook my hand quickly and in a clipped British accent said, "Howdjedoo." Then he excused himself and left.

"If you're going to be in the television business," explained Bill, "Lewis Titterton is someone you have to know. He is head of television programming for Compton, one of our agencies. He is one of

105

the top men in the business and we have great respect for his judgment. And one note of caution, Henry. Don't ever call him Lew. He'll chew you out. His name is Lewis, pronounced *Lew-is*, and don't ever forget it. The last person who called him Lew hasn't been heard from since."

He laughed and said, "Let's go over to the table so you can tell me what Terry was so impressed with."

We sat down and ordered drinks. When they arrived, Bill opened the conversation.

"Okay, shoot," he said.

"How much time do you have?" I asked. I had learned over the years that before a meeting got started it was important to establish how much time I had to tell my story. If there was only fifteen minutes, I took a different approach than if I had an hour, and the conversation could be more leisurely.

Bill looked at his watch. "I have a dinner date at 7:30. I'll leave here about 7:15. We have plenty of time. Go ahead."

I started in on my well-rehearsed pitch. Bill was interested. He interrupted me frequently with questions. I liked the interruptions because it indicated that he was listening and absorbing what I was telling him.

Finally he said, "We may well be interested in working with you, Henry. None of your competitors have ever talked with us about a plan like yours. I'm going back to Cincinnati headquarters tomorrow, and I'll talk to Gail Smith. He's my boss. If Gail is interested, then we'll talk again. I'll let you know."

I paid the check and we left together. Again I was elated. Terry Clyne was interested. Now Bill Craig was interested. Next stop was Gail Smith. If Gail agreed with them, then possibly I could get my first assignment from Procter & Gamble. And P & G was only one of some twenty-five advertisers who I planned to contact. It was a long road, but it looked as if there was a rainbow and then a pot of gold at the end of it.

A week later Bill Craig called. Would I come to Cincinnati to meet with Gail Smith and some of his other associates? There was nothing for me to prepare—just a general discussion about whether or not P & G should consider the hiring of a publicity agency to publicize the television programs which they sponsored.

A week after that I sat in one of the small conference rooms at P & G headquarters in Cincinnati. I was completely at ease. Bill

Craig's easygoing personality, his lack of formality, was duplicated by the others in the room. Gail Smith was in his shirt sleeves as were three other crew-cut, Ivy League-type young men. I repeated what I had told Terry Clyne and Bill Craig, but by this time I had done some additional homework. I knew how much P & G had spent on their sponsored television programs the previous year. I had computed the fee and out-of-pocket expenses if they decided to engage Rogers & Cowan to handle publicity for all their shows. It came to less than one-quarter of 1 percent of their total budget. I explained that this minuscule amount of money (minuscule for P & G, tremendous for Rogers & Cowan) could conceivably increase their audiences to the extent that their cost for reaching each thousand viewers could be discernibly lessened. I explained in their terms that if hypothetically it now cost them $4.00 to reach one thousand television viewers, as a result of my efforts their cost could conceivably drop to $3.90 or $3.85 per thousand viewers. With hundreds of millions of viewers involved, the savings could be substantial—so substantial in fact that they could purchase additional advertising time for the same amount of dollars that they were spending now. It was all hypothetical of course, but it made sense.

The meeting was over. They would think about it and let me know. Another week passed. Another phone call. The interest was definitely there. Would I please prepare a proposal. Here was a list of the television programs they sponsored. Without going into too many specifics, what did I think we could do for each program and how much would it cost? Would I please return to Cincinnati in two weeks and present them with a proposal. I would.

The next two weeks at Rogers & Cowan were hectic. Here was our big opportunity to break into television. The biggest advertiser in the United States might engage us to handle publicity for all their programs. It was an exciting challenge. We worked hard on the proposal. In two weeks I was back at Procter & Gamble headquarters meeting with the same informal, shirt-sleeved set of characters. We passed the coffeepot around time and time again. A secretary came in regularly to refill it. Completely at ease, I made my proposal. I finished. Questions. Answers. Meeting completed.

"We'll think it over," said Gail Smith. Bill Craig walked me to the elevator.

"It looks as though you will be doing business with us soon," he said. I thanked him. Before getting into a taxicab to return to the

107

airport, I went to a phone booth. I called George Gruskin at the William Morris Agency in Beverly Hills, and then Terry Clyne in New York. I thanked them both. I would not have gotten this far if it had not been for them.

Ten days went by. One morning my secretary, Erna, buzzed me on the intercom. "Mr. Craig is calling from Cincinnati," she said. This is it, I thought. Here is our first breakthrough into television. It took a long time, a lot of traveling, a lot of lunches and cocktail dates. But here comes the payoff at long last.

"Hello, Bill," I said. "I've been waiting to hear from you."

"I'll bet you have," he replied. I could sense by the tone of his voice that he had good news. Sure enough.

"I have good news for you, Henry. We have okayed your proposal." At long last. The big breakthrough.

"That's great," I said. "I really appreciate all your help, Bill. It would never have gone through if you hadn't pushed it. When do we start?"

"Start? Start what?" he asked. "You have a long way to go before you start. I'm giving you approval now to go to all of our agencies."

I couldn't believe it. What was he talking about?

"Agencies? I don't understand. You're the client. It's your money. If you approved the proposal, then that's all there is to it."

I paused.

"Or is it?" I asked.

"No, it isn't," he explained patiently. "The fact that we approved your proposal is only the first step. Each of our shows is handled by one of our advertising agencies. They control our involvement in the show and we never make any decisions without a recommendation from the agency. I'm going to give you a list of our shows and the agencies which handle them. Then I'll set up appointments for you to meet with Lewis Titterton at Compton, Terry Clyne at Biow, Tom McDermott at Benton & Bowles. . . ."

I couldn't hear what he was saying. It was all a blur of words and names. After all this work, after all the meetings, all the trips to New York and Cincinnati, I seemed to be right back where I had started months before. I hadn't climbed the mountain at all, I hadn't even gotten as far as the foothills.

"Hello, hello, are you still there? Henry? Were we cut off?"

"No," I replied. "We weren't cut off. I just had to pick myself up off the floor. I thought when you called that you would tell us to start to work tomorrow. It's a shock, that's all. I'll get over it."

Bill laughed.

"You want to get into television," he said. "You want to work for P & G. That's the way we play the game. Do you want to quit or do you want to play?"

"Quit? Are you crazy?" I replied. "I'm in the game to stay. I should have learned the rules a little better before the first inning. But I'm ready to go to bat now. Who should I see first?"

"Well," said Bill, "you started with Terry Clyne, so I suggest you go back to him. I don't have to call him for you. Make your own appointment. Good luck."

Madness, I thought. A multibillion-dollar company can't make its own decision to hire Rogers & Cowan. They leave it to their advertising agencies to make the decisions. And their agencies have their own axes to grind. It's going to be a long pull but if that's the way they do business, I have no alternative. I must go along. I'm certainly not going to stop now.

Before I got around to calling Terry Clyne, another phone call came in. It was from Taft Schreiber, one of the top executives at MCA, the largest theatrical agency in the world. I had become very close to the key people at MCA over the years—Jules Stein, founder and chairman at the time, the now-legendary David (Sonny) Werblin, currently President of Madison Square Garden in New York. Because we had mutual clients, we worked closely together, and our business relationship had developed into a warm personal one. I was entertained in their homes; they were entertained in mine.

MCA had just started to produce its own filmed television programs. Taft explained that they had just sold their first show to American Tobacco Company. It was titled "Biff Baker, USA" and starred Alan Hale, Jr. He and Sonny Werblin had recommended to American Tobacco and its advertising agency, Batten, Barton, Durstine & Osborn, that Rogers & Cowan should handle the publicity for the show.

He had set up a meeting for me to make a presentation at the offices of American Tobacco Company in New York two weeks from that day. He and Sonny would accompany me to the meeting. That was good, I thought. I would have friends at court. Listening to my proposal, he explained, would be Paul Hahn, President of American Tobacco, and Ben Duffy, President of BBD & O, and their staffs.

I thanked Taft for his recommendation. I would meet him in

New York on the appointed day. I hung up the phone and broke into a sweat.

Paul Hahn! Ben Duffy! Giants in the world of big business. Hahn was president of the company that at the time sold more cigarettes than any other company in the world. Duffy was the president of one of the largest advertising agencies in the world. Making a presentation to Terry Clyne or Bill Craig or Gail Smith was no problem to me, but Hahn and Duffy were different. I was in the biggest league of them all and I was scared because I knew I was going to stutter. I knew I would make a damn fool of myself. I would also embarrass my friends, Taft and Sonny. What to do? Nothing. Goddamn it. Go to work. You could do it at P & G. You can do it in this case too. I stood up from my desk, wiped the sweat off my face, took a deep breath, and walked into Warren's office to discuss with him the presentation we had to write.

I had better forget about the stuttering. Here was another opportunity. I was no longer dependent on Procter & Gamble for my breakthrough into television. I was being brought in by the right people to see the right people—the people who had the power to say, "Okay, you've got a deal. You start getting paid tomorrow." I would not have to worry about going to the ad agency after I had made a proposal to the client. I would be seeing them both together.

I recruited some of my associates to help me plan and then write a convincing presentation. First, I would tell our prospective client who Rogers & Cowan was, then why we were particularly qualified to handle this challenging assignment. Then, surmising they knew comparatively little about how a television series was publicized, I would tell them step by step what we planned to do. Press kits, photographs, features to go to the nation's television editors. Color photography for weekend television supplements, *TV Guide,* and the other magazines which were using television news. Press previews in New York and Hollywood. Video and audio promos to be sent to station promotion managers to augment the material that they would be receiving from the network. Telephone interviews with television editors in the fifty major markets, and more and more and more and more.

After the material was written, I decided to incorporate it into a visual presentation. We prepared two-foot-by-four-foot cards, with large type, highlighting the major points to be stressed in the proposal. I planned to read the headlines that were imprinted on each card, and then expound on the subject from the total written presenta-

110

tion that I held in my hands. The visual presentation would have two advantages. It would appeal to both the visual and aural senses of my audience. After the tobacco and agency people read the headlines on each card, which would tell them the subject to be discussed, they would be prepared for me to outline it for them verbally in detail. As I finished discussing the subject that was on one card, I planned to flip it aside and present a new subject on the next card.

It also would have another advantage. Preparing for the worst, I figured that the cards would distract everyone while I stuttered and struggled my way through the presentation.

The presentation was completed in the allotted two weeks' time. We placed it carefully in a packing case. At the airport I checked it through with my suitcase and boarded the plane for New York.

Panic time. The fear was back. I started to sweat again. Why was I doing this? Why didn't I just remain in Hollywood with my comfortable business, where by this time I could handle the stuttering problem with comparative ease. Who needed all this torture? Goddamn it. *I* needed it. I was going to lick this fear . . . even if I did make an idiot of myself.

Why did stuttering remain after all these years such an inexplicable problem? For some unknown reason, I had managed to get through my Procter & Gamble meetings without the anguish I was having now. I had gotten stuck on a word occasionally, but it hadn't bothered me. Maybe it was because I had been dealing with easygoing shirt-sleeved middle management people. But this was different. I knew it was silly but I obviously had a psychological hangup about meeting with company presidents. Somewhere deep in my psyche, I had been saying, "What right does a punk kid from Irvington, New Jersey, have to make a presentation to the President of American Tobacco Company?" Was I that insecure? I guess I was.

The plane arrived in New York. An hour later I checked into the Madison Hotel. Exhausted, I went right to bed but I couldn't sleep. I tossed, turned, tossed, turned. Too hot. Too cold. The covers went up to my chin, then they were tossed aside. I envisioned Mr. Hahn and Mr. Duffy laughing as I stuttered my way through the presentation. I finally came to a decision. To hell with it. I wasn't going through with it.

I decided to call Taft the next morning. I would tell him that I had taken suddenly ill—pneumonia, or pleurisy. I was so sick that my doctor had advised me to return to Los Angeles immediately and check right into a hospital. I would apologize for the unforeseen turn of events. Probably Taft and Sonny would recommend another office to handle publicity for "Biff Baker, USA." I didn't care.

It must have been 4 A.M. when I finally fell asleep. Then the telephone rang. I looked at my portable alarm clock—it was eight o'clock. Taft was on the line. He would have one of his office boys pick up the heavy presentation and easel which I had brought with me on the plane and bring it down to American Tobacco Company. I should meet him and Sonny at his office at 9:30. We would take a taxi downtown together in plenty of time for our ten o'clock appointment. I tried to interrupt him, but I couldn't. He was talking too quickly. Then he hung up.

I never had the chance to tell him that I was too sick to make our appointment. I crawled out of bed and staggered to the bathroom. What a ghastly sight. I was a pale green color. I dragged myself into the shower. The water was hot. I tried to soap myself, but I couldn't —I didn't have the strength.

What for? I kept asking myself. Why am I doing this to myself? Screw that goddamned mountain that I wanted to climb. It's not important. It's not worth it. I want to get the hell out of here. Who needs television? Why can't I just stay in Beverly Hills and live the good lush life? No, I was stuck. I just couldn't do that to Taft and Sonny. I had to go through with it.

I dressed, gulped down a cup of coffee, and shuffled myself around the corner to the MCA offices at 598 Madison Avenue. They were waiting for me.

Sonny took a look at my pale green complexion and said, "What's the matter with you? You look terrible. Are you sick?"

"N-n-n-no," I mumbled. "I'm all right. I j-j-j-just had a bad night." We taxied down to the American Tobacco offices on lower Broadway. In the reception room I felt as if I were in a Victorian setting. Nothing seemed to have changed since the turn of the century. The receptionist had probably been there as long as the furniture. She recognized Werblin and Schreiber as they stepped off the elevator, and promptly told them that Mr. Schullinger wished to see them for a moment before the meeting got underway. I was pointed in the direction of the boardroom where I was to make my presentation.

I opened the door, and looked around. I didn't believe it. I had seen this in the movies, never in real life. It was a scene out of *The Hucksters* or *Executive Suite*. I was in a huge paneled boardroom. In the middle of the room was a fifty-foot-long walnut table. Around the table were thirty-six cushioned chairs. In front of each chair was a yellow lined pad, a sharpened pencil, and a water glass. Neatly placed from one end of the table to the other were eight cut-crystal water pitchers. On the walls were oil paintings of distinguished, stern-looking gentlemen who must have been the presidents and chairmen of American Tobacco Company from years past. At the end of the room where I was standing was my easel with the Rogers & Cowan presentation cards placed neatly on it. The MCA office boy, as planned, had arrived before we had and had done his job well.

I took all of this in in a moment. Nope. I just couldn't do it. It was too awesome, too overpowering. I could not possibly stand up there and give a presentation to all those people who would be occupying those chairs in just a few minutes' time. The fear of stuttering surged up in my guts. I felt nauseous. I began to sweat. I felt droplets slipping down the sides of my body from my armpits. Okay, that's it. I'm getting out of here right now. I'll tell the receptionist I suddenly took ill. Let someone else read the presentation. I moved toward the door, but at that moment it opened.

Sonny and Taft walked in first. They were followed by an army of Brooks Brothers dark-suited, white-shirted gentlemen. I was introduced to each of them, who shook my hand and then walked to his appointed place at the table. It all seemed to be planned with militarylike precision. They seemed to be clicking their heels as they shook my limp, wet hand, and then goose-stepped to their chairs. Of course they weren't. I thought I was going mad. How could I get out of this? I couldn't.

I was introduced to Al Stephens, Karl Schullinger, Herminio Traviesas—name after name—blurred face after blurred face, all thirty-four of them.

Finally Taft said, "Henry, meet Mr. Ben Duffy, President of BBD & O, and Mr. Paul Hahn, President of American Tobacco Company."

I hastily wiped my wet hand on my trousers and gave them each a handshake. As I shook Mr. Hahn's hand, I experienced for the first time in my life a sensation that I had heard and read about a thousand times. My knees actually shook. I felt my whole body tremble.

The thirty-four gentlemen stood behind their chairs. Sonny and Taft stood beside their chairs which were away from the table, on either side of the easel. I stood in front of the easel. Mr. Hahn and

Mr. Duffy walked briskly to the far end of the boardroom. Mr. Hahn sat down at the head of the table; Mr. Duffy sat at his right. The other thirty-four men slipped quietly into their chairs. Sonny and Taft sat down. I was the only one left standing in the room.

Mr. Hahn cleared his throat as a sign that he was calling the meeting to order. He looked at me. "You may begin, Mr. Rogers."

"Th-h-h-h-hank you, M-m-m-m-m-ister Hahn," I replied. Everyone turned their eyes to me. They waited.

"G-g-g-g-gentlemen!" Getting out that one word had taken my breath away. I gasped for air. My hands were wet as I gripped the written presentation which I would refer to if I could ever get started. Now I felt the sweat dripping from the inside of my thighs. I took a deep breath.

"Gentlemen," I said it again. This time it came out smoothly. "I want to thank you for giving me this opportunity to tell you about Rogers & Cowan and what we hope to accomplish through our publicity and promotion efforts on 'Biff Baker, USA.' "

I had gotten through the first sentence. I stepped to the side of the easel and read the first three headlines. Then I got stuck on a word. I couldn't go any further. I felt my face flush. My lips tightened up. My throat constricted. At first the word wouldn't come out, and then suddenly it burst forth.

I looked around. I wanted to run. I looked for the smirks that I expected to see on their faces. I listened for the snickers which I was certain were there. But there were no smirks. There were no snickers. They just sat there. They were waiting for me to get started again. Maybe they know what I'm going through, I thought. Maybe they're not bad guys after all. Maybe each one of them has had to make a presentation like this at one time. Maybe they were frightened too. Except that they don't stutter. I do.

I stumbled through the presentation. It must have taken an hour instead of the half hour it should have. It seemed like twelve hours. For a few minutes I would talk fluently, then I would get stuck on a word. It seemed an interminable length of time until I could get the word out, although it was probably only a few seconds. I would get embarrassed. I wanted to tell everyone that I was sorry to put them through this ordeal. But it wasn't an ordeal for them. They seemed to be listening intently. It was just an ordeal for me.

Finally it was all over.

"Thank you, Mr. Rogers," said Paul Hahn. "Do any of you gentlemen have any questions for Mr. Rogers?" There was silence.

"Well," he said, "then that winds it up. We can all get back to work now."

I stood there. I was a failure. I had blown it. I had had the perfect opportunity to really break into the big time and I had blown it. I was just plain stupid to let that stuttering get the best of me.

Everyone stood up and began to leave. Taft and Sonny stood beside me saying good-bye to everyone as they left. I tried to keep a smile on my face to hide my mortification. Finally, Mr. Hahn approached. He extended his hand and shook my still-clammy one.

"Nice presentation, Mr. Rogers. Congratulations on a job well done."

I couldn't believe it. A good job? A job well done? He was just being kind. It was a catastrophe.

Mr. Duffy was next. He turned to Taft and Sonny and said, "If you fellows have no other plans, let's all go to lunch. Mr. Rogers deserves a good lunch. He's had a tough morning." He smiled at me. I smiled back at him—weakly.

I could see that he understood what I had gone through.

The four of us went to 21. When the captain came over to take our orders, Mr. Duffy pointed to me and said, "Give Mr. Rogers a double martini—he needs it." We all laughed. They all knew that I had been terribly shaken by the experience and they wanted to put me at ease. I drank my double martini quickly. I could feel my muscles relax, and I began to feel a little giddy. No mention was made of the morning's presentation. The conversation had taken a different turn. What was going to happen to the Dodgers this season? I joined in the conversation. I spoke fluently. Suddenly I started to laugh. I guess I was a little drunk, but felt fine.

"What's so funny?" asked Taft. They all looked at me.

"I was just thinking," I replied, "I should have had that double martini *before* I made the presentation." They all laughed.

It was at that moment that I learned something that has served me well ever since that day. I must talk about my stuttering, not try to hide it like some dreaded disease. I must have a sense of humor about it. If I laugh at it, and laugh at myself, then people will laugh with me. If we're all laughing, then the fear disappears.

A few weeks later, there was another telephone call from Taft Schreiber. BBD & O and American Tobacco Company had decided to engage Rogers & Cowan to handle publicity for "Biff Baker, USA."

We had made the breakthrough. We were handling a television series for a national advertiser. We were into a new phase of our business.

The phone call did more than get Rogers & Cowan into the television business. It got me over my fear of stuttering. Even though the double martini experience had taught me to laugh at my affliction, I would still have retained my stuttering complex if I had been turned down by American Tobacco. I would have felt that I had failed because of my speech, not because of the content of the presentation. It would have inhibited me for the rest of my life.

And what happened with all those meetings I had with the Procter & Gamble agencies? Lewis Titterton, the British gentleman from Compton Advertising, was the first to come through when he engaged us to handle publicity for a half-hour dramatic series titled "Jane Wyman's Fireside Theater." This, together with "Biff Baker, U.S.A.," our show for American Tobacco Company, at long last put us into the television business. A few years later we found ourselves handling all the Procter & Gamble shows, and all the General Foods shows, the "DuPont Show of the Week," and different series for Prudential Life Insurance, Interstate Bakeries, Colgate, and Lever Brothers. Our position in the television industry was secure, but I always remembered that it was American Tobacco Company and Procter & Gamble that had brought us into television, and it was because of my American Tobacco experience that I made the most important discovery of my life. Stuttering would not hamper the development of my business or my personal life. I had learned to laugh at my handicap.

CHAPTER 11
Dog Food and Movie Stars Are Much Alike

If someone had said that to me back in the forties and up through the early fifties I wouldn't have believed it either. But now I know better. Dog food and movie stars are much alike because they are both products in need of exposure. When a message about or from them is to be conveyed to the American public, when the movie star wants to tell the public about his new movie, or when Ralston Purina wants to introduce a new dog food product, they both do it, or at least try to do it, through the same channels.

Indisputably, the most effective channels today are the television talk shows—Mike Douglas, Johnny Carson, Merv Griffin, Dinah Shore, and the hundreds of local television panel and game shows throughout the country. That certainly was not the case when I started out in the public relations business.

When I represented Rita Hayworth forty years ago, I decided that a cover story in *Look* could most effectively help in launching her career. Today, given the same situation, I would probably decide that an appearance on the Johnny Carson show might be even more effective in getting across the idea that a new star was about to be born. It is not easy, of course. I must still convince Johnny's producer that the girl is not only beautiful and on her way to success as a film star, but that she can also be provocative and witty in a conversation and an entertaining guest on his show.

Even though I earned my credibility many years ago, and have been responsible for placing many, many, successful guests on "Tonight" over a period of years, the producer still will not take my word that the young lady can hold her own in a conversation with Johnny Carson on the show. If he is interested in my idea at all, he will arrange to have some of his staff members do a preinterview with the girl before he and Johnny agree to accept her as a guest on the show. Although it means a lot of work for the public relations person, if the client appears on the show it will pay off a hundred times more effectively than a hundred Louella Parsons interviews in reaching the public.

Today we work closely with television. When a client has a point

to be made, whether it is to help promote his new movie or to un-
selfishly promote something about which he or she feels strongly
(as Marlo Thomas did in her television appearances boosting the
Equal Rights Amendment), we seek the cooperation of the "Today
Show," "Good Morning America," Johnny Carson, Dinah Shore,
Mike Douglas, Merv Griffin, Phil Donahue or Irv Kupcinet in Chicago. The hosts of these shows are always looking for important
personalities to appear as guests on their show.

Their producers or talent coordinators constantly call Rogers &
Cowan for Paul Newman, Steve McQueen, Ali McGraw, Marlo
Thomas, Ben Vereen, James Caan, Nick Nolte, and many of our
other important star clients to appear as guests.

The problem is that in many cases, the clients who they want to
have on the shows have no interest in making an appearance at that
time. In contrast, the talent coordinator is not particularly anxious
to have on his show those of our clients who are anxious to get on to
promote a particular product, idea, or company. There is then a
constant contest between us and the talent coordinators about setting
guests for the show. "Why should we put client X on the show," they
ask, "if you won't give us Paul Newman?" We then go on to explain
that we are not in a position to put Paul Newman on the show. He
is a very independent gentleman. When he has something important
he would like to say and is anxious to reach a nationwide audience,
he will agree to appear on one of the interview shows. He won't do it
just for no reason at all, or because we ask him to.

We are, of course, always anxious to get our corporate or "product" clients on the network or syndicated shows. It is very difficult.
The producer says, "Why should we plug your product? Why don't
you tell your client to advertise on our program and then he can
plug his product on a thirty-second commercial." However, the client
uses his advertising agency to buy advertising time. He hopes that his
public relations firm can be creative enough to get coverage for the
product within the editorial content of the show.

Just recently, as part of our total public relations program on
behalf of our client, Jockey International, we were anxious to get
important television exposure for their new line of jogging clothes.
How to do it? There are 50 or 100 or 200 different manufacturers
of jogging clothes. Why should one of the important television interview shows do a feature involving Jockey jogging clothes? It was our
responsibility to come up with the answer.

118

We went to Launa Newman, talent coordinator of the "Dinah Shore Show," and discussed it with her. She agreed that jogging was of great interest to Dinah's viewers. Dinah herself had become interested in jogging. We developed with Launa an idea for the show which she then presented to the producer of the show and to Dinah herself. If Rogers & Cowan could put together a segment for the show which would include a jogging expert and a number of important personalities who would be willing to jog on the show, then Dinah would allow us to put on a fashion show of Jockey jogging clothes, and during the course of that show, mention would be made a number of times that the clothes being shown were designed and manufactured by Jockey. We went to work.

With the client's approval, we engaged the services of James Fixx, author of the best-selling book, *The Complete Book of Running.* His expertise immediately lent credibility to the show. Jockey agreed to pay him $3,500 for his services. We then analyzed the list of our clients. Joanne Woodward had recently appeared on an NBC television movie in which she had played a marathon runner. She was already being talked of as an Emmy Award contender for her performance and she agreed that it would be advantageous to call attention to it by appearing on the "Dinah Shore Show," being interviewed by Dinah on the show, and then having Dinah use film clips of her performance. She loves to jog and agreed to jog on the show. Parker Stevenson of "Hardy Boys" fame, another Rogers & Cowan client and a jogging enthusiast, agreed to appear on the show. Hal Linden joined us too and the format of the show was completed. Someone came up with the idea to do the whole show on the Beverly Hills High School track.

On August 4, 1978, the show appeared on the air. Dinah came on screen in jogging clothes, telling her audience that she was at the Beverly Hills High School track, that the whole country was jogging or talking about jogging, and that she had decided that the time had come to devote her whole show to the subject.

She then introduced Jim Fixx as the number one jogging expert in the country. They talked about some of the sport's do's and don'ts. Then the camera switched to Joanne Woodward jogging around the track. She finally arrived at the place where Dinah and Jim had been talking and, breathing deeply, sat next to Dinah for her interview. The show proceeded and then, after everyone was interviewed, Dinah explained that people weren't jogging in old sweat suits anymore.

119

Jogging called for stylish clothes these days, so she was bringing her viewers a men's and women's fashion show of jogging clothes by Jockey.

Then, from the other side of the track, appeared a dozen male and female models running toward the cameras in their latest-fashion Jockey jogging clothes. Each one came close to the camera. Dinah and Jim Fixx described the clothes, Joanne, Parker, and Hal oohed and aahed. There were a number of references to the Jockey advertising and sales promotion slogan, "Man in Motion," which Dinah had agreed to mention because our client was anxious to get that point across. When it was all over, everyone's needs had been satisfied.

The "Dinah Shore Show" had put on a very entertaining show for its viewers. Jockey, for a very small expenditure, had received invaluable exposure for its product. The public relations firm had done its job well. It had helped the "Dinah Shore Show" develop an informative, interesting show with important guests, which every show looks for. It had rendered an important service for its client.

Readers might ask, "If Dinah Shore wanted to do a show about jogging, why didn't she have her own production staff prepare it?" The answer is that the "Dinah Shore Show" prepares five sixty-minute shows every week. The show took hundreds of R & C man-hours to prepare. The "Dinah Shore Show" production staff could never have afforded to spend that much time to prepare any one show. This then was the perfect example of the media and the public relations firm working together for their mutual advantage.

The press still plays a very important role in our day-to-day activities. We work with the nation's newspapers, the syndicates, the magazines. Yet, television gives our clients the exposure and the impact that the printed word never could.

Over the years, we learned that the talk shows and the news programs would welcome working with us if we could furnish them with newsworthy and entertaining guests. We learned that the television news reporter and the host of a talk show are in the same position as a journalist. It is impossible for him to cover every beat himself, impossible for him to come up with news every day and newsworthy guests every day. He has a staff behind him, but they always welcome outside help. Their doors are open to the public relations man who can help make their shows more amusing, provocative, newsworthy. If we want our clients to get television exposure, it is our responsibility to think first of the needs of the television program and then develop ideas and approaches for our clients that will help fill those needs.

In successive years, we introduced two new dog food products for Ralston Purina. Both campaigns involved a spokesperson who would travel to major cities and make appearances on television talk shows and news programs to promote the product.

In the formulation of such a campaign, our first responsibility is to find a person whose qualifications assure credibility with the client, the television show, and the public. These qualifications include a logical identification with the product, an authoritative, outspoken point of view on the subject in question, and an attractive, personable manner that would project easily on camera. Overall, without compromising ourselves, Rogers & Cowan must be able to assure a talk show host that this person will give an excellent interview and that the audience will love him. The person must also be "available," that is, able to give us the two, four, or six weeks it might take to make a tour around the country.

Requirements and qualifications are far from fixed. We can use an eighteen-year-old girl or a sixty-five-year-old man. We have used a former Miss Universe, a New York restaurant owner, a chef in a Beverly Hills Italian restaurant, a UCLA water resources professor, a Detroit housewife who washes her clothes with Tide, and even at one time, the President of Hunt-Wesson Foods. For Ralston-Purina, we had to meet their requirements as well as the requirements of the media. We knew that we needed someone who was an authority on dogs. The person had to have a good reputation both personally and professionally, and we were charged with the responsibility of making certain that there are no skeletons in a spokesman's closet. The person had to be respected in the community of canine fanciers, and must be willing and able to speak convincingly about Ralston Purina dog food products. Once we satisfied the needs of the client, we also had to make certain that the person we selected would be acceptable to the media. It would do us no good if the client approved someone, and then have the television producers say that our selected person was not interesting enough, newsworthy enough, amusing enough, to make a suitable guest on their shows. Whenever we search for a particular kind of spokesman, it is a long and tedious procedure. We talk to experts in the industry, we talk to the press and ask them if they know of the kind of person we are looking for. In the case of

121

Ralston Purina, we talked with the editors of dog magazines, and pet editors of important newspapers.

For the two Ralston Purina campaigns, we found two perfect spokespersons to travel the country and promote the product. The first was a Hollywood dog trainer who was enormously effective in launching one of the new Purina products. He had credibility because he was an authority on dog training. He was acceptable to television programs because he told wonderfully amusing anecdotes about his dogs' experiences working in Hollywood movies. The client liked him because he was well spoken and lent credibility to the product as, fortunately, he had long used Purina foods to feed his dogs. The trainer agreed to accept $250 a day for a fee, and it was arranged that he would make appearances in twenty cities in four weeks—one city a day, five days a week.

The product introduction tour was most successful. Our dog trainer appeared on an average of three television programs and four radio programs in each city and did two newspaper interviews as well. Our public relations media campaign on television and radio acted as a supplement to the blitz advertising campaign which Ralston Purina launched simultaneously in each city featuring spectacular in-store displays in supermarkets in each of the twenty cities. The product was launched.

The second person was equally qualified but even more provocative—a woman who readily filled all the necessary requirements and qualifications.

One of my New York associates called me from New York to tell me that he had discovered a dog psychiatrist who had agreed to act as a traveling spokesperson for the new dog food product. I was not aware that there were dog psychiatrists. It was just too good to be true. I knew that television talk shows would love the idea of having a dog psychiatrist as their guest. It was a funny, provocative, and newsworthy idea, exactly what a talk show host looks for all the time. Then I was told what the major thrust of the interview would be.

"Listen to this," said my associate. "She says that there is nothing wrong with a dog that misbehaves. It's the owner. She doesn't give therapy treatments to the dog. She gives them to the dog's owner."

"Does she speak well? Can she handle herself well on a television program?" I asked.

"She not only speaks well," my associate replied, "but she's funny. She reminds me of Joan Rivers. When she was telling me about some

122

of her experiences I just couldn't stop laughing."

"She sounds perfect. Make an appointment to bring her to St. Louis to meet the Ralston Purina people. I'm sure they will approve her, but they should have an opportunity to see her in person before we ask them to do so."

As I thought, the client approved, and the dog psychiatrist made a triumphant tour of the country, promoting the new Ralston Purina dog product on television talk shows all the way.

The public is never aware when the creative brain of the public relations man is responsible for something they watch on a television program. A few years ago, we conducted a public relations program for AT & T designed to convey to the public that they are an EOE—Equal Opportunity Employer. The women's liberation movement was under way and the militant NOW group was charging that AT & T did not employ a sufficient number of women. Having a debate which goes "Yes, we do," "No, you don't," doesn't do any good. We had to prove our point—and one night Johnny Carson helped us do just that. Our research had indicated that there was a growing trend on the part of the telephone companies throughout the country which comprise the Bell System, to hire young women and train them to become linemen—or, in present parlance, linepersons. Further research turned up the fact that Pacific Telephone in San Francisco had a young, pretty, vivacious, eloquent woman in its employ working as a lineperson. Yes, she climbed telephone poles all day long. Someone in the office said, "Wow, wouldn't she make a great guest on Johnny Carson's show." Another said, "I've got it. She'll teach Johnny how to climb a telephone pole." We went from there.

First, a telephone call to the public relations man at Pacific Telephone in San Francisco. We told him of our idea. Could he make the young lady available? Would she agree to go on the "Tonight Show"? Could she teach Johnny Carson how to climb a telephone pole? Was it possible to bring two telephone poles into the NBC studio in Hollywood and affix them to the floor so that they would be climbable? The public relations man said he would call us back. He did the next day and gave us affirmative answers to all our questions.

I called an old friend, Fred de Cordova, producer of the "Tonight Show." I told Fred our idea. He laughed. "It's a funny idea," he said. "Let me talk to Johnny and see what he thinks. I'll let you know." Fred called back. "Johnny loved the idea. If you can arrange to set up the telephone poles on our stage and get the young lady down from

San Francisco, we have a spot open next Thursday night." I agreed, and we began to set up the arrangements.

The following Thursday night, in the middle of his show, Johnny Carson informed his audience, "Tonight we have the most unusual guest in the entire history of our show." After a short introduction, the curtains parted and out stepped our lady lineperson. She was dressed in her regular work clothes, blue jeans, a workshirt, a white hard hat with Pacific Telephone imprinted on it, spiked shoes, and an enormous leather belt with hooks attached. She was carrying another pair of spiked shoes, another hooked leather belt, and another white hard hat. The studio audience was silent. They had no idea what was about to happen.

"Tonight," Johnny said to his studio audience and millions of viewers throughout the country, "I am about to realize one of my life's ambitions. I am about to learn how to be a telephone lineman."

At that moment, four telephone company maintenance men walked on stage carrying two telephone poles and proceeded to set them up. In another moment, Johnny sat on the floor, took off his shoes, and put on the spiked shoes which the young lady had handed him. The audience started laughing. The camera moved quickly to Ed Mc-Mahon screaming with laughter and slapping his knees with both hands. The camera returned to Johnny. He was on his feet again; the young lady had fastened the hooked belt around his waist and placed the white hard hat on his head. The camera moved close in on Johnny. He gave the audience one of his typical quizzical looks as though to say "How did I get into all of this?" The camera pulled back. The girl looked thoughtful and competent. Johnny looked ridiculous, which was the intent. The audience kept laughing.

"Well, young lady, what do I do now?" asked Johnny.

"It's really very simple, just watch me," she replied. She unhooked her belt, wrapped it around the telephone pole, spiked one shoe into the pole, then the other, shifted her weight, lifted the strap, and in three seconds she was eight feet up the pole.

Johnny's mouth dropped open. He looked up. He looked at the audience. "Oh, no," he mouthed to the audience, "not me." He started to walk off the stage, clip-clopping his heavy spiked boots.

"Come back here," said our composed young lady. "Do you want everyone to think you are a coward?"

Johnny turned around, and walked back slowly, clip, clop, clip, clop, to his own telephone pole. The camera closed in on his deadpan

124

look. "Yes," he mouthed to the camera, "I'm a coward." Gingerly he unhooked his belt, wrapped it around the pole, lifted his right leg up to the pole. He jammed his spiked shoe into the pole, looked at the audience, and smiled.

The audience applauded. Now came the problem. How to get the left leg off the floor and on to the pole. He grabbed the pole with both arms and tried to get his foot off the ground. He couldn't do it. He sent agonized looks out to his audience while they laughed and applauded his clumsy efforts. Finally our Pacific Telephone lady, who had been encouraging him from atop her pole, resignedly climbed down. She unfastened her belt, and walked toward the struggling Johnny. She kneeled beneath him, placed both hands on his rump, and heaved his body upward. Johnny triumphantly lifted his left leg, placed the spiked shoe into the pole, and there he was, on the telephone pole, belt wrapped round in proper fashion, both feet in place, at least a foot off the ground. He laughed, took off his hard hat and waved it at the audience. They gave him a standing ovation. Enough was enough. The girl helped him down off the pole, and they walked together across the stage.

Johnny took his proper place behind his desk, and the young lady sat down in the interview chair. He began to interview her. She told him quickly about her early life, then about how she got her job with the telephone company, and how she was taught to climb the poles and make line repairs. Then Johnny asked the key question and she answered as we expected her to.

"And how does your salary compare with your male counterparts?" asked Johnny.

"Why," she replied, "my salary is exactly the same as the men's. I do the same job and naturally I get the same salary. And I have the same opportunity for advancement as they do."

Her segment on the show was completed. Rogers & Cowan had dramatically and effectively told millions of television viewers, through her appearance, that the telephone company was an equal opportunity employer, that women had the opportunity to get jobs at AT & T that were previously regarded as the exclusive prerogative of the male gender, and that when they did get one of those jobs, they were paid the same salary as a man. Achieving this was the crux of our responsibility to our client. AT & T was more than pleased with this one example of what we were doing to create a favorable climate for the company by telling the public that they gave equal job opportunities to women. In the next week, AT & T received hundreds of favorable letters, complimenting them on their employment policy, which proved to our client that we were helping them to achieve their objective.

Our print campaign, I felt, was not nearly so effective. You can read an article in the newspaper that says AT & T is an Equal Opportunity Employer, but it will never make the same impact on you as will the sight of a pretty young girl talking to Johnny Carson on the "Tonight Show," telling him about her job and the fact that her salary is equal to that of the men who perform the same job that she does.

 There is no doubt that today television is the most effective tool that the public relations man has in getting across his client's message to the public.

CHAPTER 12

Brassieres, Bouquets, and Murphy's Law

When Mr. Murphy stated that "If something can go wrong it will," his law was based on his experiences in the aviation business. He didn't know that it could also be easily applied to the public relations business.

I have learned that in planning a campaign, a promotion, or an event, I must project ahead and think through every situation that can go wrong, and be prepared for it to go wrong. This kind of thinking is essential to every aspect of our unpredictable business. Let there be no surprises. Still there are, and there always will be. And when there is a surprise turn of events, when something does go wrong, I simply step back and assess the situation in a new light. Yes, sometimes I'll concede it was Murphy's Law winning out again and leave it at that. In other cases, when something goes wrong, it can bring surprisingly serendipitous results, and we're ready to accept these with no questions asked. A good example of this was our campaign for the Hidden Treasure Brassiere—where a stunt we planned went all wrong and the end results could not have been better.

For many years I never thought of expanding our business into corporate public relations, financial relations, and product publicity. I was a product of show business, and had been led to believe that the corporate world looked down its nose at those of us who frequented Hollywood movie studios or Shubert Alley. It wasn't until later that I was told by the late Ben Sonnenberg that he had started his distinguished public relations career as a Broadway press agent. The move from the movie business into television had been a natural, easy transition for me, based on the accurate assumption that television was just another form of entertainment, on a small screen at home instead of a large screen in a theater. For a public relations person with my background, it was easy to predict success in television. Yet I never would have dreamed that a show business background was ideal training for representing the blue chip companies of the world. In the mid-fifties, just as television was becoming an important factor in my business life, I was literally pushed into corporate public relations and product publicity.

127

One night at a dinner party in Beverly Hills, I was introduced to a good-looking, well-groomed, smiling, suntanned New Yorker named Henry Plehn. We exchanged pleasantries for a few minutes and then he began a conversation that was to change my thinking about the public relations business from that very moment on.

"I understand you're a big wheel in Hollywood," he said. There was something provocative, not quite insulting, possibly combative about his remark and manner.

"I'm not a big wheel at all," I replied. "I'm in the publicity business in Hollywood, and I guess we're fairly successful."

He smiled. "I know you're the most successful publicity man in the movie business," he continued, "but you're not very bright."

What was he driving at? I didn't even know the guy. How did he know whether I was bright or not?

"There is a whole world out there waiting for your talent and your contacts. The streets are paved with gold and you're too dumb to get your head out of the clouds and pick it up."

Oh come on, I thought, this guy is just too corny.

"What world is that?" I asked. He was beginning to annoy me. What was he driving at?

"The world of business," he replied. "Product publicity, corporate public relations. Your Hollywood experience is invaluable. There are hundreds of companies, all over this country, all over the world, which would be interested in talking to you about their public relations problems. Many of them will quickly realize that the techniques you have learned can be applied effectively to the world of business."

I perked up. Maybe he's not corny after all, I thought. This man may be on to something. Why have I never thought of this before?

I nodded and asked him to continue. He did. He told me of the opportunities that lay in store for me, and the fact that it would be possible for me to charge substantially higher fees in the business community than I could in Hollywood.

"In fact," he said, "if you're interested, I have your first client for you."

"Who is that?" I asked.

"Me," he replied.

"Who are you?"

"I'm the President of Peter Pan Foundations. We are in the bras-

128

Who launched whose career? The author and Rita Hayworth, forty years
after the ingenious publicity campaign that was such a resounding success
for them both.

At home with Joan Crawford, watching a movie in her private projection room, with director Vincent Sherman at right.

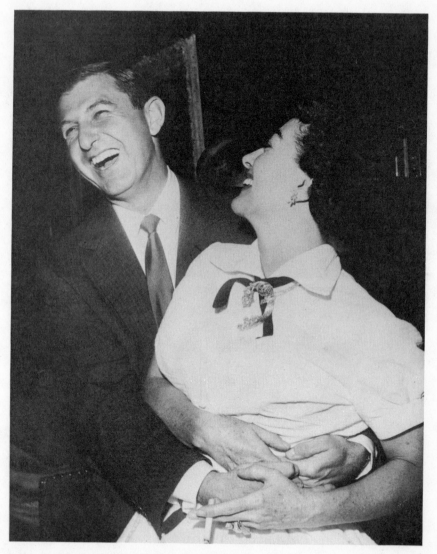

I thank Joan Crawford for the surprise party she gave on my fortieth
birthday . . .

. . . and dance with her daughter Christina, then sixteen. Little did we know then what horrors Joan's children had weathered with their "Mommie Dearest."

Olivia de Havilland wins her Oscar for *To Each His Own* and I am
convinced I have the Midas touch, thus setting myself up for a hard fall.

On the roof of the Mark Hopkins Hotel in San Francisco, client Jane Wyman takes a relaxing break with the author during a whirlwind publicity tour.

Being in the publicity business has some rewards: holding the beautiful
Maureen O'Hara in my arms.

Many years after our ominous confrontation in the McCarthy days, John
Wayne and I let bygones be bygones.

June Allyson whispers pretty words to her favorite publicist.

With Audrey Hepburn, very much "My Fair Lady," on the
set of the movie at Warner Brothers Studio.

The author, wife Roz, Audrey Hepburn, and then-husband Mel Ferrer
relax at the Hollywood Bowl.

The author with peripatetic Danny Kaye in Moscow on his State Department tour.

Danny Kaye relaxes in his dressing room after a television show, greeted
by Roz Rogers, the author, and other well-wishers.

One of the highlights of my career, serving as Press Officer to Prince Philip on his goodwill tour of America. Performing introductions at one of countless receptions (above); briefing Prince Philip before a press conference (top right), and sharing an informal moment together with Roz in Palm Springs (lower right).

The Duke of Bedford, flanked by the author and wife Roz, in front of Woburn Abbey, after their tiff was settled.

siere and girdle business. If you are interested, I would like you to handle our account."

"We-e-e-l-l," I hesitated, "I'm not quite sure what I could do for you."

We chatted for a few minutes and I agreed to meet with Mr. Plehn the following week at his offices in New York. He would tell me all about his brassiere business and I would then decide whether we should take on this challenging new assignment.

When I met with him again, Mr. Plehn explained to me that his design engineers had just developed a new model padded bra which could do more for a woman's shape than Mother Nature could ever have imagined. He had named it "Hidden Treasure." The reaction from department store buyers was very enthusiastic, and Mr. Plehn said that the merchandise would be available to the public in about six weeks' time.

Although it was not yet clear to me how I could make the American woman conscious of Peter Pan bras in general and Hidden Treasure in particular, I agreed to take on the client. This account seemed to me to present a challenge and that intrigued me. We determined a fee arrangement, and as we shook hands before my departure, Mr. Plehn said, "I have great confidence in you, Henry. I know that your show business background will enable you to do a job for us that no other public relations office here in New York can do. I know, I tried four of them before I approached you."

It was kind of Henry Plehn to be so complimentary, but I had not yet developed a plan for him. I called a meeting in our New York office where we racked our brains as to what could be done to launch a publicity campaign for the Hidden Treasure bra. Our thinking was routine. We would write press releases for fashion editors and send them around the country with photographs and drawings. We could contact the women's foundation editors of the fashion magazines and show them the new design, pointing out what it could do for the woman who did not have an ideally shaped or full bosom. I was not at all inspired.

Then came the breakthrough. I had long discovered that many of my best ideas come from meticulously reading the morning newspaper, always trying to relate my clients to what is happening in the news. That morning was no different than the others and yet suddenly there it was, the word "bra" leaping right out of an Associated Press story with a Miami dateline. The Miami telephone company had apprehended a number of its female employees who had been caught stealing ten-dollar rolls of quarters. They had stuffed these rolls of quarters inside their bras and left the offices every night without being noticed. It had taken many weeks before they were finally caught.

I smiled. Here was our opportunity to bring the Hidden Treasure bra effectively to the attention of the public. If all the Miami telephone girls were forced to wear Hidden Treasure bras, they could no longer steal those easily stacked rolls of quarters. The heavily padded Hidden Treasure bra was designed in such a way that it made it impossible for a woman to push a roll of quarters down inside it. It was wired, top, bottom, and sides, and even if a woman managed to push a roll of quarters down inside, it would be too painful for her to keep it there for very long.

The idea fell into place. We would send a Peter Pan representative, a beautifully endowed young lady, with 100 Hidden Treasure bras, to Miami and have her present them as a gift to the manager of the Miami telephone company. She would explain that his troubles would be over if he arranged for each of his girls to wear the Hidden Treasure bra instead of the one she had been wearing. I felt certain that the media, which had given the original story an important play because of its amusing implications, would give the solution to the problem an equally important play.

The first step was to find the right woman. I remembered meeting just such a candidate at a party a few weeks before. She had talked with me because she was an aspiring actress and felt that this Hollywood publicist could help her. I got her telephone number from my friend who had hosted the party, and in a few minutes I was talking with her. I told her what I had in mind, and that she would get a lot of publicity if she went to Miami as a Peter Pan representative. I explained to her that we would alert the press and local television stations to meet her at the manager's office when she presented him with the Hidden Treasure bras. She would have to take her blouse off to demonstrate how closely and firmly the bra fit, but that shouldn't offend her sense of modesty in the slightest, as the bra would cover her more thoroughly than did her swimsuit. She agreed to participate and I was ready to get the client's approval of our plan. I called him, told him about the story which had appeared in print, and explained to him what we intended to do based on what I had read in the paper. He loved it.

146

"Henry, I just knew you would come up with something as brilliant as this. I'm sure no other brassiere manufacturer or public relations office representing a brassiere manufacturer would have ever thought of such an ingenious idea. Go ahead, Henry, send the girl to Miami. I'll send the bras over to your office in assorted sizes."

"Mr. Plehn, thanks for the compliment, but you're part of this. You have to call the manager of the telephone company in Miami, tell him that you have solved his problem, and that if he approves, your representative will be in his office tomorrow morning."

"Give me his name and telephone number and I'll call you back."

Ten minutes later my new client confirmed that the manager had agreed to see Barbara at ten the following morning but did not promise to supply his young ladies with the Hidden Treasure bras. He would have to think about that.

I wasn't going to wait for him to decide. We alerted Barbara to get ready for the trip to Miami. Then we called the Miami newspapers, the wire services, and the Miami television stations, and alerted them to our plans. They thought it was funny and newsworthy and agreed that it would be an amusing follow-up to an already amusing story. They agreed to cover Barbara's meeeting with the telephone company manager the next morning.

Barbara arrived in our office the afternoon she was leaving for Miami. We briefed her on what she was to do. We rehearsed her as to what she would say to the manager, and what to say to the media. We gave her a roll of quarters. Sure enough, she couldn't slip it into her Hidden Treasure bra. She was ready. She put the carton of bras under her arm and left for Miami.

"Call me after it's over," I said to her. "You should be finished with everything by 10:30 and I'll be eager to hear how it goes."

At 10:40 the next morning Barbara was on the telephone.

"Well, what happened?" I asked.

Barbara hesitated. "Let me start from the beginning. When I arrived at the telephone company and walked into the reception room of the manager's office, it was jammed full with reporters, photographers, television commentators, and cameramen. They all gave me a big hello, but when I told the manager's secretary who I was and that I had an appointment at ten o'clock, she said she was sorry but I couldn't see her boss. She explained that when he discovered that his office was filled with the press, waiting to photograph him with me, he had changed his mind. He had decided that it was all a publicity stunt for Hidden Treasure bras and he wanted no part of it."

I groaned. Our whole plan had fallen apart. "Well, what happened then?" I asked anxiously. "Was that the end of it?"

"No. When the reporters heard what the secretary said, they told me that it was still a good story for them. Maybe even better than if the stunt had worked. I went out into the hallway with them, and they interviewed me. I told them exactly what I had planned to tell the manager. When the time came for me to show them how the roll of quarters would not fit into my Hidden Treasure bra, I took off my blouse. You should have seen their eyes pop. You've never seen so many flashbulbs go off. Then when I tried to slip the roll of quarters into my bra, one of those fresh reporters said he would be glad to help me. Everyone laughed. I laughed too, and just said 'No thank you.' And that's about it. In a few minutes it was all over."

"Barbara, it sounds just great! You did a wonderful job and I really appreciate it. I'm sure you and Hidden Treasure will get a lot of publicity coverage in tomorrow's papers. I hope it helps your career. We gave you an expense advance before you left, and your fee for two days' work will be in your apartment mailbox when you get home, with an added bonus."

The *Miami Daily News* ran a photo of Barbara with the whole story that afternoon; the *Miami Herald* picked it up the next morning. All the evening news shows in Miami carried it, and the network news ran it that evening. All the New York papers and the Associated Press and United Press ran stories about the Miami telephone company, Barbara, and the Hidden Treasure bra, and their versions of the story also appeared in hundreds of newspapers throughout the county.

Henry Plehn and I had lunch the next day.

"My telephone hasn't stopped ringing since yesterday afternoon," he said. "Our salesmen from all over the country have been calling. Buyers and merchandise managers from the leading department stores have been calling. My wife says all of her friends and her family have been calling. Everyone is talking about Peter Pan's Hidden Treasure bra. You and I will be working together for many years, Henry; Rogers & Cowan is what Peter Pan has needed for a long time."

"Henry," I replied, "I'm delighted you're pleased. But I'm pleased too. I'm also grateful to you, because as a result of your pushing me

148

into it, we're now in a new business—product publicity."

We did represent Peter Pan for many years. And as a result of Henry Plehn's telling me one day that I wasn't very bright, product publicity has been one of the major factors in the Rogers & Cowan business ever since.

The Peter Pan publicity stunt, and it was a stunt rather than a long-range program, had not gone according to the original plan. The manager of the telephone company had not seen our young lady with her supply of Hidden Treasure bras, nor were the telephone company employees wearing the bras, which was the original intention. Fortunately, our representative went ahead on her own and put on her performance for the press, and they responded the way I had hoped. We got as much publicity coverage as we would have if the plan had gone according to schedule.

Sometimes, however, we are not that fortunate. There are times when something goes wrong and, as a result, an entire project, an entire campaign, goes down the drain.

When I am asked the difference between advertising and public relations, I explain that advertising is an exact science and public relations is an inexact science. A simple example of this theory as it applies to advertising is that the agency with the approval of the client prepares an ad. The copy, layout, and color are spelled out in advance, and it appears in the magazine or newspaper exactly as planned. The agency pays for the ad's publication, and is reimbursed by the client with 17.6 percent added as its fee.

In a public relations program, media placement becomes part of the overall assignment, but the public relations man has no control over what appears in print. He doesn't pay the media, and is consequently subject to the media's will in determining the fate of the information which has been submitted. A press release on a corporation's earnings statement may be cut in half by the editor because of lack of space. A press release announcing a new product may be rewritten entirely by the editor and the rewrite may put a completely different emphasis and consequent meaning on the announcement.

I have always felt that Murphy's Law was written for the public relations practitioner. It has many versions, chief among which are "If something *can* go wrong it will," "If anything can *possibly* go wrong, it will." There is, however, only one version of Sullivan's Law, which states simply that Murphy was an optimist.

I illustrate this observation by using the example of Warren Avis,

149

one of our clients. Mr. Avis, founder of Avis-Rent-a-Car, sold his business many years ago, and went on to become one of the nation's leading entrepreneurs. He is in the real estate business, has ranching interests, conducts an Institute of Psychological Research in Ann Arbor, has written three books, and also runs Avis-World-Wide Flowers.

Avis-World-Wide-Flowers was his brainchild. It works like this. Instead of following normal procedures in ordering flowers, the purchaser simply telephones 800–648–AVIS, gives his order and his credit card number to the girl who answers, and the flowers are delivered the same day—in most cases—to any city in the United States. In addition to affording his customers convenience and prompt service, Mr. Avis also prides himself in selling flowers well below the market price.

We started our campaign to bring Avis-World-Wide-Flowers forcibly to the attention of the American public by staging a news conference at the Biltmore Hotel in Los Angeles. It was well attended by reporters and newsmen from the *Los Angeles Times* and *Herald Examiner, Wall Street Journal,* Associated Press, *Business Week,* four radio and three television stations. Mr. Avis is a newsworthy personality and, because we are conscious of his name as a result of our constant exposure to Avis-Rent-a-Car, his activities have always been of interest to the media.

Mr. Avis stepped to the microphone, introduced himself, and told the media representatives about his new business enterprise. The reporters made their notes, the television cameras whirred, and the radio microphones picked up the voice of our distinguished client. One of the major points stressed was price advantage.

"Because of our marketing methods," stated Warren Avis, "we are able to undercut the prices of other florists or florist delivery services. For instance, the price of long-stemmed roses ranges in different parts of the country from twenty-five to thirty-five dollars a dozen. Our price is fixed at $17.95 a dozen. And that price applies to any city or town in the country." After a short question-and-answer session, the news conference was over.

That evening I had been invited to a cocktail party which was being given in Warren Avis's honor. A moment before the seven o'clock television news came on, I asked him to come into the library with me. The NBC Channel 4 news commentator had attended our conference earlier that day, and I was anxious to hear whether he used the Avis story, and, if so, how it would be handled. The commentator came on screen, and sure enough when it came time for a summary of the local news, there was Warren Avis telling the story of the Avis-World-Wide-Flowers business. The film had been well edited to cover all the important points. The telephone number 800–648–AVIS was stressed as was the fact that roses cost only $17.95 per dozen as against the normal price of $25 to $35. Warren and I were elated.

Then Mr. Avis went off camera and the news commentator came back on. "Mr. Avis's remarks about his new business impressed me so much," he said, "that I decided to send roses to my lady friend just before this program went on. I dialed 800–648–AVIS just as I had been directed to do, and the operator answered. I gave her all the information she asked for, and then I asked her how much were the roses. She replied, twenty-five dollars a dozen! I canceled my order. And so goodnight for Channel 4 News in Los Angeles."

The news show went off. I looked at Warren Avis. His usual ruddy complexion had paled. "What the hell happened?" he exclaimed. He walked briskly to the telephone and dialed 800–648–AVIS. "Who is in charge there?" he asked. The operator answered him. He turned to me. "The son of a bitch is out to dinner," he said. He then talked to the operator. She knew nothing. She said that her job was to quote the prices that were in front of her—and yes, the price of roses was twenty-five dollars a dozen.

Warren was furious. So was I. His integrity had been impugned. So had mine. An hour later the telephone rang. The man in charge had returned from having his dinner. He made some lame excuse as to why the operator had been quoting a $25 price that day instead of $17.95. Warren ordered the price to be changed back to $17.95 immediately. An hour later I called and ordered some roses. The price was $17.95. But it was too late. The damage had been done. We telephoned the news commentator and told him what had happened. We were hoping that he would clarify the situation on the eleven o'clock news, but he didn't. The Warren Avis story had to give way to other fast-breaking news.

So, once more Murphy's Law had come into play in the public relations business. But we are not yet finished with Murphy's Law and Avis-World-Wide-Flowers.

A few months later *Time* agreed that Warren Avis's new business and some of his other activities were sufficiently newsworthy to warrant an article in that illustrious publication. A reporter from the "Business" section, having been thoroughly briefed by one of my associates in advance, interviewed Mr. Avis in his New York Fifth Avenue apartment. Shortly after, the editors sent a photographer up to the apartment as they planned to illustrate the article with at-home photos. A week later we inquired and were told that the article was to appear the following Monday.

We were delighted. Such an article would certainly have a significant effect in generating public interest in Avis-World-Wide-Flowers. I called Mr. Avis to tell him the good news and we then impatiently waited for the appearance of the latest issue of *Time* on Monday morning. When the big day arrived, I looked through the index to find the page number of the "Business" section. I looked and looked but it wasn't there. Maybe they had put it in another section. I looked, page by page. The story wasn't there.

I called the reporter who had done the interview. "I hate to bother you," I said, "but I'm curious as to what happened to the Warren Avis article?"

"It was killed at the last minute," he replied.

"Why? What happened?"

"The Pope died."

"I know the Pope died," I said. "But what has that got to do with the Warren Avis article?"

"We had to kill eleven pages in order to make room for the story on the Pope's death. The Avis story was one of many that were dropped," the reporter explained.

"Will it run next week?" I asked.

"I have no idea," was the reply.

The story on Warren Avis never did appear in *Time*. By the following week, other business news had emerged that the editors regarded as more important and Warren Avis was forgotten.

Of course, Murphy's Law did not always apply to Warren Avis. We have had many successful experiences with him and to this day he continues to be an important client of Rogers & Cowan.

Since brassieres and bouquets came into my life, I know that there will always be a Murphy's Law at work. Sometimes it does not hamper the effect of a particular effort, as was the case with our Hidden Treasure bra promotion many years ago. In other cases, such as the

152

campaign tactics for Warren Avis's flower service, it completely scuttles our plans. Public relations is far from being an exact science, but I have learned to accept the fact that the best-laid plans often go awry, and that the best way to absorb the shocks is either to look for something good in a bad situation or let it rest and move on to the next challenge without a moment's hesitation.

CHAPTER 13
I've Heard Some Kookie Ideas in My Time

I have conceived and executed hundreds of publicity and public relations programs over the years, but the ones that are remembered and continue to be discussed by my friends and in business quarters are the funny, kooky, insane, incongruous ideas that catch the fancy and appeal to the sense of humor of the media. When I was engaged in 1966 to take Prince Philip on a tour of the United States, the *London Express* page 1 headline blared, "The 'Octopus' Men Boost Philip's Tour." The article then went on to explain that "the firm is Rogers & Cowan which once publicized a waterproof watch [Timex] by strapping one on an octopus." By such deeds does a public relations firm become recognized.

When a client calls to say that there is an important news announcement to be released, our job is easy. We learned the rudiments of this part of our job many years ago. We know how to write a news release so it is acceptable to the media, and we know whether a particular story is geared to the financial editors, the movie editors, the television press, or the city desk.

The true problem in public relations arises when the client has nothing that is particularly newsworthy to announce, and it then becomes our responsibility, in accordance with the program that we and the client have already agreed upon, to create situations, promotions, stunts, ideas that will be picked up by the media, and help us to achieve our clients' objectives.

Warren Cowan is the most creative publicist in the world—in my purely subjective opinion. I think I'm pretty good too. However, neither of us depend on our own creative juices to come up with ideas for every client. We bring in our associates and have brainstorming sessions, and we are open to anything that they come up with. Usually, as a result of our putting our heads together, we come up with something that is right for the client, and that will be of sufficient interest to the media to enable us to take our campaign for the client forward another step.

At Rogers & Cowan everyone is free to speak up. I've heard some kookie ideas in my time, but I have also learned to listen very care-

154

fully to what is said, and to who says it. Some of the best, most original campaigns have come from the unlikeliest corners of the conference room. A good example of this was our memorable campaign for the "Jack Benny Show."

Lever Brothers, the sponsor, engaged us to handle publicity for the Jack Benny television series. Lever Brothers ran commercials for a number of their different products on the "Jack Benny Show." It was important to them to reach the largest possible audience, as the greater the audience, the greater the potential for increased sales of its products. It has long since been agreed that continuing publicity coverage on a television series is important in keeping the ratings at a high level. The network press information departments do their best to give high visibility to all their shows. Most advertisers who sponsor series or what we call "specials," find it is advantageous to engage a public relations organization which is a specialist in television to supplement the activity of the network press information department. Hence, Lever Brothers was a client of ours at that time; we handled publicity for the television series which they sponsored.

Jack Benny had already been a television star for many years and it was a challenging assignment to come up with a fresh idea to stimulate the press to give important coverage to his new television season. We started with the premise, "Let's think of something that will reflect everything that Jack Benny stands for." From there we proceeded to the point where we decided to have a celebrity-press party to usher in the new season. Something new? Something different which reflects the Jack Benny character? Should we have another celebrity give a party in honor of Mr. Benny? The Mayor? The Governor? This discussion took place at a staff meeting in our Beverly Hills office. Ideas were tossed back and forth and time wore on with no results. Then suddenly, an unfortunately long-forgotten associate held up his hand and timidly said, "How about having Jack Benny host a party at the Automat?" What a perfect idea. I almost kissed him.

Most of the Automats have long since departed from the New York scene. In those days, they were an institution. Horn & Hardart's Automat was a chain of restaurants where food was displayed behind glass doors. In order to get the dish you wanted, whether it be a ham sandwich, scrambled eggs, beef stew, or chili and beans, you merely put the designated amount of money, twenty cents, thirty-five cents, fifty cents, all in nickel, dime, and quarter change, into the slot alongside your preferred dish. The glass door would then open automatically; you would take your dish, pick up your silverware, and walk over to an empty table where you could comfortably eat your breakfast, lunch, or dinner.

The association between Jack Benny and the automat was perfect. The Automat was known as the cheapest restaurant in New York. Jack Benny had built a character for himself over the years that was based on the fact that he was the cheapest man in Hollywood. The press was accustomed to going to celebrity parties at 21, Sardi's, the Waldorf, and a dozen other recognized elegant restaurants and hotels in New York. For Jack Benny to host a party at the Automat was an inspiration.

I called Irving Fein, Jack Benny's manager at the time, and told him the idea. He laughed. "I love it," he said. "I'm sure Jack will love it too. I don't know why we never thought of it before."

I then called Sam Thurm, Lever Brothers Vice-President in charge of advertising, our client, to get his approval. "It sounds good," he said, "Do you think you can get press coverage on it?"

"I'm so sure of it," I replied, "that if we don't I'll pay for the party out of my own pocket."

"Don't be silly," said the client. "Do you have enough money in your budget to pay the costs?"

"Of course we have," I answered. "We have enough for a party at 21; this party will cost 10 percent of what we had originally planned."

"Go ahead," said Sam, "and good luck."

Jack Benny gave us a formidable list of all his celebrity friends in New York; we added to it press, television, and radio reporters who we felt would give us coverage.

What kind of an invitation would we send? A penny postcard, of course! We wrote the invitation for Jack. It said, "Over all the years I have had the reputation of being the cheapest man in Hollywood. I always resented this and have now decided to refute this unwarranted charge and prove that it isn't true. Please join me at a party I am giving on the occasion of the launching of my new television series on —————— evening —————— at 8:30 P.M. at Horn & Hardart's Automat on Fifth Avenue and Forty-Fifth Street. Dress— Black tie for the gentlemen, long dresses for the ladies. Please RSVP my office at 486–7100. Sincerely, Jack Benny."

The invitations went out and every important celebrity in New York responded immediately. They knew and liked Jack and it sounded like fun. Jack was kidding himself again, taking his professional reputation of being a cheapskate, a reputation that he had carefully nurtured over the years, a reputation that had been the subject of many hundreds of television and radio shows over the decades, and was capitalizing on it with a party he was giving at the Automat, the cheapest-priced restaurant in New York. The press responded because they knew that this would not be an ordinary press party, that there would be all sorts of celebrities invited. They knew that there would be plenty to write about, because Jack had always had the reputation among the media of being a newsworthy personality.

One of the columnists wrote, "It looks as though this may be the funniest of all television seasons for Jack Benny. The deadpan violin-playing comedian already has everyone in New York laughing with his penny postcard invitation to a party he is hosting at the Automat to prove to his friends that he's not a cheapskate after all."

On the night of the party, Jack, Irving Fein, some of my New York associates, and a number of people from the CBS press department arrived at the Automat about an hour early.

"What is the routine?" asked Irving. "What do you want Jack to do?"

"It's very simple," I said. "Jack, you stand here behind the cashier's stand. There will be 150 rolls of nickels stacked up here in front of you. As each person arrives, you will greet him, and hand him a two-dollar roll of nickels. All you have to say is, 'Have a good time.' You might want to mention that when they run out of money they can come back for another roll of nickels, but ask them not to come back too often."

Jack laughed. He got right into the swing of it. He saw that a bar had been set up on one side of the room, and a dance orchestra on the other. He could see that his elegant, wealthy guests would enjoy themselves in what was for them a totally incongruous atmosphere.

A half hour later the television camera crews arrived followed shortly by the television editors, gossip columnists, news reporters, and press photographers. Promptly at 8:30 the elite of New York's social, political, and show business world began to arrive, the men dressed elegantly in black tie, the women in their Givenchy, Dior, and Balenciaga gowns, sparkling with expensive jewelry. Jack stood behind the cashier's stand, solemnly handing out two-dollar rolls of nickels to his elegant guests. His straight-faced, deadpan expression occasionally broke into a smile. Everyone was laughing, drinking, dancing, putting coins into slots to get their dinner; the party seemed to be a smash hit.

Irving walked over to me at one point in the evening. "I'm curious about something," he said. "Let's go outside and see what kind of cars these people arrived in." We walked outside. Now we both started laughing. Parked outside the Automat, lined up on Forty-fifth Street on both sides of Fifth Avenue were chauffeured Rolls Royce, Cadillac, and other such limousines. We had never seen such an incongruous sight in New York, and we tipped off the news photographers and television news that this might give added color, another dimension, to their coverage. They agreed. Soon the chauffeurs and their limousines were being photographed as much as were Jack and his celebrity friends inside.

The next day there were headlines and photographs in newspapers all over the country. The television news shows all carried it. "Jack Benny launches new television program with a party at the Automat," "Jack Benny proves he's not a cheapskate by hosting celebrity party at Automat."

Rogers & Cowan had *made* news.

Brainstorming has paid off on any number of other occasions.

Once, in 1956, when Frank Sinatra was about to start work on his first western, *Johnny Concho*, United Artists had engaged us to handle publicity for the movie. This was at Frank's request, as he was one of our clients at the time. Frank Sinatra's first appearance in a western was somewhat newsworthy but it certainly wasn't earthshaking. How were we to bring to the movie added attention? Warren and I paced up and down the office one day trying to think of something, tossing this and that idea around fruitlessly. Suddenly Warren stopped and held up his hand, always the magic sign that inspiration had struck.

"I've got it. Let's get one of the big western stars to act as technical adviser on the picture."

"Great, maybe John Wayne or Gary Cooper might go for the idea."

"We had better ask Frank what he thinks before we go off half-cocked," said Warren.

"You're right," I replied, "I've an appointment to see Frank at the studio this afternoon. I'll discuss it with him."

158

That afternoon I sat in Frank Sinatra's dressing room on the movie set, going over business with him. Finally, as diplomatically as possible, I came up with our idea for promoting the movie. "Now here is another idea that Warren and I came up with this morning. We think you need a technical adviser on this movie. Let's face it, you're more at home in a dinner jacket than in those western duds you're wearing and you know that you're not the fastest gun in the west, even though Sammy Davis has been helping you with that fast-draw routine of his."

Frank laughed. "You're right, Henry. What do you have in mind?"

"We would like to try to get Gary Cooper or John Wayne to work with you as a technical adviser on this movie. The press will eat it up. It could be one of the high points in the campaign."

"Come on now, Henry, you're crazy. First, they wouldn't do it. Why should they? Second, this is a low-budget picture. Where would we get the money to pay them?"

"In our opinion, Frank, Warren and I both think that either one of them might regard it simply as fun, and that they would be delighted to be associated with you. No one's talking about money. This is strictly for laughs. We'll bring one of them over to the set one day, to help teach you how to handle a gun, place your hat on your head at the right angle, and walk properly in those high-heeled boots you're wearing. The whole thing will take an hour. We'll tip off the press and they'll be on hand when it all takes place."

Frank looked at me. "Do you really think that great stars like Cooper or Wayne would really do that—for me? Why would they?"

"I *think*, Frank, that there's a good chance they regard you as a giant star too."

Frank shook his head. "I don't get it, but if you and Warren think you can set it up, go ahead. You have my approval."

I left the dressing room and called Warren.

"Frank okayed the idea of the technical adviser. The ball is now in your court. I'm on my way back to the office."

Twenty minutes later I walked into Warren's office. He was all smiles. "I spoke to Gary Cooper. He agreed to do it!"

"Did you have to talk him into it?" I asked.

"Talk him into it? No, not at all," was Warren's reply. "He kept asking me, 'Does Frank really want me to do it.' It's the old story, Henry. We've seen it a hundred times. Gary Cooper is as impressed with Frank Sinatra as Frank Sinatra is with Gary Cooper."

A week later Gary Cooper, accompanied by Warren, walked onto the set of *Johnny Concho*. Frank was waiting for them. I had thirty-six members of the press waiting too. The two giants of the movie world shook hands. They had never met before. The press descended on them.

For weeks afterward the press all over the world reported that Gary Cooper had volunteered to act as technical adviser on Frank Sinatra's first western movie, *Johnny Concho*. The articles were illustrated with photographs. Again, Rogers & Cowan had *made* news.

Ideas like bringing Frank Sinatra together with Gary Cooper do not come from the stratosphere. Usually every idea we develop to *make news* stems from some experience that we have had in the past. Public relations is a continuing learning experience, and we constantly use the basis of ideas that have worked for us in the past, to develop news-making promotions for our clients in the present. In the Frank Sinatra-Gary Cooper case, we had drawn on our past experience that bringing together celebrities, particularly those who contrast with each other, is always of interest to the press. Bringing together a popular singer who was about to do a western movie with one of the world's most important western film stars, was something that we just knew would result in page 1 stories.

The incident had an aftermath. Gary Cooper was so impressed with what we had done that, shortly after, he hired Rogers & Cowan to represent him. We continued to represent him for many years, right up until his untimely death.

We have generated news events, literally hundreds of them, over the years, and we are constantly trying to think of new ones. The media is always willing to cover new, provocative, amusing, and unusual events. And the coverage they give to them is beneficial to our clients.

Recently, Warren had an idea that we called "The Billboard in the Sky," which we used to promote a movie, *The Cheap Detective*. We leased the rooftop of Bell Industries, a company that had offices near the Los Angeles International Airport. On the roof of the building we had painted in enormous white letters *The Cheap Detective*. For a month, two million people flying in and out of the Los Angeles Airport saw it, and the media, including *The New York Times*, AP, and UPI, all reported it as an ingenious new way to promote a movie.

Out of another brainstorming session came one of our most successful ideas for our client Danny Kaye, and his favorite charity. Danny Kaye has been closely associated with UNICEF for many years. At one point they approached him to make a nationwide tour of sixteen cities to promote their "Trick or Treat" fund-raising program just prior to Halloween. Danny was eager to participate but did not have a full three weeks in his schedule which such a tour would normally take. He turned to us, and we came up with an idea. Danny was a close friend of William Lear, the man who had designed and engineered the Lear Jet. Danny himself had been an inveterate flyer for many years, and, in fact, had just gotten his jet pilot license, which authorized him to fly his own jet. Working out all the details with the UNICEF people, we figured that if he flew his own plane, supplied by William Lear, he could visit sixteen cities in one and a half days, instead of the three weeks originally estimated for the tour.

With everything proceeding on schedule the UNICEF people in New York arranged with their chapters in each of the tour cities to have hundreds of school children at the airport meet Danny when he flew his plane into each city. The press, television, and radio in each city were all alerted: "Danny Kaye will arrive in your city at 10:25 A.M. to give a fifteen-minute press conference at the airport to announce the forthcoming 'Trick or Treat' UNICEF fund-raising drive in your city." At 8:00 A.M. one bright October morning, we held our first press conference at the Newark Airport, where the tour was launched. At 8:15, Danny and his Lear copilot taxied the five-passenger plane down the runway and readied it for takeoff. I was in the backseat with Paul Edwards of UNICEF. At 8:20 we were airborne and twenty minutes later we arrived in Philadelphia. At noon the following day we arrived in Los Angeles, the tour completed and all sixteen cities across the country visited for UNICEF.

Media coverage had been excellent. Local UNICEF chapters were most enthusiastic. We had made news again, and this time for a worthy cause. Danny was particularly pleased a few days later when he was told that proceeds from the "Trick or Treat" campaign were 25 percent higher that year than it had been the year before. Danny did his Lear Jet city-hopping tour for three years in succession. Each one was an enormous success—all the result of a clever idea that had popped up at Rogers & Cowan and that we had guided to great success.

The job of the public relations man is usually to manage the news that emanates from his client. There are times, though, when no news exists and that is when we rack our brains to make news.

In our office brainstorming sessions which are held regularly on behalf of our clients, all sorts of ideas are kicked around all the time. Occasionally one of them can be developed into a meaningful promotion for a client. Creative thinking in itself is not the answer; there are lots of ideas that come to mind but only a few that fit our requirements for a given campaign. Kooky as it may sound, each idea is considered and then weighed carefully against certain criteria: it must conform to the client's objectives, it must fit within the allocated budget, it must be of potential interest to the media, and finally it must have the desired effect on the public—get them to see a movie or tune in to a television program, make a contribution to UNICEF, or react in whatever way we and the client hope they will.

A painter gets great satisfaction when his latest work is hung in a museum. A writer is gratified when his book gets on the best-seller list. A lawyer smiles and eats a hearty dinner that night when the judge rules in his favor. I enjoy similar gratification and satisfaction when a kooky idea that we develop in one of our brainstorming sessions is so successfully planned and executed by us, that the client calls and says, "Henry, your people really did a great job for me. I appreciate it."

CHAPTER 14
Walking the Tightrope

As a public relations man, my contacts with the media are crucial if I am to serve my client effectively. Our relationship is based on trust —that is, the press, television, and radio must trust me as a reliable source of information. If I issue an earnings release on behalf of our client, Continental Telephone Company, the *Wall Street Journal* and other media outlets which carry financial news must regard me as an accurate source of news, and must recognize the importance of the press release which I hope they will run the following day. There must be an open, reciprocal working relationship between me and the media. If there is a breakdown in that relationship, I can no longer properly service my clients.

It is in this relationship with the media on one side and the client on the other, that I am constantly walking the tightrope. I am constantly trying to find the balance between serving the client and serving the media. Usually the rope holds firm and steady and there is no problem. Occasionally it begins to sway, the wind begins to blow, I lose my balance and fall off. In each case, I must guard against losing the goodwill and trust of the journalist or the broadcaster. There are hazards in every business, but the problem of falling off the tightrope on the wrong side of the media is that I have no way of climbing back up unless Mr. Media gives me his approval. He calls the shots and I am dependent on him—in most cases I have been treated fairly, occasionally not.

Fortunately, I have only fallen off a few times over the past forty years. I was unable to get my clients into Hedda Hopper's column for many years because she unfairly accused me of double-crossing her. Associated Press in Los Angeles once barred Rogers & Cowan from servicing news to them on our clients because of an incident involving Frank Sinatra, but a few months later, Hubbard Keavy, head of the bureau at that time, relented and agreed that we had been given a bum rap. When he was editor of *Esquire* many years ago, Clay Felker barred us from his publication because he claimed that one of our young associates, who has long since gone on to another career, had lied to him. Many years after that, when Mr. Felker set up *New York* and *New West* magazines, he still regarded Rogers & Cowan with a wary eye.

Is Rogers & Cowan beyond reproach in its dealings with the media? Of course not. We have made mistakes over the years. When we deal with the responsible media, we usually manage to come to an understanding with them which is satisfactory to everyone, but when we come into conflict with certain representatives of the media who are less than honorable, less than ethical, less than responsible, we are helpless. We throw up our hands in frustration, and say to our damaged client, "There is nothing we can do." The client says, "I'm going to sue them." I suggest that we seek legal counsel, knowing full well that his dedicated lawyer will never allow him to file a suit for libel. The odds are a thousand to one that he could ever win it.

The day after the John F. Kennedy Inauguration, I received an irate call from Washington from Frank Sinatra, who was our client at the time. I was in New York.

"Did you see that story in the *New York Daily News*?" he asked. I told him that I was reading the *Times* report of the Inauguration and had not gotten to the *News* as yet.

"I'll hold on," said Frank. "Read the color story on page 3 of the *News*." I hurriedly grabbed the *News*, turned to page 3, and quickly scanned it. There it was. In their reporting of the Inauguration, a paragraph was devoted to Frank Sinatra's drunken behavior in the reviewing stand during the ceremonies. I got back on the phone.

"Jesus, Frank, what did you do? How could you get loaded at the Inauguration ceremonies? President Kennedy is your friend!"

"For Christ's sake, Henry, why the hell do you think I'm calling you? I wasn't at the Inauguration ceremonies. I wasn't in the reviewing stand. I decided not to go at the last minute. I stayed in my hotel. There were a dozen of us here in my suite. We watched the Inauguration on television. Henry, call that son-of-a-bitch editor at the *News* and demand a retraction."

"Just a minute, Frank. You're not kidding me," I asked. "You really mean it? You weren't even there?"

"Henry, there were a dozen people there. I'll sue the bastard. Each one of them will testify in court."

"Okay, Frank," I replied. "I'll get on it right away. I'll call you back."

I called the *New York Daily News,* and asked for the city desk. That is proper procedure. A voice answered, "City desk." I introduced myself, and then told them why I was calling. One of his reporters who had covered the Inauguration must have made a mistake. Frank Sinatra wasn't in the reviewing stand—he hadn't attended the Inauguration ceremonies. I would appreciate it very much if he would run a retraction, also on page 3, in tomorrow's paper.

There was a pause. The man on the city desk asked me to wait a moment while he went to talk to someone else—obviously someone higher up. He returned to the phone in a moment.

"Sorry," he said. "We're not going to do anything about it. We won't run a retraction."

"Excuse me, sir," I said very politely. "You ran a story in this morning's paper which is obviously untrue. Mr. Sinatra has twelve witnesses who will state that he was not at the Inauguration. You also said he was drunk. This is damaging, harmful, and could make for a lot of trouble for Mr. Sinatra. Your reporter made a mistake. He probably saw someone in the crowd who looked like Sinatra, and thought it was him. Anyone can make a mistake. All we're asking you to do is correct your mistake. That's not unreasonable, is it?"

"Look, fella, I don't think you understand. We're not doing anything about this. We're not running a retraction and we're not admitting we made a mistake. You see, we don't like Frank Sinatra here at the *News*. We took good care of him today. If he wants to sue us, let him sue. We'll see how far he gets."

He hung up.

I called Frank. I was as furious as he was. We set up a conference call with his lawyer who was in Hollywood. Would Frank sue? The lawyer told us both to calm down. He would think about it until the next day. The days went on. The lawyer finally convinced Frank that it would be useless to sue. It would take years before it got to court. It would cost hundreds of thousands of dollars in attorney's fees. When it was all over, it was doubtful whether Frank could have proven damages. We were powerless. We were dealing with a journalist to whom journalistic integrity was unimportant. Over the years, Frank Sinatra has had similar experiences with the press. When occasionally he loses his patience and lashes out, or speaks his mind, I understand. The *New York Daily News*, fortunately for the public relations man, is a more honorable publication today.

One day a magazine editor called me to say that it was time to do an article on Audrey Hepburn. She had assigned a prominent writer, Eleanor Harris, to do the interview.

I told her that for a lot of reasons Audrey did not want to do any magazine articles that year, and I begged off. She was insistent. I told her I would think about it. Eleanor, who had been a friend for many years, called. She, too, tried to influence me.

The conversations went back and forth for a number of days, and then I made a mistake—I finally capitulated. After all, one man has little chance against two women.

I called Audrey. I told her that I realized we had decided not to do any magazine interviews that year, but this was a different case. Both the writer and the editor were friends of mine. It would be a very up-beat, constructive story. I would arrange to stall publication for six months. That would coincide with the release date of her latest motion picture, and, all in all, it was a constructive, logical recommendation. She reluctantly agreed.

She did the interview—in fact, she did a series of interviews with Eleanor Harris.

Some six months later the story appeared in the magazine. It was prejudiced, unfair, and often untruthful. I was shocked; I had been double-crossed.

I wrote a letter to Eleanor Harris and a copy to her editor, which ran as follows:

> *Dear Eleanor:*
> I always knew that some day a beautiful woman would get me into trouble. I was right.
> If you remember, I had originally rejected your request to do an Audrey Hepburn piece for *Ladies' Home Journal*. Then I succumbed to the charm and beauty of you and your editor. I just read the story. I have been double-crossed.
> You and I both know that your name is attached to a dishonest article. I am sure that your first version, which your editor obviously rejected, was a completely honest one. It was so honest that the magazine didn't want to run it. They evidently didn't believe that Audrey Hepburn was really such a nice person. They evidently didn't believe the results of the research you had done, and they evidently didn't believe the quotes you got from all the people you interviewed. . . . They just decided that it wouldn't sell magazines.
> When your editor turned down the piece, you were faced with the problem of how to make the story acceptable. You then came up with the gimmick that made the editors accept it. You said to yourself, "No one can be that nice. It is evidently all an act.

Audrey Hepburn has done a superb job of fooling me and everyone around her. I'll take the same story, tell my readers that she is all these wonderful, wonderful things, but imply throughout it that she is really a phoney, and that her whole life is one big phoney act."

You relate a series of anecdotes, all pointing to the fact that Audrey Hepburn is a remarkable woman, but, just to make sure everybody knows it is a phoney act, you throw in little zingers like "It's that princess bit again." Then, "heroically long suffering."

You then say that she is "almost too good to be true as an actress, a wife, and a homemaker." Your authority for this statement is some unidentified ghost who says that she "isn't true."

That's my comment on the story. I have been deceived. My client has been maligned. There is nothing I can do about it except tell you how I feel.

I never received a reply to that letter. The editor knew that a bitchy story would sell more magazines than an "up" one. The writer was forced to do the rewrite as requested or she would not have received her fee. Who is to blame? Economics, I guess. The editor is pressured by her publisher to sell more copies. She knows that a critical story on Audrey Hepburn will sell more copies than a flattering piece. The writer has worked for two or three months on a story, and now there is a possibility that she will not get paid for her efforts. She must compromise her integrity in order to obtain her financial reward. I neither condemn nor condone such practices. Each of us has to live with his own conscience. I have tremendous respect for the media. I work with them every day, but I soon learned that mixed in with the good guys who are in the great majority, are some rotten apples who make life for the public relations man more difficult than it should be.

The late Mike Connolly, who wrote the gossip column for the *Hollywood Reporter*, was an irresponsible man. I went to see him in his office one day and factually proved to him that a scurrilous item he had printed on Kirk Douglas, one of my clients, the day before was 100 percent untrue. I asked him for a retraction. He refused. "I never retract an item I've printed. It doesn't matter to me whether it's true or untrue. It's my policy. No retractions."

A few weeks after that incident occurred, I went to see him again about a false remark he had made about Shirley MacLaine. Again he refused. I called Shirley and told her that I was helpless. "Don't

167

worry about it, Henry," she said. "I'll take care of him myself." And take care of him she did. She walked into his office, looked at him, and requested he "Stand up." He did. She pulled back her Irish arm, clenched her Irish fist, and belted him, right in the chin. She walked out with a big grin on her face.

Recently a publication printed a syndicated article about our client Marlo Thomas which stated that she had spent $50,000 on shoes in one year in a Beverly Hills shop. The piece was picked up by many papers across the country. She was furious, indignant. The item was an outright lie and she found it humiliating, in light of her altruistic efforts on behalf of ERA and other progressive women's causes. Marlo regards herself as a responsible woman first, and an actress second. She wants to be regarded by others as a responsible woman, and this kind of ridiculous item seemed to refute her efforts. On her behalf we attempted to get a retraction. It was refused. Out of frustration, Miss Thomas wrote an article on the subject in which she made a plea for responsible, honest reporting.

We were impressed with it, and tried to get a respected publication to publish the article. No one would. I can only assume that they did not want to get involved in a battle that was not theirs, or possibly they did not want to admit to their readers that irresponsible, dishonest reporting exists in these United States.

Ladies' Home Journal ran an article in a recent February issue called "Celebrity Valentines." The article dealt with what Valentine's Day meant to the stars—people whose well-publicized love affairs often seem larger than life. The article included the supposed Valentine's Day experiences of two of our clients, Ali McGraw and Robert Wagner. Their comments were innocuous, unimportant, certainly not malicious, not libelous. What was wrong? Why did we object? It was all a fabrication. It was all a lie. The writer had never talked with our clients; the quotes were made up of whole cloth. The incidents had just never happened. We called the present editor, Lenore Hershey, a woman of integrity. A retraction was not important, nor even called for. We just wanted her to know that she had been bilked by an irresponsible reporter. "Thanks for telling me," she said. "I'll never use that writer again."

In another case the *National Star* ran a story with a headline that ran: "Ali McGraw reveals the new man in her life and says, 'I know it's really love.'" The article was written by Robin Leach.

In it the author stated, "She told the *Star* in an exclusive interview."

Ali McGraw never gave the *Star* an interview—much less an *exclusive* interview.

The article went on to quote Larry Spangler, Sue Mengers, and Candice Bergen with revealing details about Ali's "hottest new romance." None of them had ever given interviews to Robin Leach or any other *Star* reporter.

All of this does not mean that the media is corrupt, dishonest, and unprincipled. It just means that some individuals are. It does not mean that all of us in public relations are honorable and noble. Just some of us are. The journalist and the public relations man—both of us are just human beings.

Most of our dealings are with responsible media, media we trust and respect. Usually there is a smooth working relationship between the public relations man, the media, and the client, but the very nature of the business makes it inevitable that things can go awry very easily—and do. We don't have a media-client crisis every day, but time and time again, situations which we expect will go smoothly, go instead against all our expectations. Here are a few examples of what can happen, and occasionally does.

We call a news conference for a client, and expect that the media will cover and accurately report the news that the client plans to announce. In most cases, that is exactly what happens, but there are instances where:

1. The media doesn't show up. Very embarrassing for us. We may have miscalculated the news value of our announcement and the media at the last minute decides that it is not important enough for them to cover.
2. A reporter at the news conference asks our client a provocative question which the client resents. He blows his cool, saying things he shouldn't, and the result is unfavorable rather than favorable media coverage the next day.
3. The media misinterprets our press release and the remarks of our client, and the result is that an obscure part of our story becomes the lead and what we regarded as the primary thrust of our announcement is literally ignored.

We send out a press release. It is usually treated in a responsible fashion. There are times, however, when:

1. It is completely ignored by the press. A world-shattering event has taken place the same day and our release winds up in the

169

editor's wastebasket. The client is disturbed and says that he thought even the outbreak of World War III should not have prevented the press from using his news announcement.

2. The rewrite man on the newspaper sees a different thrust to the story and rewrites it so that when it appears in print it is difficult to recognize as the release we had issued.

3. Ten minutes after the media has received our release, the client calls to say that some unforeseen circumstance has arisen and the story must not be released. When we tell him that it is too late, he pleads impending bankruptcy if we are unable to stop the presses—which we can't.

When we set up an interview for our client, it usually achieves the desired result. The reporter is pleased because he has gotten a good story, and the client is pleased because he has been quoted accurately. But there are times when:

1. The client shows up for the interview but the reporter doesn't, even though we had confirmed the appointment with both of them an hour before.

2. The reporter appears but this time the client doesn't. An hour before he had said that he would be there.

3. No story appears because the reporter says that the client didn't give him anything sufficiently newsworthy to write. The client demands to know why we have wasted his time.

4. The article appears and the client is furious because he says he has been misquoted. (The reporter usually has the article on tape but the client complains anyway that the troublesome quote has been used out of context.)

5. The article appears and the client is accurately quoted but he is upset anyway. His wife doesn't think he came off in a favorable light.

The tightrope keeps swaying all the time, back and forth, back and forth, and I always have to be ready to perform the balancing act. The client must be served, but we owe an equal responsibility to the media. The following is an example of my proving to a journalist that Rogers & Cowan feels just as strong a responsibility to the media as it does to its clients.

Vernon Scott, a UPI correspondent who has been a friend of ours for twenty-five years, interviewed an Exxon consultant for us recently in connection with a project we were handling for this largest company in the world. We expected a favorable article, but instead, it excoriated the company. We expected terrible repercussions from our client but fortunately they made no complaint. Exxon and the other oil companies have received so much bad press in recent years that they have become inured to it. When I asked Vernon a few months later, when we met at a party, why he had written such a supercritical article, he answered, "That's the way I saw it, Henry. I knew you and your client wouldn't like it, but my responsibility is to UPI." I had no argument with my friend. He called it the way he saw it, and that is the chance that the public relations man always takes when he works with the media.

Of course we try to hedge our bets all the time. There are certain publications which are known to do hatchet jobs on personalities, and these we avoid. If they want to do a story on one of our clients, we avoid, evade, stall, and do everything we can to keep the client away from them. Sometimes they outsmart us. They do the story anyway, without even interviewing the client. They talk with people who know the client, and patch together a story in this way. There is nothing we can do about this. We are helpless and the clients know it.

There are certain free-lance writers who also do hatchet jobs. We avoid them as well. We make certain that they do not have access to our clients, but we can do nothing to prevent them from manufacturing an interview with a client.

What do I do when something goes wrong? An interview turns out badly, a press conference has not developed as we had planned, or a press release has not appeared as we had written it. What do I do? First, I don't cop a plea, I don't make excuses, and I don't try to blame anyone else. I usually say to the client, "We tried our very best and it just didn't come off as we had planned. We don't publish the newspaper, and we don't control what gets into print. Even though we are professionals, things occasionally go wrong when you deal with the media, and unfortunately, this is one of those times." I find that most clients, being professionals themselves, realize that in their business too situations get off the track at times. They accept what I say, and we go on to other matters.

Other times I say, "I'm not going to make any excuses. We goofed. We made a mistake. We handled this situation badly, and I apologize. We have represented you well for many years, and although I don't excuse mistakes made by our organization, I do hope that you will.

171

I'm going to do everything I can to make certain that something like this will never happen again." The client usually accepts this honest approach.

There are times when we don't come off that well. Recently we did an interview with a client that turned out badly. We had tried to stop him from saying derogatory things about his own customers. He persisted. When the story appeared in print, his boss was furious—and rightfully so. Our client had to figure some way to take himself off the hook so—he fired us. That is the nature of the public relations business.

The relationship between the public relations man, the media, and the client is always a delicate one and requires walking the tightrope every moment of the working day. It is the most challenging, most gratifying, and most frustrating aspect of the public relations business.

CHAPTER 15

Conflict of Interest:
An Ordeal in Murky Waters

Everyone in the service business at some time or another finds himself faced with a conflict of interest; it is as common a problem in the public relations business as it is in advertising, law, accounting, or any other "service" occupation. I cannot very well try to sell you on buying Ivory soap with one hand while I am holding a bar of Lux in the other. I would not think of representing Jaguar if I represented Mercedes. I would turn down Estée Lauder as a client if I represented Revlon. Those are obvious cases. The problem arises, however, when conditions are not as clear-cut as those described above, but rather murky, with no definite guidelines, no rules, to go by. In the murky conditions, I must rely upon my own business judgment, my own standards, my own code of morals.

My strategy is always to try to project the possibility of a conflict of interest in advance, before I take on a new client. In other words, if a prospective client appears at the door I make the decision then and there about whether there might be a conflict between the new client and someone presently represented by Rogers & Cowan. I use my own judgment and if I feel there is no conflict, I go on and try to conclude an arrangement with the prospective client. If I feel that there might be a conflict and I'm not sure, I then go to my present client and discuss it openly. It is most likely that the client will assure me there is no conflict and that I should go right ahead and pursue the prospective client. In that case, in my next conversation with the prospective client, I tell him about the present client, explain that both of us believe that there is no problem, and we proceed from there. On the other hand, if the present client had thought there was a conflict when I presented the situation, I would have gone along with my client's wishes, and no longer pursue the new one.

This clear procedure is easy to follow, but there are times when a client does not agree with my decision as to whether there is or is not a conflict of interest. When we represented the Polly Bergen Company, a cosmetics and fragrance firm, we also represented Vivian Woodard Cosmetics. We had represented both companies for a number of years. It was my reasoning that there was no conflict of interest because the Polly Bergen cosmetics were sold in leading department stores, while the Vivian Woodard products were sold door-to-door, similarly to Avon. We believed that the woman who buys her cosmetics and fragrances from a door-to-door representative rarely if ever buys those products in a department store. Hence, no direct competition.

Because the two companies were not competing for the same cosmetics dollar, I felt sure there was no need to tell Jack Levin, President of Vivian Woodard, that we represented Polly Bergen at the time when he was about to become our client. If we had represented Avon cosmetics, a direct competitor, we would have told him automatically that we could not represent him. Unfortunately, and unforeseen, Vivian Woodard felt that there was a conflict.

Levin called me one day many months after we had taken on his account.

"I understand that you represent the Polly Bergen Company," he said.

"Of course. Is there a problem?"

"Yes, there is," said Jack. "I cannot accept your representing a competitor."

I explained to Jack why Polly Bergen was not a competitor, but he did not agree with me.

"Please make a decision, Henry. You can represent either Vivian Woodard or Polly Bergen. You can't represent both."

I discussed it with Miss Bergen and she agreed with my point of view.

"Of course there is no conflict," she said. "We are both dealing in different marketplaces. As far as I'm concerned, Henry, I don't mind at all if you continue to represent Vivian Woodard."

When I got back to Jack Levin I told him, "I feel as strongly as you do about conflict of interest. If I had felt that the two companies were directly competitive, I would never have started to represent you. I'm sorry, Jack, I have no choice. If you feel that I am in conflict, then I must resign your account. If it's all right with you, we will wind up everything at the end of the month."

Jack and I agreed that there was no compromise, and we stopped our representation of Vivian Woodard, even though they were a bigger company and paid us a higher fee than the Polly Bergen firm. It would have been easy for us to give up the lesser-paying client, but I had no choice but to stay with Polly Bergen.

174

My reasoning was simple. I had long since decided that there was no conflict. One client agreed with me, the other didn't. If I had decided to go with Woodard, it would have been an admission that Jack Levin was right. In my judgment he wasn't and I had to back up the decision I had originally made.

There are other instances where the client feels we are in conflict and we don't. Sometimes he is adamant as was Jack Levin, and at other times he recognizes our position and agrees that we can proceed with both clients.

Some twenty-five years ago, we represented Dinah Shore and Doris Day. Dinah's primary public appeal was in radio at the time, later in television. Doris was essentially a movie star and a very important one. Dinah's then-manager felt that if we represented Dinah we should not represent Doris. We felt that he was being overprotective of his client. Was he saying that if we represented Dinah Shore we should not represent any other female vocalist? We felt that we should not be penalized just because we represented Dinah Shore. He finally agreed that we were right and that he was being overly protective of his client's interests. We continued to represent Doris Day and Dinah Shore for many years.

There are also cases where we take a second look at a situation and agree that the client is right and we are wrong. Such a situation arose very recently, where we decided that the client was right. Mike Douglas, the television talk show host, is an important and valued client. He and his wife Gen are two of the loveliest, warmest, and most reasonable people I have encountered in the world of show business, and I was surprised therefore when I received a complaint one day from Mike's business manager.

"Mike is very upset," he said. "He cannot understand how you can represent him and Merv Griffin at the same time."

I was very confused because I knew we didn't represent Griffin.

It must be understood that there has long been an intense rating competition between Johnny Carson, Mike Douglas, Dinah Shore, and Merv Griffin. Carson is a bit apart from the battle because he has that late-night spot, but the other three shows are syndicated, and constantly compete for ratings, sponsors, and the best time slots on stations throughout the country. A station in Cleveland doesn't have enough available time to carry all three shows so it decides on one. That leaves the other two competing to get on the other two available channels in the city. One channel might have available time;

the other one might not. It happens, then, that one of the trio is squeezed out of Cleveland. Then, to compound the problem, Mike Douglas might be aired at 5 P.M. on one channel, and Merv Griffin at five o'clock on another. Which show will the viewer tune in? Who will emerge the winner in the rating battle? These are not idle skirmishes. Millions of dollars are involved because advertisers invest their money in the shows which have the largest number of viewers. Thus the intensity of competition between talk show hosts can be readily understood.

"We don't represent Merv Griffin," I said. "We wouldn't represent Merv as long as we represent Mike. We know that would certainly be a conflict of interest."

"Henry," he replied, "you should know what is going on in your own organization. I'm telling you that you do represent Merv Griffin."

"I don't know what you're talking about," I said, "but I'll check it out and get right back to you. I'll talk to Warren. Maybe there is something going on that I don't know about."

I walked into Warren's office and asked, "Do we represent Merv Griffin?"

"Of course not," Warren replied. "What are you talking about?"

"I don't know. It's very strange. Vinnie Andrews just called to say that Mike Douglas was very upset because one of our competitors told him that we were representing the 'Merv Griffin Show.'"

Warren paused reflectively and leaned back in his chair.

"Christ," he said. "Now I remember. It's that Columbia deal."

"What Columbia deal?"

Warren reminded me about a special project deal we had just made with Columbia Pictures. Now he elaborated on it. "It is a three-month assignment, but I didn't go into detail when I told you about it. I never got around to telling you just what the assignment entails."

"I don't understand," I said. "What does Columbia Pictures have to do with Merv Griffin?"

"Wait a minute and I'll tell you. Columbia set up a promotion with Merv Griffin where Merv will devote three full shows to 'Columbia— Today and Yesterday.' They will try to get all the people who were big stars at Columbia years ago to appear on the show and air film clips of them before Merv does the interviews—and then they'll bring it up to date by getting the stars of all their current movies to appear. Then they will show scenes from the current films, and the three shows will be a series of terrific plugs for all the upcoming Columbia

176

productions. Great idea. Merv went for the idea because he'll get a lot of star guests who would normally be difficult for him to get, which could mean higher ratings for his show."

"That's all fine, Warren," I answered, "but what has all that got to do with us?"

"Columbia hired us to help line up the talent to appear on the show and then to publicize the shows. Oh, shit, there it is. It never dawned on me. That's why Mike thinks we're handling the 'Merv Griffin Show.' We are going head to head against the 'Mike Douglas Show.' By getting stars to go on Griffin and then promoting those shows we're bringing added viewers to Griffin and possibly taking viewers away from Mike. What do we do now?"

"There's only one thing to do," I replied. "Call Columbia and tell them we can't go through with the deal."

"How can I do that?" Warren said. "We just signed the contract today. It's so damned embarrassing."

"There's only one way to handle it," I said. "Call Bob Cort at Columbia and tell him the truth. Tell him we made a mistake. Tell him about our conflict of interest, and explain to him that we have to tear up the contract. He'll understand. In fact, he'll respect us more for it."

"You're right," Warren replied. "I'll call him now. I must admit that I never thought about a possible conflict of interest. If I had, I would never have made the deal."

I walked out of Warren's office. In a few minutes he walked back into mine. "It's done," he said. "I called Bob. He understood. They'll hire another office to handle the assignment."

I picked up the telephone and called Vincent Andrews. I told him what had happened and how we had quickly resolved the problem.

"Mike will be very pleased," he said.

"I'm going to call Mike myself," I said. "I want him to know that, even without the phone call from you, it would have quickly become apparent to us that we were in a conflict of interest situation and we would have walked away from the Columbia deal."

I called Mike and told him the whole story. He was most understanding, and very pleased with our quick resolution of the problem.

Then there was the case of Dean Martin and Jerry Lewis. They had been one of the most formidable comedy teams in the history of show business. When they split up there was much publicized bitterness and recrimination on both sides. Shortly after the announced

177

breakup, we received a call from Dean's agent. Would we be interested in representing Dean Martin? Of course we would. Warren had a meeting with Dean and a few days later, Dean Martin was added to our client list. A month later a call came in from Jerry Lewis, who was also interested in our representing him.

I had a meeting with him at Columbia Studios where he was preparing a film. He knew that we represented Dean. He didn't mind, even though a bitter feud had developed between the two men. We talked for an hour and then decided that we should both think it over.

I went back to the office and talked with Warren.

We both agreed that here was a definite conflict of interest. This show business feud appeared as though it would go on for many years, and we would be right in the middle of it. We couldn't win. The next day I called Jerry.

"Warren and I talked about it," I said. "We feel very uncomfortable in telling you this, but we feel that as long as we are representing Dean, we should not represent you. You said you didn't mind and thought there was no problem. We haven't even discussed it with Dean and we have no idea how he would feel about it. The fact is that Warren and I believe that if we were to represent you both, we could not act fairly toward both of you. We appreciate your thinking about us, but it would be better for everyone if you hired another publicity representative."

Jerry responded very favorably. He preferred to have us represent him, but he appreciated and respected our position. We have represented Dean Martin for some twenty years and although we continue to have a pleasant personal relationship with Jerry, we have never represented him.

Bob Hope was about to engage a new publicity firm after he'd had a falling out with his former representative. I telephoned him for an appointment but he did not return my call. Later I was told that he would not consider Rogers & Cowan because we represented Danny Kaye. His thinking was that if we represented Danny, we could not do him full justice. In contrast, we were engaged by Milton Berle at the height of his career, and he never felt that there was a problem in being represented by the same firm that represented Danny Kaye.

The conflict of interest situation is clearer in the corporate world. We could not very well represent General Motors and Chrysler. We could not represent Ford and Chrysler. We represent DMC-12, the

178

new John DeLorean sports car, but we would not represent Porsche or Corvette, who are direct competitors. Yet, we would have no compunction about representing DMC-12 and Fiat or Volvo or Volkswagen, because we would not regard them as direct competitors.

Our policy of representation in the soap business would seem to be contradictory, but it always made sense to us and to our clients. At one time we represented Procter & Gamble, Colgate-Palmolive, and Lever Brothers, simultaneously with no conflict. There was no conflict because we did not represent the companies, or their products—we represented the television programs which those companies sponsored. Our job was to generate publicity for the shows so that the ratings would climb to the highest-possible level. Hence Procter & Gamble engaged us to handle "The Rifleman" and other shows knowing that we represented the "Jack Benny Show" and "Father Knows Best" for Lever Brothers.

There would have been a conflict if, for example, "The Rifleman" was in a competitive time slot against "Father Knows Best." If "The Rifleman" is on NBC Tuesday night at nine and "Father Knows Best" airs on CBS Tuesday night at nine, then we are in direct conflict with ourselves. We cannot very well tell audiences to tune in both shows. Our responsibility is to get the largest share of audience for the show we represent. In order to do this, we must take viewership away from the other two networks. If and when such a situation ever arises, we must resign from one or the other of the shows.

In the product area, the situation is murky at times. As a result of our handling television programs for Colgate, I became very friendly with David Foster, at that time head of the Household Products Division of that company. Later, Mr. Foster's astute sense of marketing elevated him to the position of Chairman and Chief Executive Officer of the company, but then he was just a division head. David engaged us to handle publicity and promotion for his "Name the Ajax White Knight" contest. The White Knight was to make a tour of the United States, white armor, white horse, and all. Our responsibility was to get maximum publicity out of his appearances, thereby helping to increase the sales of Ajax. Mr. Foster went on the tour with the White Knight and in every city we also set up press interviews for him.

As the clippings began to pour in, I became increasingly uncomfortable. David Foster, in his interviews, was helping to promote Ajax, but he was also rapping Procter & Gamble, his most formidable competitor. We were representing four television shows for Procter & Gamble at the time, and were working on two product assignments. Were we in conflict? I didn't know. The situation was not clear in my head. I felt I needed clarification and guidance.

I called Al Halverstadt, at that time advertising Vice-President of Procter & Gamble. We had known each other for many years. I had entertained him in my home, and he had entertained me in his home in Cincinnati.

"Al," I said, "I have a problem and need your advice. I know how busy you are, but if you can spare me a half hour one day this week, I would really appreciate it."

"Henry, you know my door is always open to you. How about nine o'clock tomorrow morning?"

"I'll be there," I replied, and I hung up fast. I had long since learned that important executives do not have time for personal amenities on the telephone. Their policy is get on and get off fast.

I took a 7 A.M. plane from New York to Cincinnati, and entered Mr. Halverstadt's office promptly at nine o'clock.

He offered me coffee, which I accepted. As we both sipped our morning stimulant, he listened attentively as I told him what was troubling me. At one point he interrupted.

"Oh, you're responsible for those David Foster articles. My salesmen have been sending them to me. I was wondering who had set them up."

I continued and finally finished telling him the whole story.

"My problem is that I don't know whether I am in conflict of interest or not. I am not handling any competitive products; you long ago approved our handling television shows for Colgate and Lever provided they were not in competitive time slots, but this situation is different. I really don't know what to do. I need your advice."

Mr. Halverstadt replied, "I can't tell you how to run your business, but you are dealing in a very sensitive area when one soap executive is blasting another soap executive in print, and you represent both companies. It's very sensitive but you must make your own decision."

With that he gave me a knowing look. I knew what he was saying.

"You've told me what I wanted to know. I'll make a decision, and I'll drop you a note telling you what it is."

I stood up ready to leave.

"Sit down, Henry," he said. "I have a few more minutes. Tell me,

180

what product assignments are you handling for us now?"

"We are handling Tide and B-B-B-B-B-B-onus." My stuttering had returned again. I was having troubles with the "B," and couldn't say Bonus without getting stuck on the word.

He asked me to tell him what we were doing on each of the products. I did, but every time I had to say the word Bonus, I was in trouble. I couldn't get the Goddamned word out of my mouth. When the interview was finally over and I got up to leave, Havy, as we called him, got up from his desk, to walk me out of his office.

He put his arm around my shoulder.

"Incidentally," he said, "if you continue to have trouble with Bonus, you let me know. We like you around here and don't want to give you any problems. If you still stutter over that word, we'll just change the name of the product!"

We both laughed, and I left. That afternoon I called David Foster who was back in New York. Our Ajax White Knight campaign was coming to a close and David had asked me to do presentations, laying out campaign outlines, for two new product assignments he had in mind for use.

"David," I said, "I feel very uncomfortable about my relationship with you and Procter & Gamble. We have represented P & G for many years, and are on many continuing assignments for them. I feel that our representation of you, with the exception of the television programs, presents us with a conflict of interest. I wanted to tell you that I don't feel that I can do those presentations for your two new products that we talked about last week."

David Foster accepted my position good-humoredly. He said, "Okay, Henry, we'll do business again some time in the future. Call me the next time you're in town and we'll have a social drink or lunch."

I agreed. That same day I wrote a letter to Halverstadt, telling him that I had decided to give up representation of all Colgate products while Rogers & Cowan continued to do business with Procter & Gamble.

There have been many times when a decision hurts me economically, and I feel a momentary twinge of doubt. Have I done the right thing? The answer is inevitably yes. I have found over and over again that growth is never retarded if a person follows the dictates of his own conscience, the dictates of his own sense of morals and ethics.

Still with the "on again, off again" nature of public relations the

181

business of a conflict of interest gets even murkier, as was the case recently with Warren Avis, the founder of Avis-Rent-a-Car. He had sold his business many years before and had gone into other business ventures that were equally successful. When he engaged us to handle his latest enterprise, Avis-World-Wide-Flowers, the business was not well managed. Mr. Avis had not given the time it required because of his other interests, and because of his preoccupation with a lawsuit which had been brought against him by Norton Simon, the present owner of Avis-Rent-a-Car. The suit sought a court ruling to prevent Warren Avis from using his own name in the flower business or, for that matter, any other business. Avis, furious because someone was demanding him to forsake the use of his own name in business for the rest of his life, countered with a $300,000,000 lawsuit against Norton Simon, its president David Mahoney, and its advertising agency, Doyle Dane Bernbach.

The battle lines were drawn. Avis hired the litigious attorney Roy Cohn to handle his case. Cohn, having recently taken on a class action stockholder suit against Henry Ford, was not afraid of facing up to corporate giants, and the fight began to shape up as a long and an ugly one. As it developed I became Warren Avis's confidant. While we were still using our best public relations efforts to help his ailing flower business, I became more and more deeply involved in the lawsuit, participating in strategy meetings to discuss how best to counter the Norton Simon lawsuit and what strategies Avis should take in pressing his own against the giant conglomerate. The battle between the two business tycoons, Warren Avis and David Mahoney, became the main subject of discussion at the best restaurants, the biggest boardrooms, and the best dinner tables in New York.

By the fall of 1978, nothing was settled. Moreover, it was obvious to both Warren Avis and me that the flower business was not working and any efforts we might put into promoting it would be wasted until Warren reorganized the business. In his own words, he explained that he felt we had done all we could and that because there was also a lull in the lawsuit fracas and nothing for us to do on that front for a while, it was time for a hiatus in our business relationship. I agreed with him, and that was that. We make many of our deals with a handshake; there are often no formal contracts and hence no formal terminations. In the case of Warren's flower business and the lawsuit, perhaps at a later date there would be something new to pick up on again, but for the time being there was no way

182

to know for sure. We had certainly had other instances where a hiatus had marked the final end of our relationship with a client, even if the term implied only a temporary separation. I certainly could not and would not count on Avis to come back as a client.

Several months passed.

In early January of 1979 I was lunching at the Four Seasons in New York when I noticed David Mahoney sitting at a table nearby. I did not know whether he remembered me, but we had been introduced on a number of occasions, none in any way connected with Warren Avis. After I paid my check, I decided to stop by his table to say hello.

"Excuse me," I said, "I'm Henry Rogers. I wanted to introduce myself. We've met before."

"Of course, Henry, I remember you," said the dynamic Mr. Mahoney, with a flashing smile. "It's nice to see you again."

"I would like to come by and see you one day at your convenience," I said. "May I?"

"Of course. Any time, call my secretary. She keeps my calendar. Tell her I said she should set up a date for us to get together."

I thanked him and left the restaurant. When I first spotted David Mahoney, I immediately thought that I should talk to him about public relations representation. There had been rumors that Norton Simon was thinking about engaging a new firm. I would not have approached him during the period that we were active with Warren Avis, particularly because of their litigation, but time had gone by and I had not heard from Warren. I felt that there was now nothing to prevent me from pursuing the Norton Simon account.

The following day I called David Mahoney's secretary and asked for an appointment. Some ten days later I met with him. Yes, he was interested in engaging a public relations firm. Yes, he had heard good things about Rogers & Cowan and would be interested in our thinking as to how to solve his public relations problems. He would like us to prepare a presentation for him. First, I should meet with one of his associates who would brief me on Norton Simon's public relations needs. I left the meeting elated by the possibility that we might soon be representing Norton Simon, one of the nation's most prestigious billion-dollar conglomerates. Certainly the company would be a feather in the R & C cap.

Out of the blue, Warren Avis called a few days later. He was back in New York and would like to see me. We made a date for late that afternoon, and as I walked to his Fifth Avenue apartment, I found myself wondering what he wanted, hoping it wasn't to renew our business association. I hoped we could continue our personal relationship, which had included many good times together, but if he wanted to renew our client-public relations connection, then I would tell him about my meeting with David Mahoney, that Norton Simon would most likely soon become a client, and, if so, that Warren would certainly feel uncomfortable about becoming a client of Rogers & Cowan again.

Our meeting confirmed my worst fears—Warren was ready to become a client again. I told him about Norton Simon and explained that from my standpoint I could represent both clients only with the proviso that neither one expected me to render any public relations services which involved the lawsuits. That would be a conflict of interest, in my estimation.

Avis objected.

"No, Henry," he said, "I want you to represent me in matters directly related to the lawsuits. There have been a number of new developments that require your assistance, and it is just impossible for you to represent us both. In fact, I'm really surprised that you even had a meeting with David Mahoney without discussing it with me first."

"I don't understand," I replied. "Why should I have discussed it with you? You are no longer a client. We stopped representing you a number of months ago. It would certainly have been construed as a conflict of interest if I had met with Mahoney during the time that you were a client, but you aren't a client any longer. I had no qualms about having that meeting. Your name never came up when we talked. If it had, I would have told him about our relationship, that you had been a client, that you were no longer a client, but that a fiduciary relationship still exists between us as far as I was concerned, and I was morally bound not to discuss with him anything I knew about the two lawsuits."

"I thank you for that," countered my friend, "but you're mistaken on one important point. You say I am no longer your client. That isn't true. I've always been your client. We were just on a temporary hiatus, but I am now ready to begin paying you again. That's why I called and suggested that we get together today."

I had never been faced with this kind of a problem before. I genuinely felt that I had the right to represent Norton Simon and that I also had the right to reject Warren Avis as a client if he insisted that there would be a conflict of interest if I were to represent both. Warren did not agree with me. He felt that I was morally bound not to represent his enemy, that he had been a long-paying client, and that just because he had gone on a hiatus from us for a few months, there was no reason for me not to regard him as a client. A moot point and a unique situation. To him, it was unethical for me to move from one battle camp to the other while the war was still raging. Was he right or was I right? I really didn't know. I would have to think it through.

"Warren, at this moment I don't know what to do," I said. "I value your friendship, but I also value the fact that Norton Simon could be one of the most prestigious and profitable clients that Rogers & Cowan has ever had. If the deal worked out for me, and I have every reason to believe that it would, we would handle corporate relations for the company. Then if all went well the prospects are very good that we would represent as separate clients the various companies that Norton Simon owns—Max Factor, Hunt-Wesson Foods, Somerset Importers, and all the rest, including," and I couldn't resist laughing at this point, "Avis-Rent-a-Car."

Warren laughed too. "That would be ironic," he said. "I can see the great potential for you, but you just can't represent us both. It's a matter of ethical business practice on one side, and making a quick buck on the other."

"I'll need some time to think about it," I concluded. "I'll sleep on it and will call you tomorrow."

"I hope you make the right decision," said Warren as we shook hands at the door.

"I hope so too," I replied ruefully.

The door closed behind me, and as I walked down Fifth Avenue back toward my apartment I faced a real dilemma. What to do? What would other public relations men in my position do? That wasn't the point. What was *I* to do? There was no one else for me to lean on, no one whose advice would help me make my decision. The Norton Simon account was the juiciest plum in the public relations world. Just the corporate account alone would pay us into six figures, and if any of their companies came our way, which was likely, this could easily be the most important client Rogers & Cowan had ever had, both from the financial and prestige standpoint. But I had to weigh all those heady thoughts against representing Warren Avis. Warren was not even a company; he was an individual entrepreneur. He wanted to renew his association with us immediately, but how long would it last this time? Not long, I surmised. There just wasn't that much for us to do for him. It would always be an on-and-off relationship. But was that the important point? If I weighed my decision on the basis of which client was to pay the most money or who was the most prestigious, there was no contest. It was Norton Simon, far and away. But was that a basis on which I was to make my decision? Not at all. Rogers & Cowan is a very successful public relations firm. We don't have to make business decisions solely on the basis of financial considerations. In this case there were other considerations. It was an issue of personal loyalty—not money. That was the area in which I felt most uncomfortable about making a decision. What was right and what wrong for me? I owed Warren my loyalty; he had confided his plans to me. There was a $300,000,000 lawsuit at stake. While I knew that I would never betray Warren Avis to David Mahoney, how could Warren know that? Did Mahoney know about my representation of Avis, and was that the reason for his interest in me? I didn't have any answers, and yet I really didn't need any.

I knew I had made my decision. I had to stay with Warren Avis and give up the prospect of representing Norton Simon.

I called Warren and told him of my decision, and then I called Mahoney and explained why I had to bow out. A number of months later the two principals in these lawsuits settled their differences. Predictably our representation of Warren Avis went on another temporary hiatus. David Mahoney, in the meantime, had engaged another public relations organization to represent his interests.

It was an expensive decision to make, but I had no doubt at all that I did what was right—for *me*.

The murky problem of conflict of interest continues and it is unavoidable. In each case, I must make a decision as to what is right for me. The murkier the waters, the more the decision rests on personal judgment, the less on professional considerations. Again, just as with any other service profession, the human factor rises up time and time again in matters of making difficult choices, particularly when they involve the complicated matter of conflict of interest. Personal loyalty and mutual trust are more important to me over the long run than all the lucrative deals I've ever made, and that may well be why I sleep soundly at night.

CHAPTER 16

I'll Even Recite a Mantra to Get a New Client

In any service business, getting new clients is crucial to success. Despite all our best efforts, clients do leave for any number of reasons, and a constant new influx of clients is required in order to compensate for the erosion. After all these years, the ongoing effort to get new clients is second nature to me. That's the way it has to be if I am to stay with or move ahead of the competition.

Because we operate in so many different areas of the economy, our competitors are a varied lot. There are only a few competitors in the entertainment world and it is interesting to note that most of them started their careers in public relations with Rogers & Cowan. They learned their techniques and approaches from us, and we are often told by clients that presentations they have received from one or more of our competitors are very similar to the one they accepted from us. In order to try to keep a step ahead of them, there are six of us in our Beverly Hills office constantly seeking out new clients, four in our New York office, and two in London. Our sheer size gives us an advantage, yet it presents us with a disadvantage as well. There are some prospective clients who prefer to go with one of our competitors because they are concerned that they will not get the same degree of personal attention from an organization as large as ours. When we get an opportunity to refute that argument, we suggest to the prospective client that he call a number of our clients and ask them whether or not they receive personal attention from us. Actually there is enough public relations business in the world of entertainment for us and all of our competitors, and we don't worry too much about them —as long as we continue to get *more* than our fair share of the business. It can readily be seen that Rogers & Cowan is not an organization to sit back and rest on its laurels.

In the world of corporate public relations, the competition is much more formidable. In entertainment we rank number one; in corporate PR we rank number twelve, and we go up against the giants in the public relations business, all of whom are headquartered in New York. In corporate public relations, a large percentage of our business comes from the firms which understand that our show business background gives them certain advantages that they will not get from our competitor who confines his activity solely to corporate public relations. There is a sufficient number of such companies that we pursue and get as clients to make the corporate public relations end of our business continually profitable.

We can divide our clients into two categories—the long-range client whom we continue to represent for many years, and the client who engages us to handle a specific project. The project might take three months or three years, but we know that at some point our assignment will be completed. As examples, we were engaged by IBM to handle public relations for a Bicentennial exhibition which they funded. "The World of Franklin and Jefferson," an exhibition designed by Charles and Ray Eames, opened at the Petit Palais in Paris, traveled to the Warsaw Art Institute in Poland, then to the British Museum in London, the Metropolitan Museum in New York, the Chicago Art Institute, the Los Angeles County Museum of Art, and the Anthropological Museum in Mexico City. This was a thirty-month assignment, and involved our London, New York, and Los Angeles offices. It was our job to work closely with the Bicentennial Commission and the Eames organization to ensure proper publicity coverage for the exhibition, to work with all interested parties to stage opening press reception and social events, and at all times to protect the interests of our client, IBM.

With similar obligations, we were engaged by SCM Corporation to advance their interests as the major funder of the Russian Costume Exhibition at the Metropolitan Museum of Art in New York, which was a three-month assignment. At this writing we are handling the public relations representation for the Folger Shakespeare Library traveling exhibition which will be seen at museums in San Francisco, Kansas City, Chicago, and New York before our two-year assignment has been completed. For this project, our clients are Metropolitan Life Insurance Company and Exxon Corporation, both of which are major funders of the exhibition. When Columbia Pictures engaged us to handle publicity/promotion on *The Deep*, it was an eighteen-month assignment. They also hired us to promote *California Suite* at Academy Award time, with the hope that our efforts would help the successful Neil Simon film win a number of Oscars. This assignment took only four months.

We have a staff of account supervisors and account executives who

188

would be almost impossible to replace. They remain on the payroll fifty-two weeks a year. Consequently, when a short-term project is completed it is essential that we have other assignments for those of our associates who have worked on it. We could not run our business if we hired and fired people as new assignments came in and were then completed.

There is also a turnover in what we always hope are our permanent clients. There are times when a client is unhappy with our efforts. At other times, despite our best efforts, his business goes sour and he can no longer afford to pay our fee.

Because the turnover exists and because our overhead keeps increasing due to inflation, it is essential that we constantly seek out new clients.

A large percentage of our new clients come to us as a result of contacts and relationships we have developed over the years. Some come as a result of our own aggressiveness in seeking out new clients.

Recently IBM called with a new assignment. Although we had not done anything for them in about two years, we had remained in touch with an occasional phone call, correspondence, and lunch dates so that the people we had worked with at IBM would keep Rogers & Cowan in mind when something new came up.

Sometimes we slip up. One day I heard an important assignment was in the offing at AT & T and I called my friend Jack Howland, assistant Vice-President, to ask him whether we could make a presentation. We had done a good deal of work for AT & T in the past and when he told me he thought the assignment had already gone to one of our competitors, I was sorry but not entirely surprised. I suddenly realized it was my own fault for not keeping in touch with AT & T continuously.

"This was a perfect assignment for you, Henry," Howland said. "I must confess that I had forgotten all about Rogers & Cowan. Why didn't you keep in touch all these months?"

This was exactly the response I expected and deserved!

In our business, we can't afford to make too many of these mistakes. The competitors are out there in the marketplace all the time, and we must be too. It is important that we keep reminding people who we know and have been associated with, that Rogers & Cowan is well, happy, and prosperous. That's what "keeping in touch" means. When I read an article that I believe will be of interest to a former client, I send it to him with a short note. He may one day return

189

to us as an active client. If I read that an acquaintance or a friend has gone on to a new job or has been promoted, I drop him a congratulatory message. If theater, concert, or baseball tickets suddenly become available, I give them to one of our business contacts.

Sometimes new business comes to us from unexpected sources. Recently I served as a consultant to the Urban Development Corporation of the State of New York. My responsibility was to counsel them on short- and long-range programing for Radio City Music Hall. When Rockefeller Center announced its intention of tearing down this unprofitable landmark, Governor Carey asked one of the state agencies, UDC, to fund the losses for a period of time, and to develop a plan to make it into a profitable venture if the state ever assumed management of it. UDC hired me as a show business expert to counsel them. One of my assignments was to seek out a person who was uniquely qualified to take over the management of the Music Hall if indeed the state did decide to operate it. My research finally brought me to Robert F. Jani, formerly head of live entertainment for the Disney organization, and who now headed up his own business as a consultant and producer of live entertainment attractions, with Disney as one of his key clients. Of all the people I had met with, I felt that Bob Jani was better qualified to run Radio City Music Hall than anyone else in the United States, and I made my recommendation to Urban Development Corporation accordingly. A few months later, Rockefeller Center changed its mind and agreed to continue to operate Radio City Music Hall for the indefinite future. Acting independently and without reference to the recommendation I had made to UDC, they hired Robert F. Jani to be President of a newly formed company, Radio City Music Hall Productions. Shortly after he took over his new role, Jani, evidently impressed with our organization as a result of the meetings he had had with me, engaged Rogers & Cowan to handle public relations for his newly named Radio City Entertainment Center. That's how we get clients—sometimes!

We do not, however, sit back and wait for new clients to appear on the scene just by happenstance. Most of our new clients come to us as a result of our aggressively pursuing new business. A few years ago, I read an article in the *Wall Street Journal* announcing that John DeLorean, formerly General Manager of Chevrolet Division of General Motors, was about to build a new sports car, the DMC-12. I felt that we were particularly qualified to represent him, because a

190

few years before we had launched another new sports car, the Bricklin. Although the Bricklin had failed for many reasons, everyone in the automotive industry knew that the car had been launched with a dynamic and flashy public relations program—just the right kind of campaign for the DMC-12 and one I knew John DeLorean would remember. I wrote him a letter explaining why he should engage the services of Rogers & Cowan, and after almost a year he replied that he was now ready for public relations representation. I met with him shortly thereafter, and we now represent DeLorean Motor Company.

The active pursuit of new clients always requires a special strategy and this really gets our creative juices going. We constantly keep a lookout for an unexpected "leg up" in any given situation, and the "leg up" usually involves a personal touch.

Paul Bloch, President of our Contemporary Music Division, and his number one man, Sandy Friedman, walked into my office one day. "We need you," said Paul. "Sandy has opened up a situation with the Beach Boys. We have both met with them, and they're thinking about coming with us, but they want to meet with you."

"You guys are the experts in pop music. You know a helluva lot more about what we can do for the Beach Boys than I do," I replied. "I'll be glad to meet with them if you want me to, but I'm curious as to why they want to meet with me."

A little abashed, Sandy stepped in. "Let me explain. The Beach Boys aren't just another pop music act. They've been successful for almost fifteen years. They're an institution. They've made millions of dollars and are used to dealing with the top honcho. They want to meet the Chairman of the Board."

"Wouldn't they be satisfied with Warren? After all, he's President and he knows more about pop music than I do."

Paul shook his head. "Nope," he said, "they want to meet the Chairman."

Actually, I would be perfectly at ease with the Beach Boys. I had known about them and their careers since they first started fifteen years before. My children had grown up with Beach Boys records, and we still had half a dozen of their old albums in our record collection. I knew that I could carry on an intelligent conversation with them because even though a large percentage of my time had been spent in corporate corridors, I had always kept up with the world of contemporary music, an important part of our overall business.

191

I laughed, "Of course I'll meet with them. When do you want to bring them in to the office?"

"You don't understand," said Sandy, "if we wait for all of them to come up here, we'll never get them as a client. We have to go to them. They're recording at a studio in Santa Monica tomorrow afternoon. If I pin them down for an appointment at five o'clock, will you make it?"

"Of course," I replied, "I'll be there." The next day at five, Paul, Sandy, and I met with the Beach Boys at the Big Brother Recording Studio in Santa Monica. I had been briefed by my associates and was ready for the meeting.

I had been told that they had been comparatively inactive in recent years. Brian Wilson, who had composed a sizable percentage of their hit songs, had a drug problem. As a result, the group had been in the doldrums. Now they were getting ready to get started again. They had just signed a new recording contract with Warner Records and were determined to get along without Brian Wilson until he had rehabilitated himself. In order to facilitate this, they had engaged a psychiatrist to live with him. They were getting ready to celebrate their fifteenth anniversary.

I was introduced to Mike Love, Carl Wilson, Dennis Wilson, and Al Jardine. They were attractive, well-spoken young men, who intelligently discussed their past career, their present status, and their plans for the future. They said that they had interviewed a number of other public relations firms but they were seriously considering Rogers & Cowan.

I perked up. Interviewing other public relations firms? Could they really consider anyone but Rogers & Cowan? Paul and Sandy were depending on me, and I knew I had better give this my *numero uno* effort. Three of the young men left, saying they would "think it over." Mike Love remained; we continued talking, and I purposely let the conversation drift into personal matters. He told me he was into Transcendental Meditation and had been for eight years. He was a teacher, had a personal relationship with the Maharishi, and was one of the leading spokesmen for the movement in the United States. It was obviously very important to him, and it triggered my thinking.

When we had completed our conversation, Mike too said he would think it over. We all walked out of the recording studio together. As we were about to say good-bye, I turned to Mike. "Incidentally, I'm very interested in what you were telling us about T.M. If you decide to become our client, we'll begin to spend some time together, and when that happens, I'll become your pupil. I'll go into T.M. if you become my teacher." Sandy chimed in, "Me too." Paul said nothing. Mike left and we stood there for a few minutes in the parking lot.

"What the hell was that all about?" asked Paul. "What were you kidding him for?"

"You mean about the T.M.?" I replied. "I wasn't kidding. We want the Beach Boys, don't we? They're considering other offices, aren't they? They wanted to meet the Chairman. The Chairman is interested enough in them to offer to go into Transcendental Meditation if they become a client. How can they resist us?"

I was right. The next day the Beach Boys' business manager called to say that Mike, Carl, Dennis, and Al had all agreed to engage the services of Rogers & Cowan. They had also agreed to pay our quoted fee.

Three days later the phone rang. It was Mike Love. "Mike," I said, "I want you to know how pleased I am that we are representing you. I know that Paul and Sandy have presented you with their 'Fifteenth Anniversary Plan' and that all of you are enthusiastic about it. I know that we're going to do a really great job for you."

Mike seemed to ignore what I was saying. "Henry," he said, "I've been waiting to hear from you."

"About what?" I asked.

"About T.M."

"What about T.M.?"

"What about T.M.?" he replied, "Don't you remember our conversation? You said that if the Beach Boys became a client of Rogers & Cowan, you would join the T.M. movement and I would be your teacher. I'm ready. Are you?"

I gulped. What the hell had I gotten myself into? It was the spirit of the chase. It was the old ego bit again. It was the wish to show the younger men in the organization that the founder of the firm hadn't lost his touch. Well, I had gotten myself into it. There was no turning back now.

"Yes, I'm ready," I said. "What's the first step?"

Mike explained that he had some twenty-five recruits lined up besides Sandy and me. He lived in Santa Barbara, but would come to Los Angeles for a weekend. He needed a place to spend two sessions with prospective members so that they could decide whether they really wanted to join up. Could he have them to my home? Could he and his girl friend stay for the weekend?

That night at the dinner table, I timidly said to my adoring and adored wife:

"Roz, there's something I have to tell you."

Roz had heard me start conversations like that before and was immediately suspicious.

"Ye-e-e-s-s-s?" she said. "Are you going to tell me that thirty people are coming to dinner tomorrow night. Or are you going to tell me that you're leaving for Peking in the morning—or are you going to tell me that we're selling the house and moving to New York? Ye-e-e-s-s-s, my darling, what do you have to tell me."

"Oh, nothing as simple as any of those logical possibilities," I replied. "Something much better. We're having house guests for the weekend."

"House guests? Who?"

"Mike Love and his girl friend."

"Who is Mike Love?"

"He's the lead singer with the Beach Boys."

"Oh? Why is he going to be our house guest?"

"Because he's going to be our T.M. teacher."

Pause.

"T.M. teacher? Whose T.M. teacher?"

"*Our* T.M. teacher. Yours and mine."

"Our T.M. teacher? Maybe your teacher, but not mine. Oh, no, that's not for me. You've been pulling these little tricks on me for forty years, but this time you've gone too far. No, no, no."

"Darling mine," I wheedled. "You're forgetting the Bible."

"What's the Bible got to do with this?"

"Don't you remember? The story of Ruth and Naomi. 'Whither thou goest, I goest.' "

She laughed. "Okay, you've done it to me again. If you want me to get into T.M., I will. Now start from the beginning and tell me all about it."

I did, and she agreed to cooperate. When she started to walk out to the guest house to prepare for the arrival of our T.M. teacher, I stopped her.

"Oh, I forgot something. Mike will have twenty-seven recruits coming over here Friday night at 8:30. Most of them will be back

194

at ten on Saturday. Nothing fancy. Just some cheese and coffee Friday night. Danish and coffee on Saturday. You don't mind, do you, darling?"

"If I were a violent woman, I'd throw an ashtray at you. As it is, I understand that you'll do *almost* anything to get a new client."

We both laughed, and then she left to prepare for our house guests.

Roz practiced T.M. for a year. I stayed in for almost two. I found it enormously helpful in creating a peaceful state of mind. As a matter of fact it worked so well for me that after a while I found that I didn't need it anymore. Before I stopped reciting my mantra for twenty minutes a day twice a day, I called Mike Love and told him that I was quitting. He understood.

We still represent the Beach Boys. Occasionally, Sandy Friedman arrives a little late in the morning. I don't mind. I know that he has been reciting his mantra.

CHAPTER 17
Give and Take—It Works All the Time

There is nothing free in this world. When I am given something, I expect that one day I shall give something in return. Give and take. Give and take. It is an axiom that works all the time. It applies to everything in life—including the public relations business.

I have found that those at the top of the business ladder are always ready to help their peers. Maybe it's because each of us wants to impress the other, or maybe it's because it makes us comfortable to know that important doors can be opened when we need help. It is a two-way street. If the head of a major industrial company runs a charity drive, he can count on other leaders in the field to make contributions because he knows that at some point he will be asked for favors too. A lawyer can always call on another lawyer friend for a favor. An actor has no qualms about asking a fellow actor to help him go over his lines. A network executive can ask another network executive for help.

Many years ago I went to see my friend Jennings Lang for some advice on a business matter that did not relate to him at all. Jennings, formerly an agent at Music Corporation of America, still works for that company but now as a successful motion picture producer for their Universal Pictures division.

Jennings gave me the advice I had sought. I went to him because he knew more about that particular subject than I did. When our meeting was over he made an interesting observation.

"I've known you for many years," he said, "and it just dawned on me that you're a brain-picker."

"You're right," I said. "I don't know whether you mean that as a put-down or as a compliment, but I take it as a compliment. Long ago I realized that I don't know everything. Fortunately, I have a lot of friends and I number you among them. If I need some information, if you know something that I don't know, I have no qualms about picking up the phone and asking you. I also expect that you will do the same if you ever need my help."

I have always asked my friends for help. My friends ask me for help all the time. I give it freely.

I might be able to help get you a job because my business has brought me into contact with so many different people in so many different positions and industries. You can help me get a new client. I can put two of our clients together in the same room, and something beneficial will come out of it for both of them.

I once introduced the President of Benrus Industries to the Executive Vice-President of Timex. As a result, Benrus sold Timex millions of dollars worth of watchcases which it was unable to manufacture itself. An advertising agency client of ours recently got a new client because the new client was a friend of mine and acted favorably on my recommendation.

Every day I help people and people help me, and it is to everyone's advantage.

In 1967, shortly after I had personally handled Prince Philip's first and only good-will tour of the United States, we convinced Margaret Gardner, who had been heading up our operation in Paris for a number of years, that there was a greater opportunity for us to build a substantial business in London than in Paris and she agreed to move to London and formally open a Rogers & Cowan office there. It was to become our international headquarters, and we named Margaret as President of our International Division.

As I arrived in London to help organize the new office, Margaret told me she had just received a call from Warren Cowan who reported that Diana Ross and the Supremes, one of our important contemporary music clients at the time, were coming to London for their first appearance in Great Britain. It was important for Margaret to launch them in a very important way. Margaret asked me if I had any ideas. I said to her, jokingly of course, "Maybe we could get Prince Philip and Queen Elizabeth to give a party in their honor."

Margaret told me to stop kidding around. This was a serious matter, and we really had to come up with something new and fresh that would alert London to the fact that Diana Ross and the Supremes were a very important American music group. My joking reference to Queen Elizabeth and Prince Philip gave me an idea. I reasoned that if a titled person would agree to host a party in honor of the Supremes, we would be assured of two types of guests at the party— London's social elite and also the top names in Britain's contemporary music world: the Beatles, the Rolling Stones, the Who, and others. Bringing rock stars together with titled society would hit front pages everywhere and the Supremes would be launched in London.

I telephoned William Heseltine, press officer for Prince Philip, with whom I had worked the previous year, and made a date for Margaret and me to see him at the palace. At 5:30 that afternoon, we were ushered into Bill's office. He most graciously offered us a drink and we began our conversation. I told him that I needed some advice. We wanted to do something special to launch Diana Ross and the Supremes in London, and while I knew it was a ridiculous idea to think that Prince Philip and Queen Elizabeth would host a party in their honor, I wondered what he thought of having the Supremes give a concert at the palace for Princess Anne, Prince Charles, and their friends. Very tactfully, he laughed off the idea. "That was a good try, Henry," he said, "but there is no chance. Forget it." I was not at all surprised. In fact, I had never expected an affirmative answer to my suggestion.

I asked him if he might know of a titled couple in London who might be willing to host the kind of party I had in mind—with the Supremes paying for the party, of course.

There was a moment of silence. Suddenly Bill said, "How about the Duke and Duchess of Bedford?" I immediately jumped up and said, "That's it, that's it . . . they're perfect."

Margaret did not understand why I had suddenly become so enthusiastic. I said, "It now makes things so easy! I know the Duchess of Bedford; I've known her for many, many years and I am certain she'll help us." I thanked our friend profusely for his suggestion, and we left.

Driving away from the palace, I gave Margaret more of the details. I had known the Duchess of Bedford for ten years before that august title had been bestowed upon her, when her name was Nicole Milanaire. She had worked for Sheldon Reynolds, a television producer, as his assistant and later as the producer of his "Sherlock Holmes" series. Since then, Nicole had married the Duke of Bedford and with that marriage had come the title, Duchess of Bedford.

I probably hadn't spoken to her for five years but now was the time to renew our old friendship. Back in the office I made a few phone calls to find out where the Duke and Duchess of Bedford could be reached. I was told that they lived some forty miles out of London at Woburn Abbey in Bedfordshire. I got the phone number, dialed through, and asked for the Duchess of Bedford. The Duke and Duchess were skiing at a French ski resort, Meribel. They could be reached there if I would like to call them. The receptionist at the Abbey gave me the phone number and I put through a call immediately. Thirty seconds later, I heard Nicole's voice on the phone. She gave me a most enthusiastic greeting. We chatted for five minutes before I had a chance to mention to her what I was calling about.

When I told her about my idea, she asked many questions. Who was going to pay for the party? I told her that Motown Records which recorded the Supremes would pay all the costs. At one point in the conversation she said, "But what's in it for me and the Duke?" "Oh, I don't know, Nicole," I replied. "Don't worry about it. You and I will work something out. We always have."

She said she would like to discuss it with her husband and asked if I would call back about noon the following day.

The following day, on schedule, I called. This time the Duke of Bedford himself answered the phone. I asked him whether the Duchess had mentioned our conversation. He said that she had talked to him about it and that it sounded interesting, but that he would like to discuss it further. Perhaps I should visit them at Meribel, to explain the details. I agreed and we made a date for lunch on Sunday.

I had no idea where Meribel was. He suggested that I fly from London to Geneva. Then, from there it would be about a two-hour automobile trip to Meribel. On Saturday night I flew to Geneva, made arrangements for a car and driver to pick me up at the hotel in the morning, and went to bed in preparation for what I expected would be an amusing, interesting day. I could picture the reactions from my friends in Hollywood when I told them that I had flown from London to Geneva and driven for two hours into the French Alps to have lunch with the Duke and Duchess of Bedford. With that thought I chuckled to myself as I went to bed.

The following morning dawned bleak and rainy. I had not brought any sports clothes with me to London, and I had no time to shop for anything. I had no choice but to dress in my Dick Carroll Beverly Hills suit, my Turnbull and Asser shirt and tie, and my British brown suede shoes, not exactly appropriate attire for a trip into ski country.

In the chauffeur-driven car I read the morning paper, and dozed a bit. When I awakened I found that the car had stopped. We were on a one-way mountain road with deep drifts of snow on either side of us. A line of cars stretched ahead and behind as far as I could see.

When I asked the driver what was wrong, he told me that we had been sitting there, on this lonely, snowbound road, for fifteen minutes. The cars were stuck because there had been an avalanche a half mile up the road. Two cars had been swept off the road by the avalanche, and the workmen were now trying to clear the way up ahead.

After sitting in the car for another half hour, I felt a wave of concern and asked the driver what he thought. He indicated that he had no idea how long we would be stuck on the road and at that point I decided that my best bet would be to get out of the car and try to convince one of the cars at the back of the line to turn around and return to the nearest town. If I could get to a phone, I could call the Duke and Duchess and tell them what had happened. I would tell them that they shouldn't wait lunch for me, and that I would join them as soon as I could.

I told the driver I would go back on foot and suggested to him that whenever he could get his car free, he should come back to the town that we had passed a few miles down the road and pick me up. He would find me in the local hotel. We agreed.

I stepped out in my elegant Dick Carroll tweeds and brown suede shoes into a three-foot snow drift. The snow was piled high on either side of the road. I plowed my way through for a half mile until I got to the last car in the line. Fortunately, the driver of that last car spoke English. I told him my plight and convinced him that there was very little use of his sitting there in the line. Why didn't he just back up for a few miles . . . there was no way to turn around on this narrow road . . . we would both go back to the little town and eventually someone would inform us when the road was clear.

That made sense to the young man. I got into the car with him and we backed up two miles. Every time we saw a car approaching we waved them back and soon there was a stream of twenty to thirty cars all backing up along this narrow, snow-clogged road.

We finally arrived in the little town. I walked into the only inn that was on the village square and asked the bartender for a phone. He laughed and told me that all the phone lines for many miles had been downed by the snowstorm. There was no chance of getting a phone call through. Now I was really stuck. I then began to think, What the hell am I doing here anyway? I am supposed to be in London on business opening an office, talking to clients, helping Margaret get the office established, and here am I in a tiny town in the French Alps snowbound with no idea of when I will get out. All of this is

200

just because Warren Cowan told Margaret Gardner that he wanted to launch the Supremes in a big way in England.

What the hell am I doing here? I kept asking myself over and over again.

I sat and I sat and I sat. I had planned arriving for lunch at Meribel at about noon. It was already well after twelve-thirty. There was an avalanche ahead of me. I was probably thirty miles away from where I was supposed to be and had no idea if and when I would ever arrive to meet the Duke and Duchess.

I had lunch with a small bottle of wine, sat there drinking my coffee, and suddenly my driver appeared. By this time it was two in the afternoon.

The driver said that even though the phone lines were down and road conditions were still a mess, he had managed to get back and pick me up. The rubble from the avalanche had been cleared away and we could now start all over again.

I got back in the car—still soaking wet from my trek through the snow hours before, and we started back. Halfway to Meribel we were in the middle of another avalanche. We were stuck once more in another line of cars. We sat. Hours later, at six o'clock in the evening, in the pitch black, a tiny buglike car with some kind of a super engine came along. It was equipped to slip past the other cars that were stalled on this road, and as it approached us, I flagged the driver down. I told him I would pay him anything if he would drive me to Meribel. He said he was going there anyway. He offered to drive me and refused to take any money.

Once again, I left my rented car and driver stuck in the snow and proceeded ahead. An hour later, at seven P.M., I arrived in Meribel. We found the hotel where I was to meet the Duke and Duchess for lunch, but now I faced another problem. The hotel fronted on an enormous parking lot piled high with three feet of snow.

Once more, the intrepid Henry Rogers with his sopping-wet clothes, climbed, waddled, fought his way through the snow until at long last I arrived at the lobby of the hotel.

Not only were the phone lines out, but there was no electricity. It was very, very dark, lit only by candles. I was told that the Duke and Duchess had waited for me until three in the afternoon, knew that I had been stuck in this avalanche, and had left word for me to meet them in their quarters whenever I arrived. Their chalet was within walking distance of the hotel, only a few hundred yards away, and I finally arrived and knocked on the door.

When it opened, there was my old friend Nicole waiting for me. She took one look and started to laugh. She called out, "Ian, Ian. Come and see how ridiculous Henry looks."

The Duke of Bedford walked to the door, took a look at me standing on his threshold, and he started to laugh too. I was a mess.

The three of us stood there and just laughed. Then they invited me in, put me in a hot tub, and gave me a change of clothes. At long last we sat down to talk about the project which we had originally discussed on the phone a few days before. It seemed like a year ago.

We talked for an hour. The Duke and Duchess finally agreed. We chose a place where the party would take place; we decided on a date. Nicole went to her personal phone book, began to make up a guest list: the lord and lady so and so, the Duke and Duchess of so and so . . . I remember her saying, "Should we invite J. Paul Getty or shouldn't we?"

The Duke said, "Oh, he's such a bore. Let's not invite him."

I knew then that if they decided *not* to invite J. Paul Getty, we were going to have a prestigious guest list. At that point I began to add to their list, my own list of film people, music people, the Beatles, the Rolling Stones, etc., etc. We finally agreed on a list of about a hundred important guests.

With business over, and a pleasant dinner completed, I announced that I was ready for bed. It had been quite a day.

"Oh no," said Nicole, "Ian and I are going to a party with some friends and we already told them that you are joining us!" So, off we went. Everyone was intrigued and amused to hear my story of my trip from Geneva, and somehow or another my Beverly Hills tweed suit and brown suede shoes in ski country always got the big laugh.

At two A.M. the Duke and Duchess walked me back to the hotel where they had reserved a room for me. Sometime during the night my driver had finally arrived. We made arrangements to leave at seven in the morning.

I had worked out a timetable. If I left at seven, and if the roads were clear, I could get back to London by noon.

At seven the chauffeur was waiting for me. Just as I was about to get in the car, he handed me a note. He said it had been on the front seat addressed to Mr. Henry Rogers. I opened up the note, read it, was completely dumbfounded by its contents—I was traumatized to say the least.

The note was from Nicole. It said, "Dear Henry: Evidently you really don't care about me or Ian or Woburn Abbey. Everything we talked about last night is off. Let's forget the whole thing. Nicole."

I couldn't understand it. It had all been so warm, so friendly, so much fun. What was it that had made her change her mind? What had I done to offend her or the Duke? Now I was faced with a real problem. What should I do? It was seven in the morning. Should I just leave Meribel, go back to London, and try to get an explanation by phone later in the day—or should I stay, wait until they awakened, and confront them in person to find out what I had done that had offended them?

For my own peace of mind I knew I had to wait it out. I had to find out in person what had made them change their minds. I asked the desk clerk what time the Duke and Duchess usually arose to go skiing. He said that they usually were heard stirring in their chalet at about noon. There was nothing I could do. I just sat down and waited.

Finally, I sent one of the hotel bellboys up to the chalet and asked him to let me know when he heard the Duke and Duchess moving about. He sat outside their door until he heard voices, then ran back to inform me that the Duke and Duchess were having their morning coffee.

I cinched my belt, pulled in my stomach, threw out my chest, bravely walked up to the door, and knocked softly. The door opened. It was hard to tell that the Nicole who opened the door that morning was the same person who had opened the door the night before. She really wasn't the same person at all. The night before, she had been warm, gracious, full of fun and life. She had put her arms around me, kissed me, and told me how happy she was to see me after such a long time.

This time I was greeted with an icy "Good morning, Henry." She asked me to come in for coffee and I did. The Duke appeared. He was not as frosty as she but he was much more reserved than he had been the night before. I told her that I could not understand her message. What had I done to offend her? And then I found out. Very qiuetly, very softly, and very patiently, Nicole asked me to repeat the original conversation we had had from London when I first called her. I repeated it almost word for word. I had remembered the conversation.

At a certain point she stopped me and said, "And then what did I say, Henry?" And I said, "And then you said, 'But what's in it for me and Ian?' "

Then it dawned on me. People help me. I help people. I had been so carried away with my mission that I had forgotten that if Nicole and Ian were doing something for me, then I was obligated to do something for them. She had given me the clue in our first conversation, but I had neglected to follow it up.

I couldn't figure out what she wanted of me. Then it finally came out. The Duke of Bedford, like many other titled gentlemen of Great Britain, found out many years before that the taxes on his magnificent ancestral home were draining him of all his assets, and unless he found a way to convert Woburn Abbey into a profitable business enterprise, he would be forced to move out and turn it over to the government. He had developed the Abbey into a tourist attraction with an animal farm, antique shops, a pub, and a guided tour of the home and its art treasures for which he charged admission. Woburn Abbey now drew literally millions of visitors a year, and generated enough income to pay the government taxes and the upkeep of the house. Such a business establishment could use public relations representation so as to attract even greater crowds. I then knew what I had to do. I agreed that in return for the Duke and Duchess of Bedford hosting a party in honor of the Supremes, Rogers & Cowan would handle public relations for the launching of the spring and summer season of Woburn Abbey—for no fee!

We kissed, shook hands, and I departed. Everything had been straightened out. I got back in the car and started to laugh. I said to myself, I have been hustled before but *no* one has ever hustled me more deliciously, more cleverly than did the Duchess of Bedford on that long, snowy trip.

The party was a *huge* success. There were headlines in every newspaper in England. Articles appeared all over the world. Record sales of Diana Ross and the Supremes in England skyrocketed. For many years the Supremes' records were in the top ten in the English recording industry. And it all happened because Warren Cowan had asked Margaret Gardner to think of an idea to launch the Supremes importantly in Great Britain.

We fulfilled our obligation. We faithfully represented the Duke and Duchess of Bedford and Woburn Abbey for the agreed-upon length of time. Since then the Bedfords and the Rogers have become good friends. Whenever we are at a dinner party together, at one point in the evening, Nicole turns to the guests and says, "Have you ever heard the story of what happened when Henry came to see us in Meribel in his Beverly Hills suit and his brown suede shoes?"

Then I think to myself, Yes, she helped me, and I helped her in return. That is the way it should be.

CHAPTER 18
It Is Better to Give . . .

In recent years we have been reading about the business practices of the late Ben Sonnenberg, acknowledged for many years as the most colorful practitioner of the public relations business. One of Mr. Sonnenberg's favorite practices was to bring together two of his most important clients for dinner at his magnificent Gramercy Park home in New York. Invariably the two clients would shake hands on some kind of deal before the evening was over, and they were both grateful to their host for having brought them together.

So, too, one of the most important and constructive roles that I can play for a client, over and above the specific responsibilities for which I get paid, is that of catalyst. When I am able to bring a client together with another client to their mutual advantage, and the result is advantageous to my clients, I am gratified because the client is getting from me a service that is more than he originally expected.

The perfect example of the public relations man acting as a catalyst on behalf of a client is an incident that took place a number of years ago with Shirley MacLaine.

It was at a time in Shirley's life when she suddenly found movie studio doors closed to her. She had scored triumphantly in such films as *The Apartment, Two for the Seesaw, Some Came Running,* and *The Children's Hour,* but one day, she awakened and found that there were no roles that were right for her. Shirley's dilemma was not unique; the doors were closed to many actresses at that time because writers and producers were not thinking of women's stories. After *Butch Cassidy and the Sundance Kid* and *The Sting,* everyone wanted to make films with and about men.

Shirley was a personal friend and had been a client of Rogers & Cowan for many years. She and I had worked on political and charity campaigns together. We had dined together. She had been a guest at my home and I at hers on many occasions over the years. I was worried about her waning career.

One day we were chatting and I expressed my anxiety.

"You're very sweet to worry about me," she said, "but don't worry about it. I've decided what I'm going to do."

"Tell me," I said as I leaned forward in my chair.

"I'm not going to sit around and wait for someone to give me a job," she replied. "You never saw me on Broadway, Henry, but I was a pretty good hoofer. No, I'm not going back to Broadway, but that might come one day. I started as a hoofer, a song and dance girl, and that's what I'm going to do again. I'm going to develop a nightclub act for myself. I'll open out of town, play a lot of different cities, and then when I decide it's good enough, I'll take it to Las Vegas. Then, maybe even back to Broadway again."

"Shirley," I countered, "I'm still worried. I don't want to sound discouraging, but you're not eighteen years old anymore. You haven't danced professionally in years. Do you know how tough it is to do Las Vegas? Besides, and forgive me for my bluntness, you're not as trim as you used to be either."

She laughed.

"I know everything you're saying. You're right, but you just watch. Shirley's mad as hell. You just watch me."

I did. I went to the rehearsal hall a few times. She was working twelve hours a day. Calisthenics, running, dieting. The excess pounds melted off her. Her arms, waistline, and legs became taut and firm. In a few weeks' time, she looked fifteen years younger than she had when she had broken the news to me that she was going to develop a nightclub act and become a hoofer again.

Shirley opened her nightclub act out of town and it was a smash hit. She took it from city to city, honing it, shaping it, improving it, getting it ready for Las Vegas. And when it *was* ready for Las Vegas, Shirley knew that her nightclub act was readily adaptable to an hour television special.

Shirley's agents arranged for the television network executives to go to Las Vegas to see her show. They all loved it, but no one bought it. They were afraid that Shirley couldn't attract television audiences. In trade parlance, the word was out that "She can't get us a rating." Finally, CBS agreed that if Shirley could bring in the show fully sponsored by an advertiser, which would mean there would be no financial risk for the network, they would accept it.

Where to find an advertiser? That was Shirley's agency's responsibility but they were at a loss. Possibly I could help. I was about to act as a catalyst—and a plan came to mind immediately.

We represented Timex, which at that time sponsored eight or ten television specials every year. I felt that the Shirley MacLaine Show was exactly right for them. I called our client and close friend, Robert Mohr, who was Executive Vice-President of Timex. He was the man who decided which television specials his company would sponsor.

"I appreciate your interest," said Bob. "But, let's go through proper channels. I'll call the people at our ad agency and ask them to go out to Las Vegas to see her show. If it's as good as you say it is, they'll probably recommend it to me. If they do, I'll buy it. It's as simple as that."

I called Shirley to tell her what had happened. The following day, three executives of Warwick, Welsh & Miller, the Timex advertising agency, flew from New York to Las Vegas to see the "Shirley Mac-Laine Show." The following day they arrived in the Beverly Hills offices of ICM. The television department of Shirley's agency was ready to make a presentation to the Timex agency as to how the Las Vegas Show was to be converted into a one-hour television special, along with the costs and other details.

I knew that the Timex agency was due to make its proposal to Bob Mohr the following day. Bob had a budget for eight shows that year. The plan was for them to recommend ten shows out of which eight would finally be selected. That evening I called Bob Mohr at home.

"What shows did the agency recommend?" I asked.

"Just a minute," replied my client-friend. "I have the list right here." He read them off to me. The "Shirley MacLaine Show" was not on the list.

"What happened to the Shirley MacLaine Show?" I asked.

"Something went wrong," replied Bob, "I asked the boys why they hadn't recommended Shirley MacLaine. They told me that although they were impressed with the Vegas show, they were very unimpressed with the presentation that ICM had made. When they weighed it against the other shows they were considering, they decided they couldn't recommend it."

There was a pause.

"Bob, you know that I never overstep my bounds in my relationship with you. I represent public relations for Timex, and I don't get involved with television programing or anything else that's not in my domain. But this time it's different. I'm going to stick my neck out. I just know that your agency is wrong. I am 100 percent sold that the 'Shirley MacLaine Show' can be the highest-rated Timex show of next season. I would like you to give it another chance. Will you agree

208

to meet with Shirley sometime in the next few days and let her tell you herself about her show? I'm sure that when you meet her, you'll understand why I'm so enthusiastic."

"My wife Mary Ann loves to meet movie stars. If you want me to meet with Shirley MacLaine, I'll have Mary Ann join us. It will be fun for her."

I called Shirley. She was devastated that her show had been turned down by the Timex agency. It was the last chance. It looked as though there wouldn't be a "Shirley MacLaine Show" on television the next season.

"We're not finished yet," I said. "We have one more chance. I'm going to ask you to do something that is completely unorthodox. I'm going to ask you to turn on your beautiful smile and sell your own show. The fate of your show has been in the hands of faceless people at your agency trying to sell faceless people at the Timex agency. You've worked too hard to leave it at that. It has to be a one-on-one confrontation. I want you to sell Bob Mohr, the man at Timex who is authorized to buy shows for his company. I'll set up a meeting. You go in and sell yourself."

"If you think it'll work, I'll do it. But isn't that unusual procedure in the television business? Isn't selling always done by the agents?"

I laughed. "It's not unusual," I replied. "It's unique. I don't know of a case where a star has ever gone in to sell herself to a sponsor. But what have you got to lose? To hell with tradition and normal procedures."

Shirley paused. "Well, it's not the most dignified approach in the world, but Goddamn it, I've worked too hard on this show not to give it every chance. I owe it to myself, and I owe it to all those other people who have been working with me for over a year. Okay, Henry, I'll do it. What's the next step?"

"I have the strategy all worked out. Here is what we do."

I told her my plan and Shirley agreed to go through with it.

Three nights later in New York I picked up Shirley MacLaine at her Fifty-second Street apartment at about 7:30. A few minutes later we rolled up in a taxi to the Regency Hotel, where the Mohrs had an apartment. When I telephoned the room, Mary Ann answered and invited us up for a drink.

As we went up in the elevator, I whispered to Shirley, "Remember, Mary Ann is the key. If she likes you, we're in. Don't worry about

Bob. He'll be paying attention, but focus in on Mary Ann."

Shirley smiled and shrugged. "No one ever told me that television would be like this, but I'm game. Lead the way."

Mary Ann opened the door. I made the introductions.

"Where is Bob?" I asked.

"He's in the shower. He got home late from the office. He'll be out in a few minutes. Where is Roz?" (Mrs. Rogers and Mrs. Mohr had become good friends over the years.)

"Roz will be joining us later for dinner, along with Pete Hamill. I just thought it would be nice if the four of us had a chance to talk quietly for a while before the evening really gets underway."

Mary Ann went to a portable bar and prepared drinks for us. I had briefed Shirley about her earlier in the day. She was an attractive young woman who had been brought up in a first-generation Italian family in this country. Unmarried, she had been Bob Mohr's secretary at Timex for ten years, during which Bob had married and divorced his wife, the same woman, three times. The loyal Mary Ann had always stood by. Then one day Bob called me and said, "Mary Ann and I just got married. I thought you would like to know." Bob had settled down happily with Mary Ann and she had left her job at Timex, but Bob still counted on her good judgment.

So here we were, Shirley MacLaine and Henry Rogers in the Mohr apartment, with the fate of the "Shirley MacLaine Show" in the hands of the former secretary.

With drinks in hand, we all sat down to chat.

Mary Ann opened up the conversation, directing it at Shirley.

"I'm just thrilled to meet you. When Bob told me you were coming up for drinks, I was really excited. You must understand that I come from a very humble background and the idea of meeting a Hollywood movie star is terribly new and exciting for me."

Shirley turned on her charm. She thanked Mary Ann for the compliment. Then she complimented her on the dress she was wearing and her hairdo and the color of her nail polish. In five minutes' time Shirley and Mary Ann were chatting together like longtime, intimate friends.

The door opened and the Executive Vice-President of Timex walked in. I introduced him to Shirley and he apologized for being late. As Mary Ann mixed him a drink, he said, "Henry has been telling me about the television special you're preparing. He told me that

I would be doing my company a disservice if I didn't hear about it directly from you. If it isn't too much trouble, I'd like you to tell me about it."

Would she like? Was it too much trouble! Shirley was rarin' to go. Like a boxer who hears the bell after having trained for the fight for a year, she pranced into the ring. She was superb. She started by describing the first scene, "talked" the lyrics of the first song, explained how the company of dancers who worked behind her came onstage, stood up, did a little dance step to illustrate the scene, then proceeded to scene two.

I looked at Mary Ann and Bob. They were entranced. How often do a businessman and his former secretary have the star of a show do a private audition for them in their own apartment? I was fascinated too. Shirley was carried away with her own performance. She quietly, without accompaniment, sang a song which was one of the highlights of the show, "If My Friends Could See Me Now." I thought that if her friends could see her now, they would have given her an Academy Award for her performance.

An hour passed and Shirley finished her audition. Mary Ann, Bob, and I spontaneously started to applaud. Shirley smiled, beamed, and simulated the bows she normally would take on the nightclub floor.

"I loved it, I loved it," said Mary Ann. Bob said, "I did too, Shirley. There is no doubt that with this material, you have the makings of a great television special. I don't know why my agency didn't recommend it."

I interrupted. "Don't be tough on them, Bob," I said, "after all, they didn't get a private audition from Shirley the way you did."

I knew the business for the evening was over. We shouldn't press it. I knew that Bob would need time to make up his mind. "Well, that finishes up the business for the evening. It's nine-thirty. I'm sure that Pete and Roz are waiting for us at 21 for dinner. Let's go."

The four of us went to 21, meeting Pete and Roz there. We had a pleasant, conversation-filled dinner. It was warm, friendly, and fun.

At one point Roz whispered to me, "I don't understand why you left Pete and me behind. Why didn't we join you and Shirley right from the beginning?"

"It was part of my strategy," I replied, "I didn't want it to become a social evening until we had finished our business. I thought you and Pete might have diverted Bob and Mary Ann's attention away from Shirley. I wanted them to feel that Shirley was giving a performance just for them. That's why I had Pete pick you up at 9:30 and bring you here."

"Did it work?"

"I don't know," I concluded. "I'll find out tomorrow."

At about midnight our dinner was over. We were standing outside the restaurant waiting for taxis and Bob turned to Shirley. "I want to tell you again how much I enjoyed the evening. I need a little time to make a decision, but I'll let Henry know as soon as I can."

The Mohrs stepped into the first cab. Shirley said to me, "Well, what do you think?" she asked. "How did it go?"

"You were superb," I replied. "You gave the performance of the year. They both fell in love with you—but I don't know what the final decision will be. Bob goes through proper channels. He'll want his agency to make a formal recommendation to him. He won't go over their heads. I don't think they'll fight him, but we'll just have to see."

The evening was over and Shirley thanked me.

Late the next day Bob Mohr called to tell me that the "Shirley MacLaine Show" was a "go." It would be a Timex-sponsored television presentation the next season. At his prompting, the agency had made the recommendation. With his approval, they had made arrangements with CBS to carry the show.

Shirley MacLaine's first television special aired on CBS the following season. It received excellent ratings and won a handful of Emmy Awards for Shirley and her associates. As a result of the success of this first show, Shirley signed a long-term deal with CBS-TV and there is a Shirley MacLaine television special on CBS every year.

What did I get out of this? I did not get paid a bonus by either of my clients for my services which were "over and above the call of duty." I didn't expect it. I got much more. I was able to confirm once more to myself that Rogers & Cowan offers a service to its clients which is beyond public relations. The ultimate objective of our public relations activity is to help our client's business, in one way or the other. There are times when being able to act as a catalyst helps the client's business even more than our public relations effort. It certainly did with Shirley MacLaine and Timex. Shirley was able to prove that she could bring to television audiences a high-quality program which attracted sufficient numbers of viewers to make it a good investment for both network and advertiser alike. Timex did get, as I had predicted, its highest-rated television special of the year, which meant that it had reached more potential buyers of Timex watches than they had reached with any other show that season. By bringing them together in the first place I had served both my clients effectively and had come away from the experience gratified that I had done an excellent job, and more than what was even expected of me. When you give more than you can get, business becomes a pleasure.

CHAPTER 19
Tolerance, Empathy, and a Sense of Humor Are Essentials

In order to retain my equilibrium in the mad world in which I live, I must be tolerant, and have empathy for those with whom I do business. If I had not fortunately been born with a sense of humor, I would have long since developed an ulcer as a result of the frustrating, emotion-stirring, laughable, tragic, humiliating, sad, happy, aggravating, and exhilarating experiences I have had over the years. In my business, life is a series of highs and lows. I am not only perpetually on a tightrope but also on a roller coaster, screaming with ecstasy as I soar headily to the top and moaning with despair as I plunge sickeningly into the pits. My impregnable defense is the sense of humor that has enabled me to shrug off the disappointments and frustrations I have experienced along with the thousand delights I have enjoyed over the years in my dealings with movie stars.

In the moments of frustration I don't stop to wait for thanks or gratitude or even sympathy. By the time a client wants to express appreciation for a job well done, I have moved on to the next job, looking for the next unpredictable challenge, another mountain to climb.

The very nature of the public relations business calls for me to face a new challenge every day, to solve a new problem, to deal with a new unpredictable client. The very nature of my business puts me in daily situations with clients that involve their emotions, their demands, their whims, their sound business judgment, their irrationality —in short, the whole complex range of talent and temperament that makes them as successful as they are in the corporate and show business world. The person who has risen to a position in his life to require the services of a public relations man is not usually an ordinary human being. His or her success has come through an inner drive combined with an unusual talent for acting, producing a movie, marketing products, or running a business enterprise. The combination of inner drive and talent makes for a colorful, enigmatic, fascinating, often larger-than-life human being whom I always find challenging to deal with.

214

What do I get out of it? In all the forty years I have been in the public relations business, I have never been bored, which is more than you can say about most businesses. This is all the reward I need. I don't want any one to give me a gold watch after forty years of service. My gold watch is the satisfaction of getting up at 6:00 tomorrow morning, anxious to get to the office because another client is waiting to have me try to solve his problem. I do not believe that this is only because I work with interesting, fascinating, provocative people, although this is undoubtedly an advantage. I believe that for anyone who recognizes it, the rewards are closely tied to one's own attitude toward his work. I look around at friends who got out of the public relations business. They were never looking for the problems, the challenges, and the unpredictable experiences that I find in my life every day. Every business has its excitements and challenges if one looks for them. No job has to be boring, no job is a dead end. Look for the excitement in any job and I believe it can be found. Performance improves with a sense of excitement, an appreciation of working with people, no matter how unpredictable they might be, without expecting thanks.

I am convinced of this, and I have had many years in the "people" business that confirm my thinking.

Of all the people whose paths I have crossed over the many years, the movie stars stand out as the most fascinating. They are more complex human beings, more enigmatic, more colorful, more exciting to be with. They are larger than life, quixotic, often irrational, and always unpredictable.

I first met Audrey Hepburn almost twenty years ago, when she was filming *War and Peace* in Rome for Dino de Laurentis and Carlo Ponti. Mel Ferrer, her husband at that time, and Henry Fonda were costarring in the film with her. Mel was an old friend who, with Audrey's agent Kurt Frings, had arranged with Paramount for us to publicize the film. Paramount suggested that I fly to Rome before the film started and get the campaign started from there. My wife Roz joined me on the trip. Mel knew we were coming and arranged for a car to pick us up at the airport and take us directly to their home. He insisted that we stay with them in their little country farmhouse overlooking the beach at Anzio rather than in a hotel.

The car drove into the little courtyard of the house and the petite heroine of *Gigi* and *Roman Holiday*, dressed in a black turtleneck sweater and black slacks and loafers, ran out to meet us. "I'm so glad you're here," she called out, and instead of the usual handshakes and "How do you do?" she embraced us both warmly, while Mel looked on smiling and waiting until he too could embrace his friends. We had never met Audrey before, and Roz and I were both enchanted. She was warm, bubbly, enthusiastic, and genuinely happy to entertain her husband's friends.

Over the years, Audrey and I became close friends. Rarely have I seen instances where men and women are truly good friends, but that was certainly the case with us. Although she has always lived abroad (with the exception of three short stays in Hollywood when she was filming *Breakfast at Tiffany's, My Fair Lady,* and *Wait Until Dark*) we have spent hundreds of hours together over the years—just the two of us. There were weekends in her home near Morges, Switzerland, when Mel was off somewhere working, or later, after they were divorced. There were long lunch hours in film studios in Paris, Rome, London, Hollywood. There were teatimes in different cities where she would happen to be. Unlike any other actress I have ever known, Audrey's career always came second. She never had the burning desire to become and remain a movie star, as do most actresses, but instead cared only for personal happiness, peace, love, her children, a husband whom she loved and who loved her. Rarely did I ever see her happy. It was no secret that her marriage with Mel was not a happy one. It seemed to me that she loved him more than he loved her, and it was frustrating for her not to have her love returned in kind. She had confided these feelings to me and a number of other intimate friends many times. She never complained but I always saw the sadness in her eyes. Audrey has rarely been happy in marital love, but she has received great joy from her children. I hope that one day the right man will come along who will give her the happiness that a woman with her ability to love truly deserves.

During the years she was married to Mel, she was Trilby to his Svengali. Although she loved acting, she wanted to work less and spend more time in private with Mel and her son Sean. She was filled with love. Mel was filled with ambition, for his wife and for himself. She was uncomfortable about doing publicity, that is, interviews and the magazine features that I continually arranged for her. Mel had pushed her into the professional relationship she had with me, and although we became close personal friends, she always bridled whenever I mentioned the need for an interview to be done or a photo session that I felt she should do.

216

I tried not to push her into a lot of publicity activity, realizing that she considered it to be an unpleasant chore. I selected only important things for her to do. Still, I performed a constant balancing act between Mel's insatiable desire for Audrey's new publicity and her reluctance to give interviews or pose for photographs.

Gradually, I realized I was being stretched to the limits of diplomacy and it could not continue. The beginning of the end of my professional relationship with them came one Sunday afternoon in their house in Switzerland where Audrey, Mel, and I had been spending a number of hours talking about Audrey's career. She was always reluctant to get into discussions of this sort and was angry with Mel and me. Mel had always resented the fact that she had given Hubert de Givenchy her name and likeness to launch his first venture into the fragrance business. *Vogue, Harper's Bazaar, Town and Country*, and other magazines all over the world were carrying a magnificent portrait of Audrey, indicating that the fragrance had been created exclusively for her. Givenchy had built a multimillion-dollar business using Audrey—without compensating her. Prior to my arrival at the Ferrer home, I had stopped off in Paris at Mel's request to meet with Givenchy's brother Claude, who handled the financial side of the empire, to discuss with him the idea of having Audrey receive some compensation for the use of her likeness. Mel had said to me, "For Christ's sake, Henry, she doesn't even get a discount on the clothes he designs for her. As for the perfume, wouldn't you think he would send her gallons of it—as a gift? She buys it herself—retail!"

I told them about my meeting in Paris. The Givenchys were amenable to working out some reasonable form of compensation.

Audrey looked at me and then at Mel. "Neither of you seems to understand. I don't want anything from Hubert. I don't need his money. He is my friend. If I have helped him build his perfume business, then that's exactly what one friend should do for another. If someone else offered me $1 million to endorse a perfume, I wouldn't do it . . . but Hubert is my friend. I don't want anything. Yes, I even want to walk into a drugstore and buy the perfume at the retail price."

As the tension began to fill the room, the doorbell rang.

"That must be Favre Le Bret," said Mel. "He said he would be dropping by about now. Henry, you're going to talk to him alone as we agreed. Right?"

Favre Le Bret was director of the Cannes Film Festival, a dynamic, aggressive man who had been almost solely responsible for making the Cannes Film Festival the most successful in the world. Audrey, Mel, and I had had an amicable relationship with him for many years. He had come to see Audrey and Mel because he wanted Audrey to attend the opening night celebration of that year's festival. Mel had asked me what I thought about it. I told him I was opposed, that there was no reason for Audrey to attend the opening ceremonies. She didn't have a film that was being screened. She did not need or care about the publicity she would get out of it. It would be obvious to everyone that she was there for publicity purposes and to take the spotlight away from other actresses who were there because their films were being shown. Neither Audrey nor I, as her advisor, had ever played those games.

Mel kept insisting I talk to him. "Le Bret is very important, and he wants Audrey very badly. Maybe someday we'll need a favor from him."

I was adamant in my resolve that she shouldn't attend the opening unless— "I'll agree," I had finally said, "if I can figure out a good reason for her to attend. Right now there is no reason."

Audrey got up. "I'm going upstairs to see Sean," she said. "You fellows decide what to do." Sean, their son, was then an infant.

Mel and I greeted Mr. Le Bret. Then Mel left me alone with him, as planned.

Favre and I were sitting in the cozy, firelit room where Mel had left us, drinks in hand, and I was giving it to him straight. "I need a reason for her to attend," I explained, "otherwise I cannot recommend to Audrey in all good conscience that she should attend your opening."

"I don't disagree with you," countered the suave Mr. Le Bret. "Come up with a good reason and we'll do it. Do you have one? Let me hear it."

"Actually," I replied, "I *have* thought of something. In fact, it's an idea that is not only good for Audrey and the Festival, but if you continue it every year, it should ensure having one of the world's most important stars appear at each one of your opening ceremonies."

"That sounds very intriguing," said Favre. "Tell me about it."

"The Cannes Film Festival should make a slight change in its usual format. During your opening ceremonies every year you should give a special tribute to one person, an actor, an actress, a producer,

218

or a director, who has made an outstanding contribution to the world of international motion pictures, to the art of international motion picures. This year it could be Audrey, who is certainly worthy of receiving the first award. Next year you could select Cary Grant or Sophia Loren or Alfred Hitchcock."

"That's a very interesting idea," replied my companion. "Let me think about it and I'll let you know in a few days." We had another drink, chatted about the most recent movie gossip, and I arose, ready to leave. I had arranged for a taxi to pick me up and take me to Geneva so that I could catch a plane to London, where I had a number of appointments the next day.

Mel came back into the room. I took him off in a corner and quietly told him what I had proposed to Le Bret and what his reaction had been. Then, when Audrey came downstairs, we kissed good-bye and I left them together with Le Bret to chat informally.

The next day, the telephone rang at 8 A.M. in my hotel room in London. A voice at the other end sobbed, "Henry, it's Audrey. I'm sorry to call you so early. I've been up all night. I haven't slept, I'm so unhappy."

"What's wrong?" I asked, suddenly worried for her. "Is something wrong with Sean?"

"No, Henry, it's you. You know how much I care about you—how much I value your friendship. I'm crying because I have decided that I don't want you to represent me anymore. I won't hire anyone else. I just can't stand any more of this. I just don't like what is happening to me, and my life and my friends."

I couldn't understand what she was talking about. I asked her.

"First you embarrassed me with Hubert. You and Mel made such a thing about his taking advantage of me, and I told you last night— I don't care. He's my friend. And last night, after you left, it was terrible. I was embarrassed. I was ashamed. I started to cry and ran out of the room. Favre Le Bret told me you had tried to blackmail him, that you told him the only way I would go to the Cannes Film Festival would be if he gave me some kind of phony, trumped-up award. Henry,"—and she was still sobbing—"I don't want you to work for me anymore. Will you still be my friend?"

I was floored. What a quick, dramatic turn of events. I really felt great empathy for her. Here was a lively, sensitive person—not a movie star in the usual sense of the word—genuinely sobbing her heart out. Although I had represented her for some ten years, she was embarrassed and frustrated about the Givenchy and Favre Le Bret situations which I had instigated, and really did not want to be involved in the complex world which is part and parcel of the motion picture industry—the intrigue, the deals, the negotiations that go on behind the scenes—and yet still did not want to break off a relationship with a man whom she regarded as a close friend.

"Of course we will be friends," I replied. "I just feel so damn badly because I caused you so much embarrassment and pain. But before we finish this conversation, you must understand one thing. You have known me for *many years*. You know how I work. You know very well that I never tried to blackmail Favre Le Bret. If he is stupid enough to interpret my proposal, which was good for him and good for you, in that way, then I never want anything to do with him again—and you shouldn't either." She tearfully agreed, and we said good-bye.

Audrey did not attend the Cannes Film Festival. We did, however, remain good friends. A few years ago we gave a dinner party at our home in her honor. She came with her second husband, Dr. Andrea Dotti, a noted Roman psychiatrist. It was a lovely reunion.

As for Favre Le Bret, I have not spoken to him since the night when I supposedly tried to blackmail him. Blackmail indeed! I had given him an idea that would have made the Cannes Film Festival increasingly important every year, and he had turned it against me. As for my professional relationship with Audrey coming to an end at that point, I had mixed emotions. It was frustrating to do what I felt was right for my client and then have it boomerang against me. The great temptation in the public relations business is to be guilty of errors of omission rather than errors of commission. If I had not met with the Givenchys in Paris, knowing Audrey's feelings about not wanting to be compensated for her perfume endorsement, and if I had merely told Le Bret, "No, Audrey won't attend your opening night ceremonies," I would have still retained her as a client. Yet, I must do what I feel is right for my client, and there will always be those times when I will face the frustration of losing a client because I have done what I felt was right for him or her.

Then there was Tony Curtis.

We started to represent Tony Curtis very early in his career, in the days when he and Janet Leigh were the handsomest and most romantic couple in town. At the time Tony had a family problem. He had moved his elderly father and mother from the Bronx when he first became successful and fixed them up nicely in an apartment, but, unfortunately, his father was very unhappy. An immigrant Russian Jew with a very heavy accent, he had been content and comfortable in his Bronx tailor shop surrounded by his own friends of similar background. The elegance of Hollywood was simply not to his liking—even more so because Tony had married a *shiksah*. Tony decided that if he could get his father a job, at least part of the problem would be solved. Where to get a job? Tony went to his agent. He said, "No." He went to his lawyer. The lawyer said, "No." He went to his business manager. The business manager said "No." He went to Rogers & Cowan. We said "Yes," because we thought it would be a generous gesture toward a client we liked and respected.

We made a job for the elderly Mr. Schwartz in our mailroom. Tony was very grateful, but he had another problem—a not-too-bright younger brother. Maybe his brother would be benefited by working somewhere. Again, Rogers & Cowan was there—we gave him a job too. Tony was eternally grateful. Then came the tragic day when Tony's father didn't come to work. With great sorrow we learned that he had died of a heart attack. A few weeks later, I called Tony's mother, who was still in mourning, and asked if I could come and see her that afternoon. Once there I told her that her late husband, Mr. Schwartz, was a Rogers & Cowan employee and was entitled to all employee privileges, among them a life insurance policy for $5,000. I then handed her a check for that amount, which we had just received from the insurance company. That night, Tony called me. "Henry, I'm so grateful to you and Warren. It's more than the $5,000. It's just that my mother was so proud that pop had been working and she was so proud that he was happy in his job. I cannot tell you how much it means to her to have the insurance money and that you took the time to bring her the check yourself. Again, thanks to you and Warren for doing so much for my family—and for me."

A number of years later, we were no longer actively representing Tony. This is not unusual in the motion picture industry. We represent a client for a number of years; then there is a hiatus until we resume again. This was one of the periods when we were on a hiatus with Tony. There was no problem, except that Tony owed us a few thousand dollars, and we had had no explanation of why he had not paid us. Much of Tony's business at that time was handled by his attorney, Marvin Meyer. On the at least half-dozen times that I had spoken with Marvin about the overdue money, I had been unable to get any sense of why we had not been paid. I finally decided to go directly to Tony. When I found out that he had just left for London, I sent him a cable care of his hotel there telling him that through his attorney I had been trying to collect the moneys due us for many months and now with much reluctance, was forced to appeal to him directly for an immediate settlement.

The next day Marvin called me. He had heard from Tony. Tony was furious with me and my cable, which was waiting for him when he arrived at his hotel. But just before that, Tony had had another unpleasant surprise—this one at London airport. In passing through customs, he had been discovered to have a cache of marijuana in his luggage. In those days, this was a serious offense. Tony was suddenly and unexpectedly in trouble with the British government. How dare I bother him with such a trivial matter as money when he, Tony Curtis, famous Hollywood star, was in trouble!!! I could not appreciate his anger at me. I was angry because he had not even had the courtesy to acknowledge his debt to us, and he was now resentful that I had had the audacity to ask for probably the thirty-seventh time for payment for past services. How the hell did I know that he was being busted at the moment my dunning telegram had arrived?

A few years later I was having dinner one night with Paul Anka in London. As we sat down at the table, Paul said, "I asked Tony Curtis to join us, but he said he wouldn't have dinner with you. What's wrong with you two?"

I laughed. "Oh, nothing important enough to talk about."

I told Paul that in our business we all have to keep a sense of humor. P.S. Tony Curtis finally paid his bill.

I have also experienced sadness in my relationships with movie stars. I remember one incident that proved to be just about the saddest and most disturbing personal experience I have ever had in my professional life. Montgomery Clift was at the height of his career when he engaged Rogers & Cowan. He wasn't looking for publicity, but for a better understanding with the press. He was embarrassed and unhappy by the way he was treated by the press and hoped that we could help him. We were trying. Monty lived in a brownstone in the East Forties in New York. On one of my frequent trips to New York I asked him out to lunch. He agreed, suggested that I come by the house, pick him up, and then we would go on to one of his favorite neighborhood restaurants, only a few blocks away.

At the appointed time I rang the door of his home. We had met a few times before, but as he opened the door and greeted me, I became suddenly aware that he was probably the handsomest man I had ever met. His thick black hair was neatly combed, his dark eyes flashed in recognition; he wore a blue oxford-cloth button-down shirt, open at the collar, no tie, grey flannel slacks, brown loafers. He smiled, welcomed me warmly, and asked me to come in and sit down. He lived with nondescript furniture, in a clutter of books and papers like any other middle-income bachelor in New York. He wanted to talk about himself and his problems, and I let him. Occasionally, I interrupted with a question. I suddenly felt like a psychiatrist, but I didn't mind. I had often played that role before, and still do. For some people, the public relations man is easier to confide in than anyone else, psychiatrists included.

Monty talked about his life as an actor and his life as a person. He was trying to keep the actor away from the person and was finding it difficult. He loved working. He loved working in motion pictures. He loved finding a script which had in it a role he wanted to play, and then wrestling with it until he had figured out how he wanted to play it. Then he enjoyed the intellectual exercise of working out his interpretation with his director and then finally enjoyed seeing himself on the screen—if the film turned out as well as he hoped it would. It all seemed completely understandable. His problem involved leading the personal life that being a movie star required. He had escaped most of it by continuing to live in New York instead of Hollywood. He hated people fawning all over him, he hated being asked for autographs, and he hated being attacked by the press because he refused to live the public life that movie stars are expected to live.

During this very articulate presentation of his personal problems, I observed that he had not offered me coffee, tea, or a drink. Although I didn't mind, I began to wonder if he'd just forgotten this simple courtesy. Finally, after an hour, he stood up and said, "Well, enough of all that for now. Let's go to lunch."

We left the house, strolled slowly in the direction of First Avenue, and entered a little, unobtrusive Italian neighborhood restaurant. There are thousands of them in New York and they all look alike—a small bar tended by the proprietor, a dining room which holds no more than thirty people, three colored plastic booths and tables for two. The proprietor-bartender greeted us warmly. "Good afternoon, Mr. Clift," he said, "glad to see you again." There was no hint of the catastrophe that was about to occur.

Monty returned the greeting, shook hands warmly with the bartender, and said to me, "Let's have a drink before lunch. I'll have a martini straight up. What'll you have, Henry?"

It all seemed so innocent. I usually don't drink during lunch. But what the hell. "I'll have a martini too, but on the rocks, please."

We each took a stool at the bar and waited for our drinks to be mixed. It couldn't have taken more than two minutes. The drinks were placed before us. "Cheers," said Monty, lifting his glass to me in salute. "Cheers," I replied. We both took the first sip of a martini.

I still can't believe what happened next. I have thought about it a thousand times since that terrible day, and sometimes I conjecture that it was all a dream.

This was Dr. Jekyll and Mr. Hyde, and Dorian Gray all wrapped into one. One sip of a martini and Montgomery Clift was drunk—not just tipsy but drunker than a Bowery derelict. From an urbane, intelligent, well-spoken, articulate young man, he was transformed into a blithering, sloppy, fumbling drunk.

I sat there, dumbfounded. Monty took another sip. I did too. Two sips and the simple martini was half-gone. Neither of us could have consumed more than one-half ounce of alcohol. He was completely sloshed. I looked at the bartender. How could he have given his customer that drink? He must have known what I did not know, that Montgomery Clift was an alcoholic—of the worst kind.

After the second sip, Monty put his arm around my shoulders. He leaned close, "Hennery, old buddy—you're my besh friend. You're the only one I can talk to, you unnerstan' me. Lesh have lunch."

Without finishing his drink, he started to get off the stool. He couldn't stand on his feet and slipped to the floor, where he lay for a fraction of a second. I was still dumbfounded. Was he kidding me or was this real? I couldn't risk waiting to find out. I reached down at the same time a waiter rushed to help him up. We both got him to his feet and we half-dragged him to one of the booths. There were only a few other people in the restaurant, and no one seemed to be paying much attention. We finally sat down at the booth. I noticed that the waiter did not offer to bring over our glasses, which had remained at the bar.

Before the waiter could bring over the menu, Monty said to him, "My friend and I'll both have beef shtew. Henner-y—the beef shtew is great. You'll love it."

He hunched over the table, bent his head, and said nothing. What was going to happen now? I wondered. I didn't have much time to wonder. The waiter brought over two bowls of beef stew. It looked delicious, the steam carrying the aroma of the beef, the red wine, and the vegetables up to my eager nostrils. I picked up a fork and was about to begin, when I looked at my companion. He had put his hand into the bowl of beef stew, had grabbed chunks of beef and vegetables with his fingers, and had pushed the whole mess into his mouth. His face was covered with gravy, his fingers were dripping. He took a deep breath, looked toward me with glazed, half-closed eyes, and then slowly, inexorably, uncontrollably, slipped off the banquette and slowly, slowly—his entire body slid onto the floor under the table.

It all happened so quickly, so unexpectedly, that I was transfixed. I was unable to stop him from sliding under the table. I was paralyzed —but only for a moment. The waiter saw what had happened. He pulled away the table and once more we helped this magnificent movie star, the brilliant actor, the pitiful figure, up off the floor. It was time for me to act.

"Let's go home, Monty," I said. "We've had enough lunch."

"Okay, Henn-er-y, ole buddy boy, you're right, lesh go home."

Without protest, he was ready to go. He knew he couldn't make it on his own. Once more he put his arm around my shoulder, this time for support. I put my arm around his waist to support him and so that he wouldn't be a dead weight. We struggled out of the restaurant and lurched along the street, back to the Clift home. A group of schoolboys on their way home from school spotted us. They started giving us long whistles. "Oh, aren't they lovey dovey!" they called out. They obviously thought we were amorous homosexuals. "Fuck off," I yelled at them and off they went. We finally arrived at the Clift house. He fumbled for his keys. Then he couldn't get the right one in the lock. I helped him and pushed open the door. "Can I help you?" I asked him. I must have sounded plaintive and helpless. "No-o-o-o," he slurred, "I'm just fine. You go on along. Thanks for the lunch. We'll do it again—shoon."

He walked in and closed the door behind him. I walked away— devastated. I was on the verge of tears.

I really didn't know Montgomery Clift. I had had only a few brief business encounters with him before that day, and I remember well only those few poignant hours we spent together at his home and at that little Italian restaurant. I never saw him again. Montgomery Clift was dead only a few months after we had lunched together, and when I heard the news I was sorry that I had never had the chance to know him better—and possibly help him.

CHAPTER 20

"Sorry, Henry," Said Prince Philip. "You Were Right and I Was Wrong."

Prince Philip was expecting me. I had just arrived at the Privy Purse door of Buckingham Palace, and I was being escorted to the office of His Royal Highness.

Walking alongside my uniformed escort, we strode up a flight of stairs lined with portraits of aged monarchs on the red brocade walls, down a long corridor, and to a closed door. We stopped. My escort opened the door and stepped back.

"Go right in, Mr. Rogers. I am sure that Prince Philip will be joining you in a few minutes. Make yourself comfortable." He disappeared down the hallway. I was in Prince Philip's office.

I looked around me. For a number of months before our appointment I had tried to imagine the office in which I was now standing. I had envisioned deep burgundy leather chairs, a magnificent Chippendale desk, exquisitely hand-carved Sheraton chairs and tables throughout the room, Gainsborough portraits on the walls, a Turner, a Constable landscape, and oil paintings of Queen Elizabeth, the Queen Mother, King George, and possibly even a family portrait of Prince Philip, Queen Elizabeth, and their children.

What I had imagined could not have been more off the mark. I had forgotten Prince Philip was a naval officer who had spent many years on duty. The furniture was simple—blond wood pieces which could have been Scandinavian. There were naval prints on the walls, model frigates on the tables, naval books on the book shelves and official-looking papers on the desk. The whole effect was Spartan, simple, unassuming—not at all like the surroundings in which I had expected to meet Prince Philip.

I was fidgety and uncomfortable. I was accustomed to movie star homes and business executive offices. This was a new experience for me. What was Prince Philip like? Was he friendly or imperious? Would he see me alone or would he have an entourage with him? Would I stutter? What kind of an impression would I make? I was confident about presenting him with the plan I had prepared, but what would his reactions be?

227

Standing there in Prince Philip's office waiting for his arrival, I reflected that at that moment I had been in business for thirty years. I had represented a myriad of different kinds of clients ranging from actors to television programs, from rock music stars to Procter & Gamble and the DuPont Company. I knew my business. I knew what to do for a client. Buckingham Palace and Prince Philip, however, was a unique experience. Was there something I could learn? What was I doing here? This wasn't exactly work. I was here because this was the kind of job in my business which I particularly enjoyed. I still enjoyed my work in the motion picture industry, but traveling out of my California surroundings to meetings in New York, Paris, and London with notable figures with whom I would not usually be in contact, had always intrigued me.

My meeting with Prince Philip had been arranged a number of months before when a call came in to my Beverly Hills office from one of Prince Philip's aides. Arrangements for a U.S. tour for Prince Philip, on behalf of Variety Clubs International and the British Board of Trade, were being made and I had been recommended to serve as press officer for the tour. After a number of meetings, I agreed to take on the assignment for expenses and a minimum fee.

Prince Philip had agreed to make this twelve-day trip to the United States, visiting Miami, Houston, Palm Springs, Los Angeles, Chicago, and New York, primarily as a fund raiser for Variety Clubs International, a charity organization with chapers all over the world rendering services to underprivileged children.

Our business had grown to the point where I could never, under ordinary circumstances, devote a number of weeks away from the office to any one client. Despite my administrative obligations, and my supervision of the activity which I conducted on many, many clients, I was ready to make an exception in this case. I regarded the opportunity of traveling with Prince Philip on a tour of the United States as something special, a rare opportunity, an exciting challenge for any public relations man. Even more important, after devoting thirty years to my business, it would be a personal experience to long remember.

I was to meet with Prince Philip two months before the tour got underway to discuss procedures and relationships with the American press, as well as the many, many other details involved in having this important member of the royal British household travel for twelve days throughout the United States. I had about forty items on the agenda I carried in my pocket to discuss with him.

The door opened. Prince Philip walked in, looking exactly as he did in his photographs, in film documentaries, and on the television news shows. I had seen him in traditional royal robes, in his numerous naval uniforms, in polo clothes, formal evening attire, shooting clothes. Now he was wearing a conservative grey suit, white shirt, maroon-and-white tie, with a sliver of white linen handkerchief peeking out from his breast pocket. He smiled warmly and walked toward me, right arm outstretched. "Welcome to London, Mr. Rogers. I'm delighted to meet you." His hand firmly clasped mine. "Please sit down." He pointed to the only upholstered piece in the room.

"We have a lot to talk about."

I felt tense. I had gained great self-assurance in first encounters as success had come to me over the years, but, somehow, meeting Prince Philip was different. Like millions of other tourists, I had stood outside Buckingham Palace and watched the Changing of the Guard. Like millions and hundreds of millions of other people throughout the world, I recalled the wedding of Prince Philip and Princess Elizabeth, the birth of Prince Charles, then Princess Anne, then Prince Andrew, all in the thousands of photos, movie newsreels, and television news shows that had been made on the family over many, many years.

"Would you like a drink," he asked. "Coffee? Tea? I have questions to ask you, and I am sure you have many questions to ask me. Sit down. Let's talk."

I had been nervous a moment before. Not now. In ten seconds, he had put me at my ease.

"Where shall we start?" he asked. He was obviously asking me to take the lead in the conversation. I was ready.

"I have an agenda, sir," I replied. "If you are agreeable, let us start with that." He agreed.

"I understand," I began, "that your normal procedure in meeting with the press is to attend a reception, where everyone stands around with drinks in their hands, and you move slowly around the room and greet everyone. Is that true, sir?"

"Yes, of course," he replied, "that is the way we have always done it. Why? Do you have a better suggestion?"

"Forgive my immodesty," I said, "but I believe I do. All of your tours around the world are related primarily to goodwill. Your trip

229

to the United States has a more practical aspect. You are going to be working very hard with the objective of raising $1 million. Those moneys will come if the people who attend the fund-raising events are enthusiastic about you and the cause you are espousing. The initial enthusiasm can be generated by the press and television coverage you receive on this tour. The amount of press and television coverage to be gotten out of a cocktail reception for the press is minimal."

"I agree with you, Henry. What do you recommend?"

"I recommend that you permit me to set up a press conference on your arrival in every city. Depending on the circumstances, we will arrange for it either at the airport or at the hotel when you arrive. I will be in advance of you all the time. I'll be there to meet you in every city as you step off the plane and I'll be with you at every press conference."

Prince Philip was thinking. He looked at me, then took a sip of his coffee.

"I've never done a press conference before. You see, Henry, we never do things like that in the royal household. It's just contrary to our policy. I do agree with you, though. This is a different situation. Fine. If you think we should have a press conference, that's agreeable with me. Incidentally, what kind of questions will they be asking me?"

"Inane," I replied. "They will be very much in awe of you, and there won't be any questions that you will not be able to handle easily."

He laughed. "That's settled then, Henry, but there have to be a few ground rules, and I would appreciate it if you would alert the press in advance as to what they are."

"Of course," I said, "tell me what they are."

"First, make it clear to them that I am not in the British government. Press outside Great Britain are often confused about what role the Queen and I play in our country. Not being a part of the government, I cannot very well answer questions about the British economy, the Tory versus the Labour Party, the Prime Minister, the union problems, and inflation. Second, I will not handle any personal questions about the Queen. Outside of that, you can declare open season and let them fire away."

I made notes as he talked. Together with Prince Philip I went through all the items on my agenda. By the time we were finished,

230

more than an hour after I had arrived, we had covered all the questions he had in mind. We were in accord.

The day after my meeting with Prince Philip, I was scheduled to meet with the Home Secretary, Sir Frank Soskice, in Whitehall. As I entered the austere government building, I was struck by the fact that although there was no longer a British Empire, I had been carried back into Victorian times. There was a huge portrait of Clive of India hanging on the wall as I walked up the broad expanse of marble stairs to the Home Secretary's office. There I once again received a warm greeting. Where had the idea ever come from that the British were cold and reserved?

I had been thoroughly briefed prior to my arrival about the Variety Club part of the forthcoming tour, and now was about to be briefed about the role the British Board of Trade would play.

After the traditional pouring of coffee, the Home Secretary explained.

"Prince Philip has allowed us to catch onto his coattails," he said. "The British Board of Trade will use the opportunity of the Variety Club tour to promote British merchandise in the United States. In each of the cities he visits, the department stores will run a 'British Week' promotion, and Prince Philip has agreed to visit one store in each city. Thus far arrangements have been made wih Saks Fifth Avenue in New York and Marshall Field in Chicago."

"That sounds logical," I said. "How can I be helpful?"

"Well," he replied, "there is really no responsibility for you here, except that I did want you to know about it. We will be getting you all the information very shortly, and you will just fit these appearances into your schedule. Oh, and incidentally, we hope you will alert the press. I am sure that Saks, Marshall Field, and the other stores which participate, will be most appreciative if Prince Philip's appearances are seen on television and covered in the newspapers."

The British always take care of business.

When I returned to New York after concluding preliminary arrangements, I evaluated my responsibilities and objectives:

> To make certain that the American press and the British press received all the information they needed in relation to the ground rules I had set up with Prince Philip.
>
> To make certain that the public was informed that the purpose of Prince Philip's tour was to raise money for Variety Clubs

International, the Playing Fields of Great Britain, and also to act as goodwill ambassador for the British Board of Trade.

To make certain that all arrangements which were the responsibilities of others were carried out effectively so that Prince Philip was not inconvenienced. I decided that if a transportation problem were not handled properly and Prince Philip were left standing on a street corner it would be my responsibility. I would not blame anyone else for the gaffe.

To make certain that the people who were responsible in each city for being the major fund raisers would have an opportunity to meet Prince Philip in person.

The tour began. For twelve days, Prince Philip and I spent from 8 A.M. until 2 A.M. together. I found him to be kindly, well mannered, amusing, witty, and intelligent, not only a great representative of the British Commonwealth but a great gentleman as well.

His aides suggested that I address him as "Sir." I did. He addressed me as Henry, which put me at my ease, immediately. I had set up a press conference in each city we visited. The British press reporters who had accompanied us didn't believe it was happening. They told me that in all the years that they had been covering the royal family, Prince Philip had never held a press conference.

A press reception is comparable to a cocktail party with a guest of honor. The press stand around with cocktail in hand and hope they will get an opportunity to meet and get a few words out of the guest of honor. In contrast, at a press conference, the principal is seated at a table with a microphone, with the press seated in front of him. On our trip, I made certain that the press was seated and settled down before Prince Philip entered the room. I would then step in front of the group, introduce myself, tell in a few words what Prince Philip was doing in a particular city, and then I would say, "Ladies and gentlemen, Prince Philip!" Prince Philip would walk into the room accompanied by a round of applause, sit down, adjust the microphone, and say, "Ladies and gentlemen, are there any questions?"

The tour started in Miami. The first press conference was held in the Fontainebleau Hotel; the first question was, "Prince Philip, how do you like the United States on this visit?" His answer, "I've only been in your country for twenty-five minutes, so I really haven't had time to think much about it." The second reporter asked him what he thought of the Beatles. The third question asked how Prince

232

Charles liked the new school he was going to. Prince Philip looked at me, obviously remembering our conversation about "inane" questions. They certainly were.

Everything seemed to go very smoothly between Prince Philip and me for eleven days. The press had been kind. Substantial money had been raised for Variety Clubs. The London papers were delivered to us every morning and we were delighted that we were getting as favorable a press in Great Britain as we were in the United States. This was a very special assignment for me. We were making headlines all over the world as we went from city to city. I had set up specific responsibilities and objectives for myself and I was succeeding.

The last morning of the trip, prior to his departure for Canada, Prince Philip and his aide, Admiral Bonham-Carter, were breakfasting in the Prince's suite at the Pierre Hotel in New York. I knocked and walked in, as was my usual custom. Instead of the cheery good morning that I had received every morning from Prince Philip, he barely acknowledged my presence, instead burrowing his nose deep into his *New York Times*. I gave Bonham-Carter a questioning look. He arose from the table and motioned for me to accompany him into the bedroom.

"What's wrong?" I asked.

"I think his dyspepsia is acting up," said the aide with a mischievous grin on his face. "Actually, he is angry because you set up a press conference for him at the airport prior to his departure for Quebec and he wasn't expecting it. You had better go in and straighten it out with him."

I went back and tried to make my explanations. The Prince cut me off sharply. "Just forget it, Henry. The damage is done. I'm really very angry. There is no way for you to cancel the press conference now, so I'll just have to go through with it." I was dismissed.

The sophisticated, worldly-wise public relations man was deeply hurt. The Prince and I had gotten along so well together. We had not become truly intimate, but we had developed a warm relationship. After a day of personal appearances and speeches, we would return to the hotel together, and the Prince would invite me into his suite for a drink. He would insist on mixing the drinks himself and I would find myself being served a scotch and soda by His Royal Highness.

"Well, Henry, how do you think the day went?" he would ask, as we sipped our drinks and relaxed.

"It wasn't too bad," I would reply. "That radio reporter who kept shoving his microphone up close to your nose, really bothered me. I tried to get him to back off a couple of feet, but he kept pushing forward, closer and closer."

"I saw you, but he was persistent," said HRH. "I always worry about those hand-held microphones. I feel that one day someone standing in back of a persistent reporter like that will inadvertently shove him, and I'll get a tooth knocked out."

The conversation would continue like that for a half hour while we reviewed the activities of the day and discussed plans for the following day.

It was heady stuff for anyone. I had felt good in my gut that I had been accepted by Prince Philip on such a close personal level . . . and now I had been summarily dismissed from the room.

I could feel my anger grow. Prince or no Prince, he didn't have to be rude. Of course I had set up the press conference for his departure day. He never told me he didn't want one. How the hell was I supposed to know? If he hadn't wanted one, he could have expressed himself last night. I was steaming mad. When the elevator arrived at the ground floor, I stopped. Hey, hold it, hold it, I said to myself. You're getting all upset because you're mixing personal relationships with client relationships. Stop thinking about it on such a personal level. You've got a job to do.

I left the hotel and was driven to the airport well in advance so as to make certain that all the proper arrangements had been made. Was the microphone working? Was the table set up in the proper place? Were the chairs arranged properly? These are the little details that the disciplined public relations man always attends to carefully before his client is presented to the press or the public. Everything was in order. Prince Philip arrived and nodded at me curtly. I introduced him. The first question was an intelligent, pointed one. The Prince gave a witty answer and there were some chuckles from the fifty or so press, radio, and television crews who were assembled. Another question. A snappy answer which brought a howl of laughter from the audience. Prince Philip was getting warmed up. The sullen monarch of a few hours ago had changed into a stand-up comedian. He was enjoying himself, and the press, writing furiously as the quips flew at them in rapid succession, as the television cameras recorded every word, and as the radio reporters kept their microphones close up to the laughing principal of the morning, were enjoying themselves too. In fifteen minutes, when the momentum had begun to wane, I interrupted, "Excuse me, Prince Philip. Gentlemen, that will be all. Prince Philip must catch a plane." Everyone left, still chuckling, and the Prince was escorted into the VIP room of BOAC where a farewell reception had been planned for him by the British ambassador.

I strolled in, feeling very good about myself at that moment. I had forgotten the personal hurt I had suffered an hour before. It was the best press conference we had had since our touring had started. I knew that we would get upbeat worldwide press, television, and radio coverage as a result. It would all be favorable to Prince Philip, Variety Clubs, Playing Fields of Great Britain, and the British Board of Trade as well. I had fulfilled my responsibilities and had attained the objectives that had been set out on that first trip to Buckingham Palace some three months before. Prince Philip was angry with me, or, at least, displeased. I felt badly about it on a personal level. For pure ego reasons, I had hoped that when he returned home, he would think not only that I had done a creditable job for him, but that he had liked me as a person.

I looked across the room. He was chatting with some people I didn't know, sipping a glass of sherry. Then he caught my eye. I saw him excuse himself, walk casually across the room, nodding and smiling to the guests as he headed in my direction. He was obviously approaching me. What would he say? I waited. We shook hands. He looked at me and said, "I'm sorry about that little temper tantrum this morning. You were right and I was wrong. It *was* proper to have a press conference before I left the country. And this one went so well. It was certainly the best one we had on the whole trip. I'm very grateful, Henry. Thank you." And then he walked away.

I was surprised. I had not expected this. I am a professional, like a lawyer, a doctor. I have a job to do. I get paid for my efforts. If I get a "thank you" for a job well done, I am appreciative, but I don't expect it. Prince Philip's selfless gesture proved to be one of the high points of my professional life.

Again, I had learned something. Admit when you are wrong. Don't try to justify your mistakes. Be a big man about it and apologize.

A few weeks later, a hand-written letter arrived on Windsor Castle stationery. It said,

> Dear Henry: Thank you so much for your letter and for sending that photograph.
> It was very kind of you to write the way you did. However, I

want you to know that in my opinion the whole thing would have been Twentieth Century chaos without your invaluable contribution throughout that extraordinary excursion!

I can only say that I was full of admiration for the way you maintained such a convincing air of patience and good temper in spite of provocations from me as well as from the press!

I can't thank you enough and I wish you all the best in the future. Yours sincerely, Philip.

Prince Philip compounded his graciousness a few months later.

Mrs. Rogers and I were invited to a garden party at Buckingham Palace. We thought forty others were also invited. There were 4,000. Out of the crowd, Prince Philip spotted us and approached. He put his hand in his pocket, took out a small package, and handed it to me. "Good afternoon, Mrs. Rogers. I am delighted to see you again." Then he turned to me and said, "Thank you for coming to our garden party, Henry. And thank you for all your help on that trip we took together." When he left, I opened the package. In an Asprey jewel box, there sat a pair of gold cufflinks, engraved with the imperial crest of the British royal family. How did he find me in that crowd of 4,000 guests? How did he happen to have that Asprey box in his pocket? I'll never know.

What I *do* know is that my experience with Prince Philip confirmed once again that I have found that the most important men are the nicest men. I have never met a rude, ill-mannered chief executive officer. The top man always has time to answer the telephone, is quick to admit a mistake, is the most considerate, and is one who is the most thoughtful about thank-you notes and little gifts.

My experiences with Prince Philip were not yet over. He figured in another event in my life, which proved that there was an exception to my rule that the most important men are the nicest men. In 1966, Darryl F. Zanuck, the famed movie producer and President of Twentieth Century-Fox Studios, was a most important man.

One day he was walking down Piccadilly in London, and stopped, aghast at the blaring poster which he had spotted on the side of the *London Sunday Mirror* newspaper truck. It said, in bold letters, "Prince Philip Says Twentieth-Fox Is Nineteenth Century Chaos." He was furious. How dare anyone say anything derogatory about his studio. He hurried to his office and asked his secretary to get him the editor of the *Sunday Mirror* on the telephone. He demanded to know what right he had to use such a defamatory statement.

"Every right in the world," replied the editor. "We are starting a three-part series this Sunday titled 'Prince Philip and I.' It's written by a Hollywood press agent based on his experiences traveling around the United States with Prince Philip a few months ago. We bought exclusive rights to the article in Great Britain. The line we are using to promote the first article is a direct quote from Prince Philip."

Mr. Zanuck hung up, and then telephoned Jonas Rosenfield, in Hollywood. Jonas was his Vice-President in charge of advertising and publicity. "Who the hell is Henry Rogers?" he yelled. Jonas told him.

"In fact, we just made a deal with Henry and his firm, Rogers & Cowan, to handle publicity on our new Doris Day film."

"You hired him?" screamed the by-now apoplectic Mr. Zanuck. "Fire the son of a bitch," and he hung up.

Jonas called me a few minutes after this conversation took place.

"Henry," he said. "I made a deal with you last week. Right?"

"Right," I replied.

"Okay," he said. "You're fired."

He was laughing. I couldn't imagine what had happened. He told me.

"If you want to work for us," he said, "you can't very well go around writing disparaging things about our company."

"I didn't say it," I explained. "Prince Philip said it. I just quoted him."

"I know," said Jonas, "that's what Darryl is steaming about. He knows you didn't say it, but he's mad as hell that you included it in your article. He's embarrassed in front of his friends."

I took it philosophically. Twentieth Century-Fox was paying us a substantial fee for handling this particular movie, and I didn't like losing the income, but there was nothing I could do about it. Possibly I should have thought about the fact that the remark would have been offensive to Mr. Zanuck, whether I represented his company or not, but I hadn't. It was too late to repair the damage that had been done to his ego.

"Oh, I guess I can't blame him," I replied to Jonas. "I brought it on myself so I can't very well complain about it."

Jonas asked me what it was all about. He had been out of the country when the incident had taken place, so I told him.

A few months before, during my jaunt with Prince Philip around the country, the itinerary had called for a visit to Hollywood, and our first stop was a luncheon in Prince Philip's honor at Twentieth

237

Century-Fox Studios. We arrived in a Rolls limousine which the British Consul-General had arranged for the occasion. Milling about the studio entrance in total confusion were hundreds of mounted horses which were supposed to have been ready for inspection as his Royal Highness, in true regal fashion, arrived on the scene. Also milling around, and not yet in formation, were a number of high school bands which had been brought together for this auspicious occasion. Between the horses and the children, the entrance to the studio was blocked.

After sitting for some ten minutes, Prince Philip suggested that we walk the approximately 200 yards to the studio entrance. In a completely undignified manner we elbowed our way through the horses and children. The sun was beating down on us. It was ninety degrees on that beautiful Southern California morning, and, as a result, we were sweating profusely.

"I'll be glad to get into some shade," the Prince said to me.

"Is this the way it used to be in India?" I asked jokingly.

He laughed. We both knew that we had better keep our spirits up, because it was shaping up as a bad day—how bad, we didn't yet know.

When we finally arrived at the site where cocktails were to be served before lunch, we found that it was outside in the blazing sun, with no shade. Good-naturedly Prince Philip accepted his introduction to a good percentage of Hollywood's famous sweating film stars who had gathered to meet him. Then it was time for lunch. I asked whether someone could put up a drape or a curtain over the head table so as to cut down on the heat, but I was told that it was impossible. At long last, what had seemed like an interminable lunch was over.

I walked up behind Prince Philip and whispered to him.

"We are scheduled to visit the Jerry Lewis set now for a few minutes, and then we can leave. At least there will be air conditioning on the sound stage." Prince Philip gave me a grim smile. He had been a good sport about it all. Two studio executives accompanied us to the sound stage where Jerry Lewis was working on a film. As the door opened we were greeted by a blast of welcome icy air. The door behind us slammed shut. We were in pitch black darkness. The lights had not been turned on and no one in our party knew where they were.

Across the far reaches of the stage, a light flickered. We stumbled our way toward it. Cables were laid across the floor, lamps and props were scattered about. We bruised our shins, cursed politely (we were in the presence of a member of the royal family), dodged and tripped and maneuvered our way toward the flickering light.

It was Jerry Lewis's portable dressing room. The door was open. It was deathly quiet in there. One of the executives, embarrassed that there obviously had been no arrangements made to greet the royal guest, called out, "Is anyone there?"

The bathroom door opened. Jerry Lewis came out, zipping up his fly.

"Who's that?" he asked casually.

He looked at the group of men standing outside his dressing room. Suddenly he spotted Prince Philip.

"What? Wha?" he sputtered. "Prince Philip, I'm so sorry. No one told me you were coming." He gave the two studio executives a withering look. What a screw-up.

"Come in, come in, I'm sorry we're not shooting a scene now. There's no one here. They're still all at lunch."

As Prince Philip extended his hand, Jerry looked at his own.

"Oops," he said. "I didn't wash my hands."

He dashed back into the dressing room. Prince Philip laughed. It looked like a slapstick scene from a Jerry Lewis movie. We all laughed, although I wasn't sure at first whether to laugh or cry. It had all been so poorly handled. At last Jerry came out of the bathroom, his fly properly zipped up, and his hands properly washed. A few minutes of conversation and we left.

We leaned back in the limousine as it took off from the studio. Driving down Pico Boulevard, Prince Philip looked back at the rapidly receding studio, then turned to me.

"Henry, that may be Twentieth Century-Fox Studios to you, but it was Nineteenth Century chaos to me."

I could only agree. Being *fired* by Darryl Zanuck was a very small price to pay for the enjoyable moments I have spent over the years telling my friends this wonderful story.

CHAPTER 21
Psyching Out the People Business

We are really in two businesses: public relations and people relations.

What do I mean by that? We don't deal with machinery. We don't deal with the money market. We don't worry about inventories. We don't get involved with union negotiations. Ours is not a capital intensive business. Ours is a *people* business. Rogers & Cowan is dependent entirely upon our ability to deal with people . . . our clients, the media, our employees, and, because a large percentage of our new clients come to us through recommendation, the total community as well. For our clients we practice *public* relations. For ourselves we practice *people* relations.

It is the human factor that determines our success. The public relations hand is the subtle, gentle hand. It must be sensitive to the feelings and the reactions of the other fellow. Kid gloves are worn all the time. There are clients who genuinely want forthright criticism. There are those who want no criticism at all. Even if forthright criticism is given, it must not be offensive. It must be constructive.

A movie producer client has just previewed his new film. I walk out of the theater, and he confronts me.

"What did you think of the picture?" he asks.

What do I say? The film was lousy. He knows it, I know it, and everyone else knows it. But what good does it do for me to tell him that it's lousy? I will just add to his grief. A rap from me about his movie at that moment might just cause him to take an extra sleeping pill later that night. I don't want to hurt him, or offend him. On the other hand, I can't tell him that his movie is great. That would be an outright lie, and he will know it. Or worse yet, he'll think that his public relations man has bad judgment. What to do?

"It's a very interesting film," I say. "It has some wonderful qualities. It's so difficult to predict in a film like this what the critical and the public reaction is going to be. Making this film must have been a great challenge for you."

My client is satisfied with my answer. I have not lied to him, nor

240

have I offended him. I have squirmed out of a ticklish situation in a satisfactory manner.

If I am publicizing the movie which I have just seen and didn't like, that presents no problem for me. It is my responsibility to publicize, not to criticize. I must disregard my own personal opinion, and concentrate on the qualities of the film which will appeal to the public. Some of my most favorite movies have died at the box office. Those I have not liked have developed into box office smashes. My personal opinion is not important.

An employee comes in and I know he will ask for a pay increase. I don't think it is deserved, but I don't want to put him down. I want to inspire him so that he leaves my office determined to do a better job than he has been doing, so that I can offer him an increase one day without his asking for it. It is a delicate situation because I don't want him to become discouraged. If my conversation with him generates an added enthusiasm, an added desire to do better, then I have handled the situation successfully.

A journalist calls. The release that he was supposed to have received an hour ago has not arrived yet. Where the hell is it? I haven't the faintest idea, but I can't tell him that. He is on a deadline, and needs it immediately. I offer to dictate it to him over the telephone. I tell him that I'll bring it down myself. At that moment the release arrives on his desk. He knows that Henry Rogers cares about him, and was willing to go out of his way to help him.

So it goes all day long. People, people, and more people. They must be handled, and in order for us to continue to be successful in our business, they must be handled carefully and with great sensitivity. It took me many years to learn that, and I am still learning every day. I still make mistakes.

Does the public relations person tell the client what he wants to hear or does he tell him what he honestly believes? It took many years for me to learn that I can be honest but not blunt. I cannot lie to a client just to agree with him. I have my own principles and standards. I can be in conflict with the point of view of the client, and express my views, but I express them in a way that will not turn the client into an ex-client. The public relations person must earn a living. In order to earn a living I must have clients. I won't have clients very long if I don't know how to "handle" the client. I can differ with the client, I can argue with him, but I must do it in a way so that the client continues to respect me—not fire me.

241

Before I learned my craft to that extent, before I learned that the ultimate in finesse and diplomacy was required, we represented Frank Sinatra. For some seven years, Warren Cowan and I enjoyed a warm, friendly, respectful, though occasionally stormy, relationship with our client, one of the greatest entertainers and personalities of our time. One day, I received a telephone call from Mr. Sinatra's attorney, Milton Rudin. He said that our mutual client had something on his mind that was troubling him. Could we all have a meeting the next afternoon? At four the next day, Warren and I arrived promptly at Mr. Sinatra's home. The singer and Milton Rudin were already waiting for us. The meeting started immediately.

"What the hell is wrong?" asked Mr. Sinatra. "I have the worst image in the world. The press keep rapping me. My reputation is going downhill more and more every day. I have the best public relations men in show business working for me, and my image stinks. What the hell is wrong?"

There was a moment of silence, which I broke. "The only thing wrong with your image is you!" I said. Tactlessly I continued. "You have been doing outrageous things, you have been making outrageous statements, you have been offending the press outrageously."

Now there was a shocked moment of silence. Frank was imperturbable. He never flinched. He asked Milton Rudin for his opinion, then Warren for his. They were much more intelligent, much subtler, much smoother than I had been in their answers. Yet, they had not lied to the client. They had been forthright. They too knew that a problem existed and had to be solved. The meeting ended after a plan of action was determined.

But we never got to execute that plan of action. A few weeks later we received a letter of discharge from Milton Rudin, acting as attorney for Frank Sinatra. The reason given was that Mr. Sinatra was cutting down on his expenses and was doing away with public relations representation. I knew the real reason. I had been honest with our client, but I had been *stupidly* honest. I had been offensive, and insulting. If I had been more diplomatic as I pride myself on being now, I would have handled the situation in a more subtle manner. Warren and I could have helped solve the Frank Sinatra "image" problem and Frank Sinatra would most likely have remained a client up to this very day. I learned something from that experience: Honesty is the best policy—but!!

Our break with Frank Sinatra preyed heavily on my mind for

many years afterward. Here was an example where I had failed badly in the *people* relations business. I had no criticism of him. I criticized myself for my lack of sensitivity and my lack of understanding of how that particular situation should have been handled. I try to learn from my mistakes. I have made many mistakes since that day, but never the same one. In the *people* relations business I must deal with a gentle and more well-informed, intelligent hand.

I believe I succeeded in dealing with Prime Minister Menachem Begin of Israel.

The word "image" has been used in our vocabulary more in recent years than in all the 200 years of our nation's history. It is a word used primarily as it pertains to public relations. We describe a person's having a good image or a bad image. A politician may have no image at all. He tries to establish a good image for himself by kissing babies, eating hot dogs at Nathan's in Coney Island, visiting slum areas, posing for photographs with crippled children, and appearing at charity and ethnic events.

It's all a matter of how a person or a company is perceived. With many variations, the perception is probably good, bad, or neutral. When it is good, the public relations man develops programs to keep it good. When it's bad, the public relations man analyzes why it is bad, and then advises his client what he should do to improve it.

An actor who is accredited in his profession can add another dimension to his image by becoming active in charity work or cultural activities. Actors like Gregory Peck and Charlton Heston command great respect for their involvement with Screen Actors Guild, American Film Institute, National Endowment for the Arts, and many other charity, community, cultural, and motion picture industry–related activities.

A business corporation may improve its image by setting up new employee benefit programs, sponsoring a Little League team, or becoming active in the local Chamber of Commerce.

A public relations man cannot wave a magic wand and thereby change the image of his client. The client, often at the instigation of his public relations representative, must do something of a positive nature, and then it is the responsibility of Mr. P.R. to bring that positive action to the attention of the particular public which the client is trying to impress.

My experience in image building, changing the image from neutral to good, or from bad to good, started right at the outset of my career. Way back in 1939, it started with Rita Hayworth, and over the years it has applied to almost every client I have represented.

It was early in 1978 that I was called upon to improve the image of a Prime Minister.

One day, Bram Goldsmith, a longtime acquaintance, and Chairman of the City National Bank in Beverly Hills, called to tell me that I would be receiving a telephone call from the national President of the United Jewish Appeal, who had just returned from Israel where he had met with newly elected Prime Minister Menachem Begin. The following day the UJA man called. The Prime Minister was scheduled to have his first meeting with President Carter on a Wednesday, some two weeks after our conversation was taking place. He and his associates were very concerned about the Prime Minister's "image." They had made a number of telephone calls to prominent people, active in Jewish community affairs throughout the country as to who was best qualified to discuss this sensitive subject with Mr. Begin, and it had been decided by this select group that Henry Rogers should be asked to help improve the Prime Minister's image. Would I agree to meet with the Prime Minister and counsel with him?

I was very flattered. To have been selected from among all the public relations men in the United States to advise the new Prime Minister of Israel on his image, on the impression that he would convey to the American public at large, to the Jewish community in particular, to the Congress of the United States, and, finally, to the President of the United States, was a very impressive honor. Of course, I replied, I would be delighted to meet with the Prime Minister. There was no discussion of fee. It was mutually understood that this would be a public service gesture on my part.

I told Mr. UJA that I would be pleased to meet with Menachem Begin, *if* the Prime Minister wanted to meet with me. I told him that I did not know whether any advice I could give Mr. Begin would affect his image in any way, that in fact I did not know at the moment what advice I would give him.

I explained to my well-meaning caller that images are not changed overnight, and repeated my theory that I could not wave a magic wand—and poof—the Prime Minister's image would change for the better. If there was a problem with the Prime Minister, and I for one did not know that there was, it would take some positive action on his part to solve it.

The caller went on to explain that the Prime Minister, when he

244

had met with him only a week before, was recovering from a recent heart attack. His cheeks were sallow and sunken, his collar was too big for him, his clothes hung on his body. The American public would not see too attractive a man when he stepped off the plane in New York in a few weeks.

"If you're talking about Mr. Begin's cosmetic image," I commented, "that's easy." Almost facetiously, I explained that on his arrival in New York, I could make arrangements to take him quietly into Saks Fifth Avenue, buy him some shirts that were the right size and two or three well-fitting suits. If his cheeks still looked sunken and sallow because of his recent heart attack, we could always get a makeup artist to improve on the Prime Minister's appearance. But, I added, I would not advise any of this.

Menachem Begin has been a firebrand in Israeli politics for more than thirty years. He had been the leader of the Irgun, the terrorist group which had given the British so much trouble in the violent years that had preceded the declaration of the State of Israel in 1948. Somehow I couldn't see a makeup artist working on this dynamic, vital man.

My caller concluded our conversation by telling me that he would be in touch with the Israeli Embassy in Washington about setting up an appointment for me to meet with the Prime Minister on his arrival in the United States. When he called a few days later, he got right to the point—he was angry. The Prime Minister did not want to meet with an American public relations man. He had more important things on his mind. My caller felt that Mr. Begin was getting off to a bad start.

The Prime Minister arrived on the Friday prior to his scheduled Wednesday meeting with President Carter. On Saturday morning my telephone rang again. Mr. Begin's advisors had convinced him to change his mind. Yes, he would meet with Mr. Rogers, the public relations man who had been recommended to him. Could I meet with the Prime Minister at the Waldorf Towers in New York on Monday morning at ten o'clock? I told him I would be there.

I had been asked to meet with the new Prime Minister of Israel on Monday morning. What would I say to him? What helpful counsel could I give him? I would think it through. I would do my best to solve the problem—if there was a problem.

I had been asked for help, and help I must try to give. I decided that I needed help myself at this point for I knew very little about

Menachem Begin. I needed to talk with knowledgeable people and so decided to call three friends and ask a number of questions. I called Arthur Krim, formerly President of United Artists Corporation, and advisor to Presidents, a frequenter of the White House, a long-time power in the Democratic Party, and an activist in Israeli and American-Jewish affairs. I then called Paul Ziffren, Beverly Hills attorney, former Chairman of the California State Democratic Committee, a man close to the influential in Washington and Jerusalem. Next on the list was Ted Ashley, Chairman of Warner Brothers Pictures. I knew that Ted was a close friend of Simcha Dinitz, Israeli Ambassador to the United States, and because of this association, was well attuned to Israeli-American relations and the complexities of the Middle East situation. They were all helpful. By late Saturday afternoon I had finished my telephone calls.

I had sought background on the man which I needed before I could make any decision. I had learned that he was not only accepted as a brilliant politician in his own country but that he knew the American scene very well. I had learned that a number of years before, as one of the leaders of the opposition party in Israel, he had toured the United States, had appeared on "Meet the Press" and "Issues and Answers," and had given numerous press conferences. This was no neophyte, unskilled and unschooled in American ways. Here was a sophisticated statesman who was far ahead of his own advisors. He knew what was right for him.

But what about the advisors who had contacted me and asked me to improve the public image of Menachem Begin. What was their motivation? What were they concerned about? Their intentions were honorable, but I believe they underestimated the intelligence of the American people, the American Jewish community, the Congress, and our President. Some of the leaders of the American Jewish community didn't like the way Menachem Begin looked. To them he looked like an unattractive little old Jew from a Polish *shtetl*. He did not look like what they thought the Prime Minister of Israel should look like. They would have much preferred the image of handsome Abba Eban with his Oxford accent, or the swashbuckling, romantic picture presented by General Moshe Dayan. They naively thought that public relations was the answer. They naively thought that a Brooks Brothers suit, and maybe a little dab of makeup before an appearance on television might change the image of the little old Jew from the Polish *shtetl*.

246

On Monday at nine I had breakfast with the President of the United Jewish Appeal at the Waldorf Astoria Hotel. We then went up and chatted for twenty minutes with Simcha Dinitz and Shmoel Katz, personal aide to the Prime Minister. I did not mention to any of them what I planned to tell Menachem Begin.

Then, a few minutes before ten, we left Mr. Katz's room, entered the elevators, and proceeded to the Presidential suite in the Waldorf Towers. As the elevator doors opened, we were confronted by a battery of men—Israeli Secret Service personnel. A few words were passed in Hebrew; they stepped aside and we were allowed to proceed down the hallway. When we came to a set of double doors, Ambassador Dinitz knocked, and a gentleman opened the door, nodded us in, and suggested we sit on a couch and chairs that were grouped on one side of the large living room which we had entered. Across the room, forty feet away, seated around a table, a number of men were talking quietly. One of them looked up and waved at us. I recognized the Prime Minister. He smiled and said, "Good morning, gentlemen, I'll be with you in a few minutes."

I looked around me. I remembered that this suite had been the stopping-off place for American Presidents since the days of Herbert Hoover. Winston Churchill had spent many days here. President Eisenhower. President Nixon. History had been made in this room. This was probably the most important, most prestigious "smoke-filled room" in the United States.

Suddenly the meeting at the other side of the room broke up; good-byes were said and the other gentlemen departed. The Prime Minister looked toward our group and immediately noticed what none of the four of us had realized. There was no place for the Prime Minister to sit. Without a moment's hesitation, and before any of us could offer to help, he picked up the chair in which he had been sitting, carried it across the room to our group, and sat down.

He smiled. I was the only person he had not met. Ambassador Dinitz introduced us, and I walked over to shake his hand. He gave me a firm grip and said, "I'm delighted to meet you. I've heard a great deal about you."

I'll bet, I thought. He had probably had both arms twisted in order to agree to the meeting we were about to have. But the Prime Minister was not yet ready to discuss his image. He wanted to tell us about a party he had gone to the night before, in the Williamsburg section of Brooklyn, where he had gone to meet with the Rabbi of the Lubavitcher sect. The wine had begun to flow, the neighbors had come in for singing, dancing, and talk, and the Prime Minister concluded by laughingly complaining, "And we didn't get back until one o'clock in the morning. What a night!"

Suddenly, he turned serious, and addressed me. "Well, Mr. Rogers, my associates have told me I must meet with you. They have told me that my image needs improving and you are the man who can do it. Tell me, Mr. Rogers, what words of public relations wisdom are you going to impart to me today?"

It was not a put-down. He was smiling when he said it. He was receptive but skeptical, obviously indulging his American advisors who had insisted on the meeting. I had my reply ready.

"Mr. Prime Minister," I said, "I am very grateful for the opportunity to speak with you. I know that you were very reluctant to meet with me, but you have listened to the counsel of your advisors. That is wise, particularly for a newly elected Prime Minister. Your advisors have told you that I am one of the most knowledgeable public relations men in the United States. They have told you that I have been active, behind the scenes, in American politics for many years, that I have supported the Zionist cause during my entire adult life. They have told you that I am intelligent in the world of public relations, and that because of this background, I am probably better qualified than anyone else to advise you on your public image. Forgive my immodesty, Mr. Prime Minister, but your advisors are right. I am the best qualified person to advise you on your image, and here is my advice."

I paused. I wanted to make certain that he was catching the nuances in my voice. I did not care whether the others did. They would find out when I finished. I looked at him. He was listening intently but the gleam in his eyes, the trace of a smile around the corners of his mouth, indicated that he knew I was speaking with tongue in cheek. I had great self-assurance at that moment. I hadn't stuttered. I knew I wouldn't. Sounding serious, I continued, *"Don't do anything about your image. Don't change anything. Don't take the advice of any American public relations expert who tries to change your image. Be yourself as you have been all your life. You are one of the most experienced politicians and statesmen in the world. For more than thirty years you have been one of the leaders of the opposition party. At long last you have been elected Prime Minister. This is no time for you to change. Your own people have given you their vote of confidence. Let me take the liberty to speak for the American Jewish community. We give you our vote of confidence too. That is my advice to you, Mr. Prime Minister."*

There was a moment of silence. I could see that everyone was taken aback. The Prime Minister smiled. Then everyone started to smile. Then the Prime Minister began to laugh. They all laughed. The public relations man had poured forth his words of wisdom. Forget it, I had said. Be yourself.

We chatted for a few minutes more, and then we knew it was time to leave. We arose, and Menachem Begin approached me. He clasped both my hands, looked at me, smiled, and said, "Thank you very much, Mr. Rogers, for your advice. I wanted to do just as you had advised me to—nothing—but my associates kept after me that I should do something. I feel better now that you agree with me."

My advice had not been given lightly. I had thought it through—painstakingly. If I had a responsibility, it was to add to his security and self-assurance—not to say anything that would give him a moment of doubt that possibly he was not following the right path. I was confident that my advice was correct.

It was gratifying for me to watch President Carter, President Sadat, and Prime Minister Begin sign the peace treaty on the White House lawn at 2 P.M. on the afternoon of March 26, 1979. The first step to a lasting peace had come to the Middle East and Menachem Begin had not changed his image since he had first come to meet with President Carter at the White House many, many months before.

One reason that we are successful in the *people* aspect of our business has to do with the fact that Warren and I fortunately complement each other's personalities. That is one reason for the success of Rogers & Cowan over the years. Warren relates better to some worlds than I do. I relate to other worlds better than he does. When a new client arrives on our scene, we usually discuss who between us should be responsible for him. To whom would the client relate better? Warren or me?

When Danny Kaye became a client some twenty years ago, Warren and I agreed that I would be the Danny Kaye man. It was a logical decision at the time. I hit it off with Danny immediately. We established a rapport. I understood that he was a very sensitive man who had to be represented in a most sensitive fashion. One must never appear to seek press coverage for Danny Kaye. It must appear as though the magazine articles, the extensive coverage which his world-wide UNICEF tours always receive, the hundreds of fans who turn out at the airports when he goes on one of his whirlwind "Trick or Treat" tours, the front-page attention when he conducts major symphony orchestras throughout the world, are all spontaneous. That is the way it must be for Danny Kaye.

He has impeccable taste. He knows exactly what is right for him. Sometimes he would take my advice, sometimes he rejected it. I never resented his rejections. He knew himself better than I did. He knew where he would shine, and where he wouldn't, and under what circumstances. He always shone with the royal family of Great Britain as an example, long before I ever met him. When I became involved with the Prince Philip tour in 1966, it was only natural that I would try to get Danny involved in some way.

Before I left for London for my first meeting with Prince Philip, I met with Danny. I told him about my impending visit to Buckingham Palace and suggested to Danny that I try to work out something that could be mutually beneficial and newsworthy as well.

"What did you have in mind?" asked Danny.

"Here is my idea," I replied. "We'll be in Hollywood for two days but only one night. That night there will be a big benefit ball, and everyone in show business will be there. The ball will be over about eleven o'clock. I think you should invite forty or fifty people—your friends—to be your guests at a midnight party you will give in Prince Philip's honor. We'll get Frank Sinatra, Dean Martin, and Barbra Streisand to entertain. It will be a sensational party. I'll quietly invite a few key members of the press. Prince Philip will have a fun evening, so will you, and the publicity will break all over the world."

Danny said nothing. He stood up, paced up and down the room for a few minutes, and then turned to me.

"Henry, you've got it all wrong. You don't understand my relationship with the royal family. I have remained close to them all these years because I never took advantage of them, I never used them for publicity. Yes, I want to do something with Prince Philip when he's here but under one condition—no publicity. Listen to me. Here is what I would like you to do. When you meet him, and if you feel that the situation is right, send him my best personal regards.

250

Tell him of our relationship. Give him a message for me. Tell him I would like him to come to my home after the ball. He will sit in my kitchen and I shall cook a Chinese dinner for him. Tell him I'll invite only a few people, and there will be no press. Tell him that when he arrives, he will take off his shoes, take off his dinner jacket, take off his tie, unbutton his collar, and eat the best Chinese dinner he will have ever had in his life. Tell him I said it will be the only relaxed fun evening he will have on the whole trip."

I smiled. Danny was right. My proposal would have been right for someone else, but not Danny Kaye. He is a unique gentleman who has always known what was right for him at any given time.

It all worked out as Danny had planned. Prince Philip was agreeable to the idea. After the Hollywood gala was over, we drove off quietly to Danny's Beverly Hills home. Danny had arrived home before. He had stripped off his black tie, had donned an old sweat shirt which he wears when cooking, and was at the door to greet His Royal Highness. The other guests had already arrived. Cary Grant and his then-wife, Dyan Cannon, Shirley MacLaine, Warren and Barbara (Rush) Cowan, Prince Philip and one of his aides, Admiral Bonham-Carter, and the Rogers. Danny said to his royal guest, "Sir, in my home I am the host and my guests do as I request. So— I request that you take your shoes off, your coat, and your tie. Come into my kitchen. Have a glass of beer and relax while I start cooking."

Prince Philip laughed and said, "Danny, I am as gracious a guest as you are a host." In a moment we were all sitting around the kitchen table, coatless, tieless, and shoeless with large schooners of beer in front of us. Danny already had his woks heated, and the food ingredients chopped. In a few moments, everyone savored the delectable aroma of shrimp, rice, beef, pork, chicken, and other delicious ingredients as they began to cook. The conversation was warm and friendly, with Cary Grant and Prince Philip exchanging jokes, as we all watched the intent master chef performing his miracles. The first dish was ready, and Danny waved aside the two servants who were waiting to serve the guests. "No, this is my party. I'm not only the chef but the waiter." He served us all quickly and then turned to the preparation of the next dish.

It went on until 3 A.M. It was finally time to break up the party, and we all left together. Prince Philip said good night to his host and all the other guests and then turned to me. "Danny was right," he said. "It was the only fun and relaxing evening I've had on the entire trip."

Danny has always been adored by important people, and as a tribute to his talent, personality, and charm, by people in different walks of life. I was privileged to be with him during the years that we worked together on numerous special occasions which still remain very important in my life.

When an actor of Danny Kaye's renown travels, it is customary that his public relations representative accompany him. Danny's travels were primarily on behalf of UNICEF and for his fund-raising activities on behalf of the Musicians Pension Funds of symphony orchestras. In connection with these activities, there were always press conferences to be set up, interviews and television news programs to be scheduled. That is the responsibility of the public relations representative; this is what I did for Danny Kaye.

We traveled together on a nine-day trip to Moscow under State Department auspices. We had lunch with five Supreme Court Justices in the Supreme Court Building in Washington and I listened while these learned gentlemen argued with Danny as to which team would win the National League pennant that year. We went backstage to watch a rehearsal of the Philadelphia Orchestra and I looked on as Danny and the eminent Eugene Ormandy stood on their heads. I had dinner in Chicago with Danny, Isaac Stern, and Nathan Milstein where the evening was spent telling disparaging stories about Jascha Heifetz. I accompanied Danny to the Newport, Rhode Island, dedication of the model of the soon-to-be-constructed John F. Kennedy Center in Washington. Dedication of the model took place at The Farm, the home of Mrs. Kennedy's mother, Mrs. Auchincloss. I was introduced to Mrs. Kennedy, Caroline, and John-John, about age two at the time, who asked me to pick him up in my arms—which I did. There were trips to London, Paris, Chicago, San Francisco, New York, Washington, and so many, many other places.

Then one day it was all over. We were in New York. The night before had been a fiasco. Danny had been named "Man of the Year" at a March of Dimes Dinner at the Waldorf. He hadn't wanted to accept the honor because it was against his policy, but one of his associates had talked him into accepting it and making an appearance.

I had opposed Danny's acceptance of the March of Dimes Award. He was being used as a shill to help raise funds for a very worthy cause. I had cautioned Danny that by appearing at the March of Dimes dinner he was breaking a policy that he had established many years before, which was to devote his charity efforts to two worthy causes. UNICEF was one, the Musicians Pension Fund was the other. He had decided, and rightfully so, that his efforts on behalf of these two causes to which he was truly devoted would be diluted if we were to accept every "Man of the Year" award that was offered to him, and to make an appearance at every charity event to which he was invited. I had denied all such requests for many years and the policy had remained firm. This time, for some unknown reason, Danny had agreed to make an exception for the March of Dimes.

He had been assured that on the dais would be such luminaries as Nelson Rockefeller, David Rockefeller, Averell Harriman, Jacob Javits, Mary Lasker, the Mayor, and a dozen other distinguished personalities of equal stature. Instead, to our chagrin, we arrived to find that the dais was occupied by a group of borscht-belt comedians. Danny was seething. It was not what he had expected, but he kept smiling through the evening.

The next morning the axe fell. He called me first thing. "Henry," he said, "I've decided that my relationship with Rogers & Cowan must come to an end. You and Warren have been wonderful for me all these years, but I don't want to have public relations representation for a while. I certainly appreciate everything you and Warren have done. Rogers & Cowan is the best, I don't intend to hire anyone else to replace you, but let's wind it up at the end of the month."

I was furious. He was giving me a bad rap. I was furious but I would not let him know it. Danny had agreed to the March of Dimes Award and now blamed me because I had been unable to get Senator Javits, Averell Harriman, and Nelson Rockefeller to sit with him on the dais. How was it my fault? His behavior was difficult for me to fathom. It was nothing new for me to lose a client—the nature of our business is that clients come and go, and there is usually a good reason. There are some times when we are unable to do a satisfactory job, and some times when we make an inexcusable mistake. In other instances, the client's business has gone bad and he can no longer afford us. But this was different. Rogers & Cowan had done an outstanding job on this client for years. I had personally been responsible.

253

I am very critical of my own performance, more so than I am of my associates, but in this case I couldn't fault myself. This was a bum rap if I ever saw one. Yet I was powerless to do anything about it. Danny had crossed Rogers & Cowan and me out of his life.

"Okay, Danny," I replied. "We'll finish up the few things which are pending and we'll wrap it up at the end of the month."

I called Warren and told him what had happened. Warren said, "Do you mind if I call Danny and try to straighten it out? Maybe your time has run out with him, and it's time for a new face. Let me take a crack at him."

"Of course I don't mind," I replied. "Go ahead. If you can get him to change his mind, good luck."

Ten minutes later Warren called back. "I think I did it. I convinced him not to discharge us until I have a chance to meet with him and discuss some new ideas. In fact, I told him that we refused to be discharged, and that if he persisted we would represent him for nothing. I think that got him. He agreed to wait, and I'm going to see him in a few days."

I was elated. "That's great. How did you do it? What did you say?"

"Henry, you never realized that in addition to music and medicine and his own career, baseball is the most important thing in Danny's life. I decided that was the key. I told him that Rogers & Cowan were the Mantle and Maris of public relations—that Mickey Mantle has just struck out (that's you) and Roger Maris was about to come to bat (that's me)."

"What did he say?" I asked.

"What did he say? He didn't say anything. He just laughed. He thought it was the funniest remark he had ever heard."

Danny Kaye did not discharge us. Warren had hit a home run and we continue to represent him up until this very day. Danny Kaye now confines his charity efforts to UNICEF and conducting Musicians' Pension Fund concerts with the world's best symphony orchestras. Warren has a much better rapport with Danny than I ever had. Danny now owns a major league baseball team. He and Warren talk baseball a lot, and when I'm with the two of them, I rarely participate in the conversation. Warren, Danny, and I all know that since I left Irvington High School, my closest relationship to baseball has been watching Gary Cooper in *The Pride of the Yankees* on the late, late show.

254

There was a time in my growing-up years that the Danny Kaye incident would have had a devastating effect on my ego. I might have accepted the fact that Danny's preference for Warren Cowan over Henry Rogers was advantageous to our business, but my own insecurities in those early years would have made it impossible for me to accept it on a personal level. Fortunately, as I have become more mature, more experienced in both my business and my personal life, I have been able to put natural personal sensitivities aside and concentrate my energies on what is good for Rogers & Cowan.

I learned early in my business career that .400 was a great batting average, but it wasn't until much, much later that I realized this applied to the personal side of things as well as the professional. I used to expect perfection from myself and perfection from those around me. It didn't work. I was in a constant state of anger and resentment. I was angry with myself because I had made a mistake, and I resented my associates because they weren't doing things the way I wanted them done. With each new year of experience, I have accepted the fact that I will always make mistakes, that I will always commit errors of judgment, and, more important, that my way is not necessarily the only way. There may be more than one way to get something accomplished. My associates may not go about solving a problem in the same way I do, but they will arrive at a satisfactory solution nevertheless. This was an important lesson for me to learn, and once I accepted the fact that .400 was a batting average to be proud of rather than ashamed of, I began to hit more home runs. I wasn't pressing as hard because I knew that it would not be catastrophic if I did not get the new client I was seeking, if that story which I expected to break on page 1 actually broke on page 6, and that Danny Kaye preferred to be represented by Warren rather than me.

There was a time when my business absorbed me totally. It stood alone at the top of my priority list—with family, health, and my own well-being falling far behind. Business is still a vital concern to me, but it shares my time and attention with those other aspects of my life which are now of equal importance. As a result of this reallocation of priorities, I am better at my job than I have ever been before. I once truly believed that the man who worked at his job sixteen hours a day was twice as effective as the man who worked eight hours a day. I believed that workaholics got more done than the average business man did. I don't believe that anymore. I have seen too many executives jump out of windows or wind up incapacitated by heart attacks, strokes, and ulcers because their minds and bodies finally rebelled against the unstinting pressures imposed on them by an all-consuming obsession with their jobs. I thank God that I have been able to set my priorities in proper order so that I can continue to work in the public relations business and the people business for the rest of my days.

Walking the tightrope becomes easier, not more difficult, as the years go by.

HM
263   Rogers, Henry C.
.R567
        Walking the tightrope

DATE DUE

DEC 4 1980		FEB 26 1982	
APR 3 1981		MAR 0 2 1984	
APR 4 1983	12/15/86		
NOV 30 1984	NOV 10 1990		
		NOV 25 1983	
			FEB 17 1989
OCT 21 1987		MAR 22 1985	

NOV 10 1989

NOV 18 1988   NOV 10 1988   JUN 14 1989   MAY 6 1992

ABBOT MEMORIAL LIBRARY
EMERSON COLLEGE
303 BERKELEY STREET
BOSTON, MASSACHUSETTS 02116

OEACQ

HM263 .R567
Rogers, Henry C., 1914-   060101 000
Walking the tightrope : the pr

0 1135 0006383 0

Emerson College Library